D0871324

Scott, Foresman

Science

Series Consultant

Irwin L. Slesnick
Department of Biology
Western Washington University
Bellingham, Washington

Program Consultant

Ronald D. Anderson
Laboratory for Research
in Science and Mathematics Education
University of Colorado
Boulder, Colorado

Reading Consultant

Robert A. Pavlik
Reading-Language Arts Department
Cardinal Stritch College
Milwaukee, Wisconsin

Special Writers

Laboratories
Alfred DeVito
Science Education
Purdue University
Lafayette, Indiana

Enrichment Features
David Newton
Department of Chemistry
Salem State College
Salem, Massachusetts

Cover: The eastern brook trout is
native to eastern North America.
It lives in ponds and small
streams.

Authors

Michael R. Cohen
School of Education
Indiana University
Indianapolis, Indiana

Bette J. Del Giorno
Science Consultant
Fairfield Public Schools
Fairfield, Connecticut

Jean Durgin Harlan
Education Division
University of Wisconsin, Parkside
Kenosha, Wisconsin

Alan J. McCormack
Science and Mathematics
Teaching Center
College of Education
University of Wyoming
Laramie, Wyoming

John R. Staver
College of Education and
College of Liberal Arts and Sciences
University of Illinois at Chicago
Chicago, Illinois

Scott, Foresman and Company
Editorial Offices: Glenview, Illinois

Regional Offices: Palo Alto, California
Tucker, Georgia • Glenview, Illinois
Oakland, New Jersey • Dallas, Texas

Reviewers and Contributors

Gretchen M. Alexander
Program Coordinator
Museum of Science and Industry
Chicago, Illinois

Daniel W. Ball
Division of Education
Northeast Missouri State University
Kirksville, Missouri

Mary Coban
Teacher
Divine Savior School
Norridge, Illinois

Thomas Graika
Science Chairman
School District 102
LaGrange, Illinois

Robert G. Guy
Science Teacher
Big Lake Elementary School
Sedro Woolley, Washington

Irma G. Hamilton
Science Teacher
Oglethorpe Elementary School
Atlanta, Georgia

Judy Haney
Teacher
East Noble School Corporation
Kendallville, Indiana

Garth P. Harris
Teacher
Lincoln Elementary School
Evanston, Illinois

Edwina Hill
Principal
Oglethorpe Elementary School
Atlanta, Georgia

LaVerne Jackson, Sr.
Science Teacher
Medgar Evers Elementary School
Chicago, Illinois

Hollis R. Johnson
Astronomy Department
Indiana University
Bloomington, Indiana

Irene S. Kantner
Teacher
Lincoln Elementary School
Evanston, Illinois

Sol Krasner
Department of Physics
University of Chicago
Chicago, Illinois

Dolores Mann
Teacher
Glenview Public Schools
Glenview, Illinois

Phillip T. Miyazawa
Instructional Consultant
Science Education
Denver Public Schools
Denver, Colorado

Anita E. Moore
Principal
George Howland Elementary School
Chicago, Illinois

Janet Ostrander
Teacher
Indian Trail School
Highland Park, Illinois

Barbara Scott
Teacher
Crown Magnet School
Chicago, Illinois

Elaine R. Seaman
Teacher
Greenbrier Elementary School
Arlington Heights, Illinois

R. A. Slotter
Department of Chemistry
Northwestern University
Evanston, Illinois

Anita Snell
Coordinator of Primary Education
Spring Branch Independent
School District
Houston, Texas

Lois Spangler
Teacher
Central School
Great Meadows, New Jersey

Carol Leth Stone
Biology Writer
Stanford, California

Johanna F. Strange
Model Laboratory School
Eastern Kentucky University
Richmond, Kentucky

William D. Thomas
Science Supervisor
Escambia County Schools
Pensacola, Florida

Dorothy Wallinga
Christian Schools International
Grand Rapids, Michigan

Les Wallinga
Science Teacher
Calvin Christian Junior High School
Wyoming, Michigan

ISBN: 0-673-42025-6

Copyright © 1986, Scott, Foresman and Company, Glenview, Illinois. All rights Reserved. Printed in the United States of America.

12345678910–VHJ–9493929190898887868685

When You Read This Book

4 Learn the science words.

1 Read the question.

3 Find the answer.

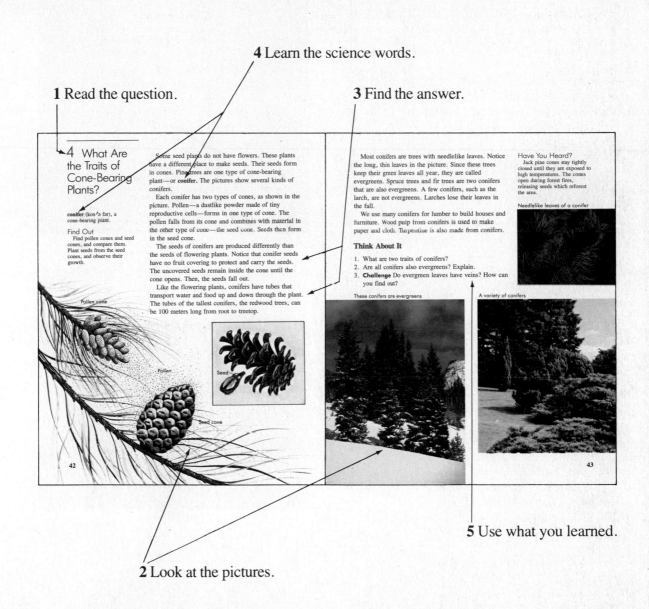

4 What Are the Traits of Cone-Bearing Plants?

conifer (kon′ə fər), a cone-bearing plant.

Find Out

Find pollen cones and seed cones, and compare them. Plant seeds from the seed cones, and observe their growth.

Some seed plants do not have flowers. These plants have a different place to make seeds. Their seeds form in cones. Pine trees are one type of cone-bearing plant—or **conifer.** The pictures show several kinds of conifers.

Each conifer has two types of cones, as shown in the picture. Pollen—a dustlike powder made of tiny reproductive cells—forms in one type of cone. The pollen falls from its cone and combines with material in the other type of cone—the seed cone. Seeds then form in the seed cone.

The seeds of conifers are produced differently than the seeds of flowering plants. Notice that conifer seeds have no fruit covering to protect and carry the seeds. The uncovered seeds remain inside the cone until the cone opens. Then, the seeds fall out.

Like the flowering plants, conifers have tubes that transport water and food up and down through the plant. The tubes of the tallest conifers, the redwood trees, can be 100 meters long from root to treetop.

Pollen cone

Pollen

Seed

Seed cone

42

Most conifers are trees with needlelike leaves. Notice the long, thin leaves in the picture. Since these trees keep their green leaves all year, they are called evergreens. Spruce trees and fir trees are two conifers that are also evergreens. A few conifers, such as the larch, are not evergreens. Larches lose their leaves in the fall.

We use many conifers for lumber to build houses and furniture. Wood pulp from conifers is used to make paper and cloth. Turpentine is also made from conifers.

Think About It

1. What are two traits of conifers?
2. Are all conifers also evergreens? Explain.
3. **Challenge** Do evergreen leaves have veins? How can you find out?

These conifers are evergreens

Have You Heard?

Jack pine cones stay tightly closed until they are exposed to high temperatures. The cones open during forest fires, releasing seeds which reforest the area.

Needlelike leaves of a conifer

A variety of conifers

43

5 Use what you learned.

2 Look at the pictures.

Unit One Classification

Unit Two The Cell

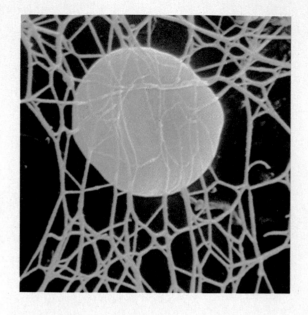

Unit Three Changes Through Time

Unit Four Matter

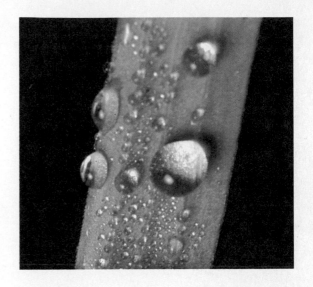

Unit Five Sound

Unit Six Light

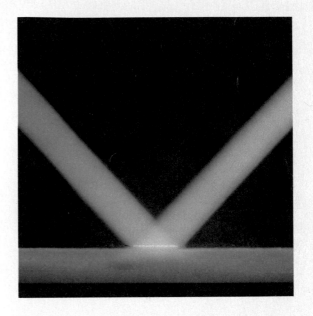

Unit Seven Solar System

Unit Eight The Environment

UNIT ONE
CLASSIFICATION

What is this weird thing
With a funny looking bill
And hind legs that stick out
    like flippers?
Though it looks like a dolphin
    It lays eggs like a chicken.
Aren't you glad it doesn't need
    to wear slippers?

Andy MacFadyen *age 9*

Chapter 1
Grouping Living Things

Imagine trying to guess which animal your friend is thinking of. With a few clues, you might be able to guess. You may already have a picture of an animal in your mind. It is a furry animal with a bushy tail, pointed ears, and a long snout. It is 60 centimeters high at the shoulders, and it eats meat. It hunts alone and is related to the dog. With these clues, you might guess—it is a coyote!

The lessons in this chapter are about the ways scientists use clues to sort and group living things.

1 Identifying Living Things
2 How Can We Tell If Something Is Alive?
3 How Is Classification Useful?
4 What Are the Five Groups of Organisms?

1 Identifying Living Things

Imagine watching *The Glob from Planet X* in a movie theater. As the Glob moves through the city, it swallows trees, cars, and even buildings. Nothing seems to stop the Glob. Bombs do not hurt it, and fire does not burn it. Finally, our hero cuts the Glob in half. But now there are two Globs! Fortunately, the Globs do not grow.

Scientists in the movie work late into the night. They compare the Glob with living things to try to discover—what *is* the Glob? Is it a living thing?

Use the clues above and what you know about living and nonliving things to decide if the Glob is a living thing.

Think About It

1. How is the Glob like a living thing?
2. How is the Glob unlike a living thing?
3. What else do you need to know to decide if the Glob is alive?
4. Draw a picture of the Glob.
5. **Challenge** In what ways are some living and nonliving things alike?

2 How Can We Tell If Something Is Alive?

trait (trāt), something special about an object or organism that makes it what it is.

Organisms produce offspring

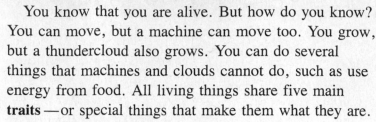

You know that you are alive. But how do you know? You can move, but a machine can move too. You grow, but a thundercloud also grows. You can do several things that machines and clouds cannot do, such as use energy from food. All living things share five main **traits**—or special things that make them what they are.

First, living things—or organisms—grow by using food to make new living material. You grow in both height and weight. A full-sized oak tree grows from a small acorn. Compare the sizes of the tree and the acorn in the pictures.

Second, all organisms can reproduce—or produce new organisms that are like themselves. Notice how much the baby rabbits look like their mother. Newly hatched lizards, tiny, young plants, and sprouting mushrooms are all new organisms that are produced by parent organisms.

Tall oak trees grow from tiny acorns

Trees use energy

Porcupine raising its quills

Third, organisms respond to their environments—or surroundings. The animal in the picture responds to danger by defending itself. A plant responds to light by turning its leaves toward the sun. When your name is called, you respond by answering or looking around.

Fourth, organisms use energy. The energy they use for growing, reproducing, and responding comes from food. A cat uses energy to run at high speeds. The plant in the picture uses energy to grow and to break the rock with its roots.

Fifth, all organisms are made of one or more small units called **cells.** The picture shows an enlarged view of cells from a tree. A cell is the basic building block of life. Cells come in many different shapes and sizes. Most cells are too small to be seen by the unaided eye. Some living things are made of only one cell. A large organism such as a person is made of billions of cells.

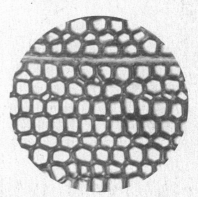
Enlarged cells of a tree

cell (sel), a small unit that makes up living things.

How Are Living Things Identified?

All organisms grow, reproduce, respond, use energy, and are made of cells. A nonliving thing might have one or more of these traits, but it will not have all five traits.

The volcano in the pictures grows when rock and lava from inside the earth build up. It uses energy to erupt. But the volcano cannot reproduce or respond, and it is not made of cells. A volcano is not a living thing.

Some nonliving things were alive at one time. Dead animals and plants are made of cells, but they can no longer grow, respond, reproduce, or use energy. Only living things grow by making cells, so we know that nonliving things with cells were once living things.

Think About It

1. State five traits of living things.
2. What is a cell?
3. **Challenge** Is a seed a living thing? Explain. How could you test your answer?

A volcano grows but is not alive

Discover!

Looking for Life on Mars

Viking 1

Is there life on Mars? Until recently people could only imagine whether life existed on that neighboring planet. In the 1970s, however, we had our first chance to scientifically investigate the question.

In the 1970s several spacecraft were sent from Earth to Mars. Some flew past and took pictures. Others landed on the planet's surface. The *Viking 1* spacecraft in the picture landed on Mars in July of 1976. Several tests were done to try to find out whether life exists on Mars.

First, the Viking lander looked for certain substances in the Martian soil. All life on Earth is made of the same kinds of substances. If life exists on Mars, we should be able to find these substances there too. But Viking found none.

Other tests were designed to investigate possible effects of Martian life. On Earth, living things change materials such as food and water in order to grow and to use energy. They change these materials into new materials. If living things exist on Mars, they probably change materials too. The Viking lander scooped up Martian soil samples to see if the soil contained any small living things. The soil was exposed to food, water, and light. In three different tests new materials were released from the soil. The Martian soil acted as if living things were present.

Some scientists think that the Viking tests show that no life exists on Mars. Others think that the question is still not answered. We might not have looked in enough places on the planet's surface. Viking was able to check only two small spots on the whole planet. We will probably have to wait for more spacecraft to be sent to Mars before we can really answer the question about life on Mars.

9

3 How Is Classification Useful?

Have You Heard?

Machines in banks can sort pennies, dimes, and other coins based on their size and weight.

classify (klas′ə fī), to arrange in groups, according to some system.

structure (struk′chər), the way parts are put together.

Organisms differ in structure

Suppose you want to buy a large can of corn. It will be much easier to find your corn on the sorted shelves than on the unsorted shelves. In a well-organized store, the vegetables are sorted into several large groups—the fresh, frozen, and canned vegetables. The canned vegetables are then sorted into smaller groups, including the canned corn. Next, the canned corn is sorted into smaller groups. In one of these groups are the large cans of corn. Sorting and grouping makes finding and identifying things easier. When you sort and group objects based on their similarities and differences, you **classify** the objects.

The living things on earth can also be classified. You might group animals by their sizes or by whether they make good pets. You might group plants by whether they are safe to eat. There are many ways to classify organisms.

Scientists use one main system to classify organisms. In this system, one way scientists group organisms is by their **structures**—or the ways the parts of the organisms are arranged. Organisms differ in structure both inside and outside their bodies. A duck and a fish have different structures, so they are classified into different groups. A duck has wings, feet, and feathers. A fish has fins and scales. Look at the picture to find other differences in their structures.

Classifying makes finding things easier

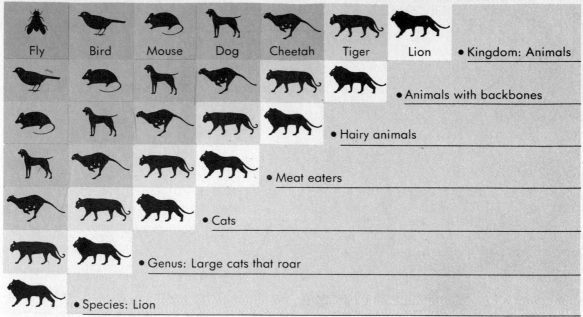

Classification of a lion

Scientists also group organisms by their food needs. Plants can make their own food, but animals cannot. Some animals eat meat, some eat plants, and some eat both plants and other animals.

Like the corn in the grocery store, an organism is first classified into a large group, and then into smaller groups. Look at the picture above to see how a lion is classified. The largest group into which an organism is placed is a **kingdom.** The lion is in the animal kingdom with all the other animals. The kingdom is then sorted, and the lion is classified into smaller and smaller groups. As the groups get smaller, the animals in each group become more similar.

The second-smallest group is the **genus,** which contains organisms that are very similar but not identical. Lions and tigers are in the same genus.

In the smallest group, the **species,** the organisms are all the same kind. A lion is one species, and a tiger is another species. Organisms in one species can produce offspring that are also able to reproduce. Lions produce lions that can produce more lions.

kingdom, a major division in the classification of living things.

genus (jē′nəs), a group to which closely related species belong.

species (spē′shēz), a group of organisms that have traits in common and that are able to produce offspring that can reproduce.

White pine trees

Pine genus

Plant kingdom

How Does Classification Help Us?

Classification helps scientists give a name to each species. Names help people keep order and compare what they know. Each species has a scientific name that no other species has. A scientific name is made up of two words, the genus name and the species name. An African lion is *Panthera leo* (pan ther′ə lē′ō), and a tiger is *Panthera tigris* (tī′gris). When scientists talk about *Panthera leo,* other scientists know exactly which animal they mean. The common name, lion, is not as clear, since African lions and mountain lions are two different species that both have the same common name, lion.

Classification also helps scientists say how they think living things are related. The white pines in the pictures are related to other members of the plant kingdom. But they are most closely related to other pine trees in the same genus. Closely related species have similar structures and food needs. If you want to learn more about an unfamiliar species, you could infer that it is like the other species in its genus.

Think About It

1. What do people do when they classify?
2. What are two traits that scientists use to classify organisms?
3. What are two ways the classification of organisms is useful?
4. **Challenge** In what ways could you classify dogs in a dog show?

Activity

Sorting and Grouping Objects

Purpose
To develop a system for classifying objects.

You Will Need
• a collection of flowers, twigs, seeds, pictures of organisms, or the collection shown in the picture

Directions
1. Look at the objects in your collection. Select 3 or more traits that you can use to classify the objects. Write them down.
2. Organize the objects according to the traits you have selected.
3. Ask a classmate to try to figure out which traits you used to classify the objects. Do not tell your classmate the system you used.
4. Think of another way to group the objects. Write down the traits you select. Sort these objects again. Ask your classmate to try to figure out your second classification system.

Think About It
1. Describe how you sorted the objects. Explain why you sorted them the ways you did.
2. How is each way you sorted the objects useful? Is one way better than the other way?
3. Was your classmate able to figure out your classification systems? Do you think it is important for a classification system to be easy to understand? Explain.
4. **Challenge** Think of two types of objects in your home or school that are sorted in certain ways. Describe the objects and the ways they are sorted.

4 What Are the Five Groups of Organisms?

Find Out

Euglena is an organism that is green like a plant, but it can move. Use an encyclopedia to find more information on *Euglena*.

five kingdoms, system of classification of animals, plants, fungi (fun′jī), protists (prō′tists), and monerans (mə nir′ənz).

Protist kingdom: diatom

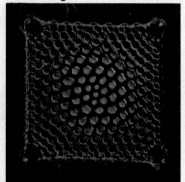

Moneran kingdom: bacteria

Millions of kinds of living things live on the earth. To keep track of them, scientists try to use one main classification system. But, even today, all scientists do not agree how every organism should be classified. At one time, scientists classified all organisms as either animals or plants. But as scientists learned more, they found that some organisms, such as mushrooms, did not really fit into either group. So scientists had to improve the classification system.

Now, many scientists use a classification system with **five kingdoms.** Animals and plants are two of the five kingdoms. The other three kingdoms are fungi, protists, and monerans. A member of each kingdom is shown below. To classify an organism into one of the five kingdoms, scientists look at the main differences among organisms.

It is possible that millions of organisms have not yet been discovered or classified. As they are classified, the system might be changed again.

Fungi kingdom: morel

Plant kingdom: daisies

Animal kingdom: monkeys

14

Bears, salmon, and seagulls are all animals

Whales, birds, insects, people, and the organisms in the picture above are all in the **animal** kingdom. Over a million species of animals have been classified. Animals can be found living in the sea, in the desert, in forests, and on icy mountains. Animals cannot make their own food, so they must get food from other organisms.

When you think of plants, you might think of trees or flowering plants like those shown here. These plants grow on land. The **plant** kingdom also includes plants that grow in water, on rocks, and even twisted around telephone wires. Most plants are green, and they produce their own food.

animals, organisms that have many cells and that cannot make their own food. Most animals can move.

plants, organisms that have many cells, that can make their own food, and that cannot move from place to place.

Trees and flowers: familiar plants

15

Mushroom: a fungus

fungi (fun′jī), organisms, such as mushrooms and molds, that are not green and cannot make their own food. [Singular: fungus (fung′gəs).]

protists (pro′tists), organisms that live in wet places and are made of one or many cells.

monerans (mə nir′ənz), very small organisms, such as bacteria.

One-celled protists

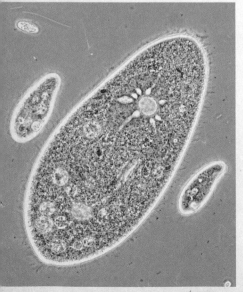

What Are Fungi, Protists, and Monerans?

The picture shows a member of the **fungi** kingdom. Mushrooms, yeasts used to make bread, and molds that grow on old food are all fungi. Some fungi look like plants, but they are really quite different. They are not green, and they cannot make their own food.

Protists live in wet environments, and many protists are made of only one cell. This picture of a protist is greatly enlarged. This protist is so small that thousands could fit in a teaspoon! Seaweed is a large protist made of many cells.

The bacteria in the picture, like most **monerans,** are each made of one cell. Monerans are even smaller than protists. Some species of monerans cause diseases, such as tonsillitis. Other species can make yogurt or cheese from milk.

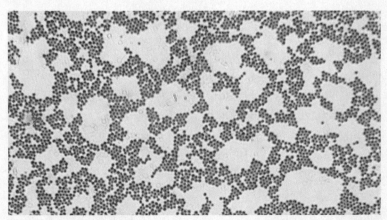

Bacteria are monerans

Think About It

1. Why did most scientists stop using a classification system with just plants and animals?
2. Name the five kingdoms, and give an example of an organism in each kingdom.
3. **Challenge** Explain why a classification system might change.

Tie It Together

Sum It Up

Imagine that you are a news reporter. Write a news story about a newly discovered organism, using the following word list.

grow	animals	scientific name
reproduce	plants	classify
respond	fungi	kingdom
energy	protists	genus
cells	monerans	species

Challenge!

1. How is a candle flame like a living thing? Unlike a living thing?

2. Can its ability to move be a good way to tell if something is living? Give an example to support your answer.

3. Compare the structures of a dog and a cat. Which differences might be used to classify them into different groups?

4. Which part of your home address is like a kingdom? Which part is like a species?

5. Scientists classify newly discovered species by comparing them to species they know. Suppose an organism is discovered on the ocean floor. It is not like anything any scientist has ever seen. Would the classification system have to be changed? Explain.

Science Words

animals	monerans
cell	plants
classify	protists
five kingdoms	species
fungi	structure
genus	trait
kingdom	

Chapter 2
The Animals

This is not a garden of flowers, but it is a garden of animals. These corals, sponges, and starfish live in shallow ocean waters. The animal kingdom includes more than the familiar animals such as dogs and cats. It also includes insects, birds, fish, people, and the organisms in the picture. You would have to travel from the bottoms of the oceans to the tops of mountains to see all the kinds of animals in the world.

The lessons in this chapter describe how the different kinds of animals are grouped.

1 Identifying Animals

2 How Are Animals Grouped?

3 How Are Vertebrates Classified?

4 How Are Invertebrates Classified?

1 Identifying Animals

Notice the variety among the animals in the pictures. An elephant is as large as a truck, and the hummingbird is small enough to sit in a soup spoon. The porcupinefish is as round as a ball, and the stingray is as flat as a pancake. Animals come in many sizes, shapes, and colors.

Ask a classmate to think of an animal and to write down the animal's name. Ask yes or no questions to find out which animal your classmate picked. You might ask if the animal is bigger than a loaf of bread or if it has four legs. Once you have guessed the animal, it is your turn to pick an animal and let your classmate guess.

You get one mark for every question you ask. The student with the fewest marks wins. If you ask questions about traits, such as size or structure, instead of guessing names, you will have fewer questions to ask.

Think About It

1. Which type of question made it possible for you to infer the name of the animal?
2. How could you reduce the number of questions you have to ask?
3. **Challenge** Besides appearance, what are other ways to identify animals?

Stingray

Porcupinefish

Hummingbird

Elephants

2 How Are Animals Grouped?

Animals are a major group of living things. Animals are classified into the same kingdom because they are alike in several ways. First, every animal, from the tiniest insect to the largest whale, is made of many cells. Second, animals cannot make their own food. They eat or take in food from other organisms. Third, most animals are able to move at some time in their lives.

No one knows exactly how many species of animals there are. Scientists estimate that several million species live on the earth. Animals live in every type of environment. The picture shows animals that live in forests, deserts, oceans, and on icy mountains. Think of other places where animals live.

Even though all animals are alike in some ways, they are different in other ways. Look for differences among the animals in the picture. Animals can have two legs, four legs, one hundred legs, or no legs at all. Some animals are furry, and others are slippery or spiny. The picture shows animals that swim, fly, or walk, and even animals that never move.

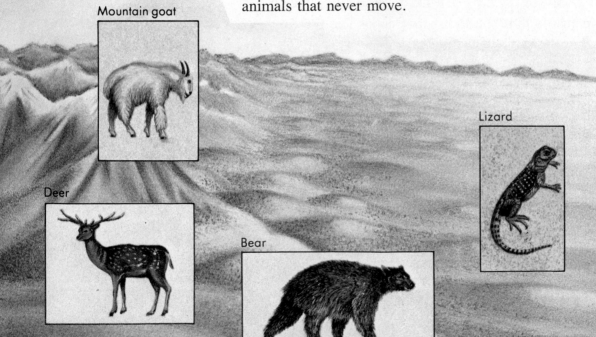

Mountain goat

Deer

Bear

Lizard

One main difference among animals is that some have backbones and others do not. Scientists divide the animal kingdom into two groups, based on this difference. **Vertebrates** are animals with backbones. You are a member of the vertebrate group. Feel your backbone running down the center of your back. Your backbone helps support your body, and it helps you move. Birds, snakes, frogs, and fish are also vertebrates. Notice the backbones in the animals shown here.

The other group includes the animals without backbones—the **invertebrates.** Insects, worms, starfish, and snails are a few members of this group. Since they have no backbones, invertebrates support their bodies in other ways. For example, insects have hard outer coverings, and snails have shells for support.

Think About It

1. How are all animals alike?
2. What are the two major groups of animals?
3. **Challenge** Could you walk if you did not have a backbone? Explain.

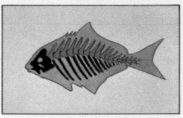

Vertebrates have backbones

vertebrate (vėr′tə brit), an animal with a backbone.

invertebrate (in vėr′tə brit), an animal without a backbone.

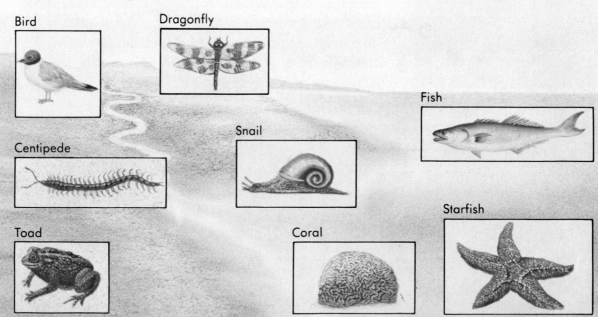

Bird

Dragonfly

Centipede

Snail

Fish

Toad

Coral

Starfish

3 How Are Vertebrates Classified?

endothermic (en′dō thėr′mik), able to keep a constant body temperature by producing one's own body heat.

mammal (mam′əl), an endothermic vertebrate that gives milk and has hair and lungs.

Bat

Dolphin

Cat giving milk to its kittens

The vertebrates can be divided into five smaller groups. In the first two groups, the animal's body temperature stays about the same even if the animal is in a hot or cold environment. These animals that have constant body temperatures are called warm-blooded—or **endothermic.** They can make heat in their bodies, and they can control how much heat they hold in. A body covering of hair or feathers helps hold the heat in. Keeping warm takes a great deal of energy, so endothermic animals must eat often.

One group of endothermic vertebrates includes the animals in the pictures. They are all **mammals,** the only group of animals with hair. Hair helps hold in their body heat. Dogs or horses have a great deal of hair—or fur. Other mammals, such as dolphins, have very little hair.

Mammals are the only animals that give milk to their young. The cat in the picture is giving milk to its kittens. Most mammals have babies that grow inside the mother. A few mammals, such as the *platypus* (plat′ə pəs), lay eggs but still give milk.

All mammals have lungs to breathe air. Water mammals, such as whales or dolphins, must come to the surface of the water to breathe.

Mammals also differ in many ways. Study the pictures to see how mammals differ in structure, size, and habitat—or where they live.

Canada goose

Ostrich

Penguin

If you found a feather, it would not be hard to guess from which type of animal it came. A second group of endothermic vertebrates, the birds, are the only animals with feathers. Feathers help keep birds warm. Notice the long feathers on the wings of this goose. It is hard to see each separate feather on the penguin because the feathers are so small and close together.

Most birds can fly, because their bodies are built for flying. Wings with feathers lift the birds into the air. Hollow bones make their bodies light. Some birds, such as this ostrich, cannot fly. Its body is too heavy, and its wings are too small.

Like mammals, birds have lungs to breathe air. But unlike mammals, all birds lay eggs. Many birds build nests where they keep the eggs warm until the eggs hatch.

Notice the different sizes, shapes, and colors of the birds in the pictures. Birds can either fly or walk. Other birds can also swim. Ducks and geese produce oil for their feathers. The oil sheds water and helps the birds float. Penguins cannot fly, but their wings help them swim underwater.

Have You Heard?

The frigate bird is such a good flier that it can dive from the air, catch a fish at the water's surface, and fly off again. The frigate's wingspread is almost 2 times as long as your height, but the frigate weighs only as much as 2 or 3 loaves of bread.

Collared lizard

Bullfrog

What Are the Ectothermic Animals?

Mammals and birds are warm-blooded animals. The three other groups of vertebrates are cold-blooded animals. This term does not mean their blood is cold. A cold-blooded—or **ectothermic**—animal produces some heat, but it cannot control its body temperature, and it has no hair or feathers to hold in the heat. The animal gets heat from its surroundings. It might sit in the sun to get warm or in the shade to cool off. The ectothermic animals have changing body temperatures. They do not need to eat very often because they depend on their surroundings instead of their bodies for heat.

One group of ectothermic vertebrates is the **reptiles,** which includes the turtles, crocodiles, snakes, and lizards. Notice the scales on the reptile's dry skin. Reptiles have lungs, and they live on land, where they lay eggs. Some reptiles, such as turtles, swim in water.

Frogs, toads, and salamanders are in another group of ectothermic vertebrates—the **amphibians.** When amphibians are young, they live in water, like this tadpole. They have gills to get air. Later in life, most amphibians' bodies change, and they live on land. The tadpole loses its gills, grows lungs and legs, and becomes a frog. Most amphibians return to the water as adults to lay their eggs.

The skin of amphibians has no covering. Some amphibians, such as this frog, have smooth, moist skin. Others, such as toads, have bumpy, dry skin.

Tadpole

24

Blue ribbon eel

Big-spotted triggerfish

A third group of ectothermic vertebrates is the fish. Fish have scales, and they live in the water all their lives. Notice how their bodies are built for life in the water. Fish have fins for swimming and gills for taking in air. Fish, like amphibians, lay eggs in the water.

Look at the variety of shapes in these fish. Another way fish differ is in where they live. Some fish live in oceans, and others live in freshwater lakes and streams.

Think About It

1. Name the five groups of vertebrates, and list three traits of each group.
2. Define endothermic and ectothermic. Which groups of vertebrates are endothermic? Ectothermic?
3. **Challenge** Reptiles are more abundant in warm climates than in cold climates. Explain.

Have You Heard?

The largest fish known is a kind of shark that is 15 m long—the height of a 4-story building.

Whitetip shark

4 How Are Invertebrates Classified?

arthropod (är′thrə pod), an invertebrate with jointed legs and an exoskeleton.

exoskeleton (ek′sō skel′ə tən), a hard outside covering that protects and supports an arthropod.

We may be more familiar with the vertebrates. But about nine-tenths of the kinds of animals in the world are invertebrates. We divide the invertebrates into many groups.

The first group—the **arthropods**—includes the animals shown on this page. There are more species of arthropods than all the other species of invertebrates and vertebrates combined.

Arthropods do not have bones inside their bodies. They have a hard outside covering called an **exoskeleton.** An exoskeleton is waterproof and is like a coat of armor that protects and supports the animal. The soft body parts are inside the exoskeleton. In order to grow, the animal sheds its exoskeleton, as the picture of the lobster shows. The animal makes a larger exoskeleton to fit its body.

The arthropods have many pairs of legs that are also covered by the exoskeleton. The exoskeleton is hard, so the legs only bend at the joints of the exoskeleton.

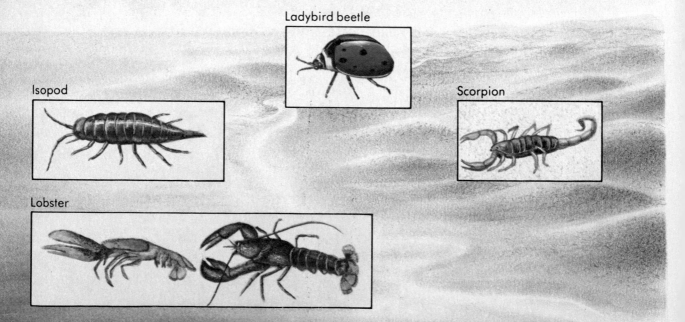

Ladybird beetle

Isopod

Scorpion

Lobster

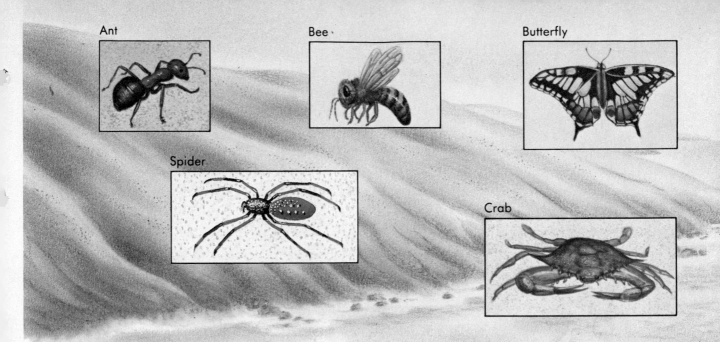

Ant

Bee

Butterfly

Spider

Crab

The arthropods are divided into several types. Insects are one type of arthropod. The ant, bee, and butterfly in the pictures are some insects you might know. You can identify an insect in two ways. All insects have six legs. They also have three main parts to their bodies, as the picture of the ant shows.

Many different species of insects live on the earth. Most insects live on land, but some live in water. The total number of insects alive at any one time might be as high as a billion billion. One reason for the large number of insects is that they can reproduce very rapidly. A mosquito can produce hundreds of eggs at one time.

Some insects are helpful to people. These insects pollinate flowers or eat harmful pests. Other insects are pests themselves. They destroy crops and carry diseases.

Besides insects, another type of arthropod includes the spiders. They have eight legs and two main parts to their bodies. Most spiders live on land.

Crabs, shrimp, and lobsters belong to still another type of arthropod. Most of these arthropods live in water, and many are important foods for people.

Have You Heard?
Insects are the only invertebrates that can fly.

Mollusk with pink foot

Starfish opening clam

Purple sea urchin

mollusk (mol′əsk), an invertebrate with a muscular foot, a soft body, and, usually, a hard shell.

How Are Other Invertebrates Classified?

The shells above come from another group of invertebrates—the **mollusks.** All mollusks have soft bodies, and most mollusks have shells. The shells protect their soft bodies. A few mollusks, such as the octopus, do not have shells. Also, each mollusk has a muscular foot that it uses for moving. Notice that a mollusk's foot does not look like your foot.

Notice the variety among the mollusks. Some mollusks live in the water, and some live on land. Oysters are mollusks that make pearls. Snails in a fish tank are another kind of mollusk.

Starfish are members of another invertebrate group—the spiny-skinned animals. Notice that the animals in this group have spines. They also have tiny tube feet that work like suction cups. They use the tube feet for moving and feeling. The starfish uses its tube feet to open a clam shell so it can eat the soft body inside. Another way the spiny-skinned animals are alike is that they all live in the oceans.

Not all spiny-skinned animals are starfish. The picture shows a sea urchin with very long spines.

Worms are another group of invertebrates. They are slender, crawling, creeping, or swimming animals. Worms have soft bodies and no legs. The worms can be divided into three types.

One type is the flatworms. The picture shows a flatworm shaped like a flat piece of tape. Some flatworms live in water. Others live inside plants or other animals and find food within the other organisms.

Another type—the roundworms—are shaped like round tubes with pointed ends. Compare the shape of the roundworm with the shapes of the other worms. Roundworms live in the soil, in water, or inside other organisms. One kind of roundworm lives in the intestines of dogs and makes the dogs sick.

A third type of worm is the segmented worms that are made of many small segments or sections. Most segmented worms live in the oceans. Some live in the soil. You may have seen segmented worms, such as the earthworm in the picture. They burrow through the soil and break it up. The loose soil then has space for the air and water needed by plants. Other segmented worms, the leeches, live in the water. Leeches get on the skin of other animals and suck their blood.

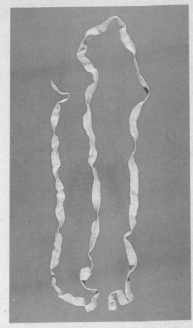

Flatworm

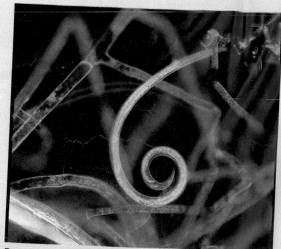

Roundworm

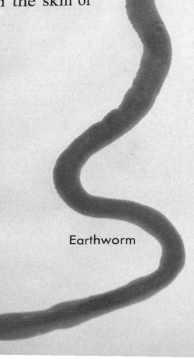

Earthworm

29

Jellyfish

Coral

Find Out
What is a coral reef, and how is it formed?

What Are Some Other Invertebrates?

The jellyfish and coral in the pictures are shaped like hollow bags. These hollow-bodied animals are another group of invertebrates. Food comes into the opening of the bag, and waste goes out through the same opening. Around the edge of the bag's opening are long stingers that can sting and capture small animals.

Hollow-bodied animals live in the oceans or in fresh water. Jellyfish and coral are two kinds of hollow-bodied animals.

Sponges are another group of invertebrates. All sponges live in water, where they stay attached to one spot and do not move. Sponges have many holes in their bodies. Tiny bits of food wash in through the holes. Wastes wash out through a large opening at the top of the sponge.

Most of the objects we call sponges and use for cleaning are made of plastic. Perhaps you have seen a real sponge like the dried one in the picture. Compare the dried sponge to the living sponge on the left.

Think About It

1. Name six groups of invertebrates, and list two traits for each group.
2. Which invertebrate groups live only in water?
3. **Challenge** How would you classify a land animal with a hard outer covering and many legs?

Living sponges in ocean

Dried sponge

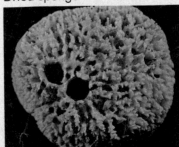

Do You Know?

The Octopus Is a Mollusk Without a Shell

An octopus can change color

Some people think of the octopus as a giant creature that they have seen in science-fiction movies. But, the octopus is a shy animal that is usually less than 30 centimeters across.

The name tells you that the octopus has eight (*octo-*) arms. The octopus uses its arms to walk on the ocean floor. Its arms are also used to capture crabs—its favorite food. The octopus bites into the crab with its strong beak and sends a poison into the crab's body.

The octopus protects itself in three ways. First, when frightened, the octopus can push water from its body in a powerful stream. This action pushes the octopus forward very rapidly, allowing it to escape.

Second, the body of an octopus has a special sac that holds a dark, inklike fluid. When a predator comes close, the octopus squirts some of this fluid and then swims away. All that the predator sees is a dark cloud in the water where the octopus was. Meanwhile, the octopus has escaped.

Finally, the octopus's body changes color when the octopus is excited or frightened. When an octopus sees a crab, patches of pink, purple, or blue appear on the octopus's skin. At the sight of a predator, such as a moray eel, an octopus changes color. Because of this change in color, the octopus seems to disappear into the background of its hiding place. Then, the eel predator might not find the octopus.

An escaping octopus

31

Activity

Designing a Zoo

Purpose
To classify animals.

You Will Need
- paper
- pencil
- colored markers

Directions
1. Make a list of animals. Include 1 or 2 animals from each group of vertebrates and invertebrates.
2. Make a copy of the map of the zoo on this page. Decide where each animal will live, and label your map with the animal's name. Group the animals any way you wish. You may use land and water environments. The animals may live indoors or outdoors. Several animals might live in the same environment. Add anything that the animals need, such as trees or islands. Design your zoo so that visitors can find each animal easily.

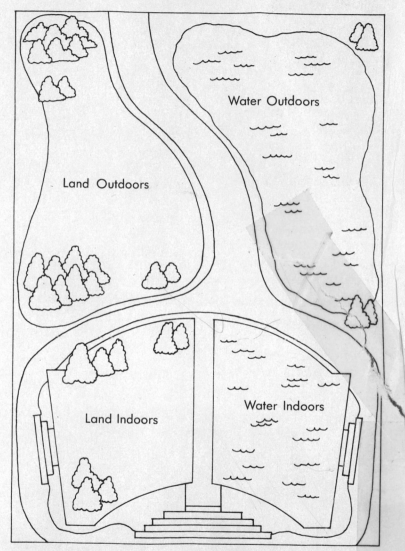

Land Outdoors

Water Outdoors

Land Indoors

Water Indoors

Think About It
1. Write a television commercial telling how the arrangement of your zoo is special.
2. How would you design your zoo differently if you lived in a different climate?
3. **Challenge** In your climate, can the ectothermic animals live outside all year? Explain.

Tie It Together

Sum It Up

Number your paper from 1 to 15. Match each description below with the correct type of animal in the diagram.

1. lives first in water, then on land
2. most have a shell
3. has slender, soft body and no legs
4. constant body temperature
5. has hair
6. has tube feet
7. has scales and gills
8. has holes where food washes in
9. has backbone
10. changing body temperature
11. has feathers
12. has bag-shaped body with stingers
13. has exoskeleton
14. has no backbone
15. has scales and lungs

Challenge!

1. How is a backbone like the poles in a tent?
2. Why is *temperature-changing* a better term than *cold-blooded?*
3. How would you classify a sea horse—an animal with fins, gills, and a backbone?
4. Suppose one insect laid 100 eggs. The new insect from each egg then laid 100 eggs. Then, the new insect from each of those eggs laid 100 eggs. How many insects would you have if none died?
5. How would you classify a sand dollar—a round, flat animal with tube feet?

Science Words

amphibian	invertebrate
arthropod	mammal
ectothermic	mollusk
endothermic	reptile
exoskeleton	vertebrate

Classification of Animals

a. Vertebrates				
b. Endothermic animals		c. Ectothermic animals		
d. Mammals	e. Birds	f. Reptiles	g. Amphibians	h. Fish

i. Invertebrates					
j. Arthropods	k. Mollusks	l. Spiny-skinned animals	m. Worms	n. Hollow-bodied animals	o. Sponges

Chapter 3
The Plants

People make use of every part of the coconut palm tree. You may have eaten the white part inside the coconut or used soap made from coconut oil. The leaves are woven to make roofs, baskets, and hats. People make a drink from the flower, furniture from the stem, and bowls from the shell.

Plants are important to people in many ways. In fact, you could not live without plants.

The lessons in this chapter will show you many kinds of plants, from towering trees to tiny mosses.

1 Observing the Plant World

Plants release oxygen that people breathe. Plants also provide much of the food we eat. Many of our clothes and homes are made from plants.

Find five objects in your classroom that are made from plants. To get ideas, note the objects in the picture. All are made from plants. Find out the plant from which each object is made. Try to find out from which part of the plant each object is made.

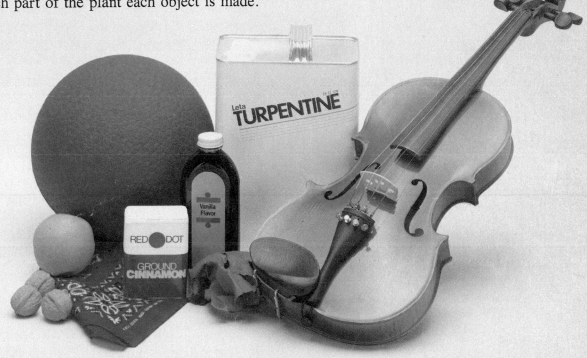

Think About It

1. Make a chart of the objects that come from plants and of the names of the plants from which the objects come.
2. Which plant products do you use every day? Which could you live without?
3. **Challenge** How would your classroom be different if it contained no objects made from plants?

2 How Are Plants Alike and Different?

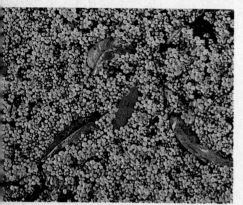

Duckweed plants

cell wall, the stiff outer covering of a plant cell.

chlorophyll (klôr′ə fil), green material found in plants and used for making food.

Plant cell

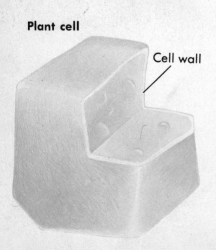

Cell wall

Redwood tree

This tree is so tall that you barely notice the man standing next to it. The plants in the other picture are so small that you could hold hundreds of them in your hand. But these and all other plants are alike in certain ways.

All plants share four traits. First, all plants are made of many cells. Like animals, no plant has just one cell. Second, a plant cell has a **cell wall** —a stiff covering around the cell, as the picture shows. The sturdy cell walls make wood hard and celery tough and stringy.

Third, plants can make their own food. To make food, plants use light, water, the gas carbon dioxide, and **chlorophyll**—a green material in the leaves and other parts of the plant. Chlorophyll gives plants their green color. The food-making process is photosynthesis.

Fourth, plants are usually fixed in one place. They cannot move around as animals do. But they can move in some ways, such as the way a Venus's-flytrap closes its leaves to catch an insect.

Fern: a seedless plant

Cherry tree: a flowering plant

Pine branch with cones

All plants are alike in some ways, but they differ in other ways. Plants differ in the ways they reproduce. Some plants, such as this cherry tree, grow from covered seeds made in flowers. Other plants, such as pine trees, grow from uncovered seeds on cones, like those in the picture. Some plants have no seeds. The fern in the picture is one kind of plant without seeds.

Plants also differ in their structure. Many plants contain transport tubes that carry water and food. Some of the tubes carry water from the roots to the top of the plant. Other tubes carry food from the leaves to the stem and roots. Some types of plants have no transport tubes. Water and food move through these plants by moving from one cell to the next.

Think About It

1. What are four traits of all plants?
2. Describe two ways plants differ.
3. **Challenge** What are other ways that plants differ?

Have You Heard?

The largest known fruit is the double coconut. It can weigh up to 27 kg—as much as a 9-year-old child.

3 What Are the Traits of Flowering Plants?

More than a quarter of a million different kinds of flowering plants live on our earth. Most plants, such as wildflowers, garden plants, and trees, live on land. Some flowering plants, such as water lilies, live in the water. Notice the variety among the flowers in the picture.

Many of our foods come from flowering plants. We grind up grains, such as wheat and oats, to make flour for bread. We eat leaves, stems, roots, fruits, and seeds from other flowering plants.

Flowering plants all have flowers, but not all flowers are alike. The drawing shows a cut-open flower. While all flowers contain the reproductive parts of the plant, other parts of the flower differ. Many flowers have colorful petals. But the flower of the maple tree in the picture has no petals. The maple flower is so small that we rarely notice it. Grasses and elm trees also have flowers that we rarely see.

A typical flower

Maple flowers have no petals

Flowers of many shapes, sizes, and colors

Inside the seed of a flowering plant is a tiny, new plant. The seed also contains food for the new plant to use as it starts to grow.

The seeds of all flowering plants grow inside fruits that cover and protect the seeds. The fruit covering also helps the seeds be carried to new places, where the seeds can grow. Animals carry some fruits, and the wind and water carry other fruits. We usually think of fruits as sweet and juicy like the apple in the picture. But some fruits, such as nuts, are dry and hard. This acorn is the dry fruit of the oak tree. The milkweed pod is a fruit that contains seeds connected to fuzzy threads.

Have You Heard?

The century plant gets its name because it only blooms once in a very long time, although not quite as long as a century. The plant produces a flower cluster on a stalk as much as 12 m high. Then, the plant dies.

Acorn

Apple

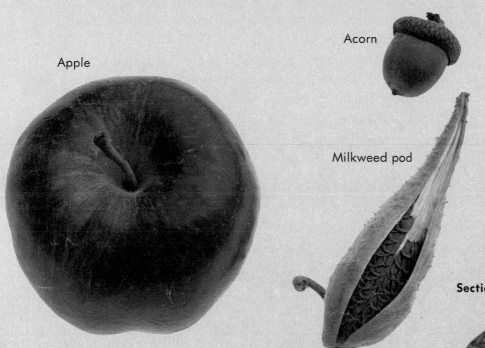

Milkweed pod

Section of a tree trunk

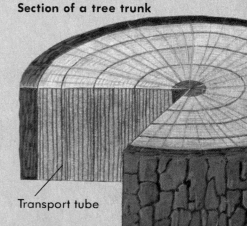

Transport tube

All flowering plants contain narrow tubes that transport water and food through the plant. The tubes in the leaves—the veins—are easy to see. Sometimes you can see transport tubes if you cut open a stem. In the picture of a tree trunk, notice that the rings are bundles of transport tubes.

Peanut

Violet

Lettuce

Dicots

How Are Flowering Plants Grouped?

Flowering plants can be classified into two groups. One group has seeds that can be split into two pieces, such as the peanut. Each piece is a seed leaf—a leaflike structure in the seed. Plants in this group are **dicots.** *Di* means "two," and *cot* is short for the word that means "seed leaf."

Notice the number of petals on the violet. Dicot flowers have four or five petals or a multiple of four or five. The veins in the leaves of dicots form net patterns, as in the lettuce leaf. Many shade trees, fruits, and vegetables are dicots.

The other group of flowering plants—the **monocots**—have only one seed leaf, as in the kernel of corn. *Mono* means "one." The flowers of monocots have petals in multiples of three, as in the lily. Veins in monocot leaves do not form net patterns, but often run in straight lines, as in the grass leaves.

Think About It

1. State two traits of the flowering plants.
2. What are three differences between dicots and monocots?
3. **Challenge** Why do you think that many flowering plants are important foods for people?

dicot (dī′kot), a flowering plant with two seed leaves in its seeds.

monocot (mon′ə kot), a flowering plant with one seed leaf in its seeds.

Monocots

Corn

Lily

Grass

Discover!

Lifesaving Plants

Pink periwinkle

Doctors are always trying to find new ways to cure sickness. Some of the newest ways of treating disease use an idea that is thousands of years old.

For a long time, people have used plants to treat injuries and to cure disease. But when chemists in the 1930s started making medicines in laboratories, some people began to think of plant medicines as "old-fashioned." Today, however, there is a growing interest in medicines that come from plants.

You may have seen the tiny pink or white flowers of the periwinkle. This plant, shown in the picture, has two chemicals that are now being used to fight two common types of cancer. These chemicals have helped many people regain their health.

Another plant, the foxglove, can be recognized by its pink, bell-shaped flowers, shown in the picture. This plant is poisonous if eaten. But, if it is used carefully, the same chemical that makes the plant poisonous can be used as medicine for people with heart problems. This medicine, called digitalis, has saved many lives.

The snakeroot plant grows in most tropical parts of the world. From the snakelike roots of this plant comes a medicine that is used to treat high blood pressure.

Chemicals from many other plants might someday be used to fight disease. American Indians and people from other parts of the world, such as South America, Asia, and Africa have used medicines in plants for thousands of years. Scientists are studying how people from all over the world use plants as medicines. They hope to find many more lifesaving uses of plants.

Foxglove

Snakeroot

4 What Are the Traits of Cone-Bearing Plants?

conifer (kon′ə fər), a cone-bearing plant.

Find Out

Find pollen cones and seed cones, and compare them. Plant seeds from the seed cones, and observe their growth.

Some seed plants do not have flowers. These plants have a different place to make seeds. Their seeds form in cones. Pine trees are one type of cone-bearing plant—or **conifer.** The pictures show several kinds of conifers.

Each conifer has two types of cones, as shown in the picture. Pollen—a dustlike powder made of tiny reproductive cells—forms in one type of cone. The pollen falls from its cone and combines with material in the other type of cone—the seed cone. Seeds then form in the seed cone.

The seeds of conifers are produced differently than the seeds of flowering plants. Notice that conifer seeds have no fruit covering to protect and carry the seeds. The uncovered seeds remain inside the cone until the cone opens. Then, the seeds fall out.

Like the flowering plants, conifers have tubes that transport water and food up and down through the plant. The tubes of the tallest conifers, the redwood trees, can be 100 meters long from root to treetop.

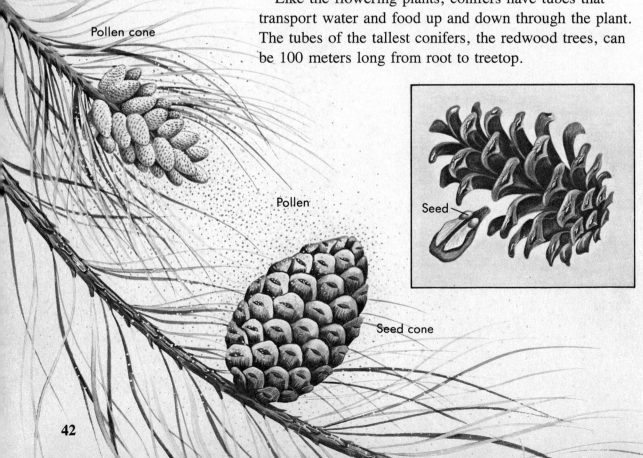

Pollen cone

Pollen

Seed cone

Seed

42

Most conifers are trees with needlelike leaves. Notice the long, thin leaves in the picture. Since these trees keep their green leaves all year, they are called evergreens. Spruce trees and fir trees are two conifers that are also evergreens. A few conifers, such as the larch, are not evergreens. Larches lose their leaves in the fall.

We use many conifers for lumber to build houses and furniture. Wood pulp from conifers is used to make paper and cloth. Turpentine is also made from conifers.

Think About It

1. What are two traits of conifers?
2. Are all conifers also evergreens? Explain.
3. **Challenge** Do evergreen leaves have veins? How can you find out?

Have You Heard?

Jack pine cones stay tightly closed until they are exposed to high temperatures. The cones open during forest fires, releasing seeds which reforest the area.

Needlelike leaves of a conifer

These conifers are evergreens

A variety of conifers

5 Which Plants Have No Seeds?

Underside of a fern leaf with spore cases

Some plants have neither flowers nor cones to produce seeds. These plants reproduce without seeds. These plants produce **spores** —tiny reproductive cells that grow into new plants. One plant might make millions of spores, but only some of the spores live to make new plants.

Ferns are one type of seedless plant. The spores of many ferns grow on the underside of the leaves, as shown in the picture. Each brown dot is not an insect, but a cluster of spore cases. Each case holds many spores.

Like flowering plants and conifers, ferns have transport tubes to carry food and water. Ferns also have very large leaves that grow from underground stems. Most ferns grow on land in damp, shady environments, as in the picture. You can find ferns growing in the woods. Ferns grow well in the tropics, where some grow as large as trees.

Ferns in a damp, shady environment

Moss is another type of seedless plant. The spores of a moss form in a capsule on top of a small stalk, as the picture shows. The capsule opens to let out the spores.

Mosses do not have transport tubes that move food and water through the plant. Instead, food and water move slowly from one cell to another. If mosses were large plants, they would dry out before water could get to the tops of the plants. For this reason, mosses are small like the one in the picture.

Like ferns, mosses live in shady, damp environments on land. They grow on mountains, in forests, and even on rocks. Often, many moss plants grow close together and look like a smooth, green carpet. The picture shows a group of mosses.

Think About It

1. List two traits of the ferns and two traits of the mosses.
2. Where do spores grow on ferns? On mosses?
3. **Challenge** Under what conditions might a plant without transport tubes grow to a large size?

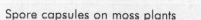
Spore capsules on moss plants

Mosses on rocks and trees

Have You Heard?
Peat is made from mosses that have been pressed in the ground for thousands of years. It is used instead of wood as fuel in Scotland and Ireland.

Activity

Experimenting with Ferns and Mosses

Purpose

To predict the growth of ferns and mosses under different conditions.

You Will Need

- soil (humus or sandy soil)
- gravel
- a clear, clean, wide-mouth, plastic or glass container
- fern and moss
- plastic wrap and rubber band (if container has no lid)
- water

Directions

1. Place a layer of gravel a few centimeters deep on the bottom of the container.
2. Cover the gravel with soil. Make the layer of soil 5–6 cm deep, as in the picture.
3. Dig a small hole in the soil, and plant the fern in the hole. Be careful not to break the roots. Gently press soil around the roots.
4. Plant the moss by gently placing it on the soil near the fern.
5. Water the soil until water seeps down to the gravel. Do not flood the plants.
6. Cover the container with a lid or with plastic wrap held on by a rubber band.
7. Your teacher will tell you to put your terrarium in one of these environments: 1) warm and sunny, 2) warm and shady, 3) cool and sunny, or 4) cool and shady. Other students will put their containers in the other environments. Predict which environment will best promote the growth of ferns and mosses.
8. Observe the terrariums every day for several days or more. Notice if the plants grow or wilt or if they change in color.

Think About It

1. In which environment do ferns and mosses grow best? Was your prediction correct? Explain.
2. How does the lid on your terrarium affect the plants' environment?
3. Count the number of spore case clusters on the underside of a fern leaf. If each cluster holds 6,400 spores, how many spores are there on the leaf?
4. **Challenge** What could you add to your terrarium to make it more like a woodland environment?

Tie It Together

Sum It Up

Number your paper from 1–12. On your paper, write the word or words that complete each sentence. The letters in the boxes will spell a hidden name.

1. _ _ _ _ _ _ □ _ _ _ _ is the coloring material needed by plants to make food.

2. A _ _ □ _ _ _ _ _ _ is the stiff outer covering of a plant cell.

3. A _ _ _ _ _ _ □ _ is found in the seed and contains food for a new flowering plant.

4. A plant with three petals, one seed leaf, and veins in lines is a _ _ □ _ _ _ _.

5. A _ _ _ _ □ has four or five petals, two seed leaves, and net veins.

6. Moss spores are found in capsules on short _ _ _ _ □ _.

7. A plant with naked seeds is a _ _ _ □ _ _ _.

8. A _ _ _ □ has spores and transport tubes.

9. The seeds of a _ _ _ _ _ _ _ _ □ _ _ _ _ _ are found inside fruits.

10. A _ _ _ □ is made in a flower or cone.

11. A _ _ □ _ _ is a tiny reproductive cell.

12. A □ _ _ _ has spores but no transport tubes.

Hidden name: _ _ _ _ _ _ _ _ _ _ _

Challenge!

1. How are plants and animals alike? How are they different?

2. Is a flowering plant with six petals a monocot or dicot?

3. How do the seeds of flowering plants and conifers differ?

4. Describe where and how seeds are formed in a conifer.

5. Compare the movement of water in a fern and a moss.

Science Words

cell wall

chlorophyll

conifer

dicot

monocot

spore

Chapter 4
Fungi, Protists, and Monerans

If you were to see these objects in the woods, you might think they were tiny birds' nests. In fact, they are alive just like the trees and animals around them! But these organisms do not belong to the plant or animal kingdoms. They belong to another of the five kingdoms of living things.

The lessons in this chapter describe three kingdoms of living things. You might be surprised to learn how much you come into contact with these organisms.

1 Growing Unseen Organisms

You live among billions of unseen organisms. They live in the air, water, and soil. They also live on objects and even inside other organisms! You can trap and grow these organisms on bread.

Take two slices of bread from the same loaf. Lay one slice flat in a clear plastic bag, and tie the end. Mark this bag *D* for *dry*. Next, carefully sprinkle the surface of the other slice with water. Place this slice in another clear bag, and tie the end. Mark this bag *W* for *wet*. Keep both bags in a warm, dark place for the next few days. Keep the bags closed. Check the bags every day, and record any changes you see through the plastic.

Think About It

1. Which bread slice shows the most changes? Describe these changes.
2. What do you think caused these changes?
3. **Challenge** Name four ways in which organisms might have reached the bread.

2 Which Organisms Are Fungi?

absorb (ab sôrb′), to take in.

Find Out

Look in magazines and science books to find pictures of the many kinds of fungi. Some examples to look for are sac fungi, cup fungi, jelly fungi, mildews, smuts, rusts, morels, puffballs, and shaggy mane fungi.

Threads grow from spores

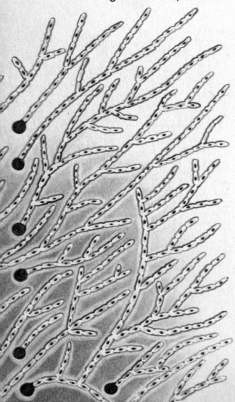

How would you classify the parts of a pizza? The red sauce comes from tomatoes that belong to the plant kingdom. Onions and green peppers are also plants. The cheese is made from the milk of an animal, a cow. But mushrooms do not fit into either kingdom.

Mushrooms, along with molds and yeasts, belong to the fungus kingdom. Altogether, there are about 100,000 different kinds of fungi on earth.

Fungi do not have chlorophyll for making food. Instead, fungi must get their food from other organisms. Fungi usually grow as fuzzy threads on dead plant or animal matter, as shown in these pictures. The threads take in—or absorb—food from the matter. As the threads absorb more food, the matter slowly breaks apart into the soil.

Some fungi grow on living things. The fungi absorb food from these organisms. One kind of fungus causes Dutch elm disease in trees. Another kind causes athlete's foot in people.

Most fungi reproduce with spores. Fungi make the spores in caps, capsules, or cases. The wind often blows the spores away from the fungi. The spores fall on dead organisms. Then, a tiny cell breaks out of each spore. As the picture shows, these cells grow into the fuzzy threads and spread over the dead organism. In time, the threads form new caps, capsules, or cases.

Fuzzy threads of a fungus

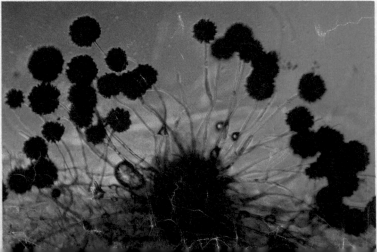

Mushrooms found in woods

A poisonous mushroom

Mushrooms are one type of fungus. Mushrooms such as the ones in the pictures above grow on lawns or near logs. Above ground, mushrooms often grow stalks that hold caps. Spores form inside the caps. But below ground, mushrooms form a wide network of threads among the plant and animal matter.

Mushrooms are different from one another in two ways. First, different species of mushrooms grow different kinds of caps, as shown in the pictures. Second, some mushrooms are safe to eat, but other mushrooms store a poison. Only mushroom experts can tell the difference between a safe and a poisonous mushroom.

Molds, another kind of fungus, are alike in these ways. First, molds look like cotton patches. Next, molds are so small that you need a hand lens to see their threads. Finally, a tiny stalk rises from each thread. Each stalk holds a spore capsule.

The spore capsules give many molds their colors. The capsules can be black, brown, gray, green, white, red, and even pink! The picture shows the brown capsules of a common mold that grows on bread.

Molds are different from one another in the places they live. Some molds live on dead organisms in the water. Others live on the **organic matter** in the soil. Still other molds can live on foods, such as fruits, seeds, breads, and soups.

organic (ôr gan′ik) **matter,** material that is part of a living or dead organism.

Find Out

Look up *fairy ring* in a library or science book, and write a short report for your class.

A close-up view of bread mold

What Are Yeasts?

Yeasts are fungi, but they are different from other fungi in some ways. Each yeast is made of only one cell. Also, yeasts can reproduce by the two ways shown here. In **budding,** a tiny cell grows out from a larger yeast cell. The tiny cell grows until it is about the same size as the other cell. Then, the cells break apart. A yeast cell can even split two or three times inside its wall. The wall then serves as a case. The new cells become spores and stay inside until the case pops open.

Some yeasts are harmful to other organisms. They can grow on plants and animals. Yeasts can cause some skin diseases in people. Yeasts can also cause some fruits to become soft and sour.

Some yeasts are helpful to people. For example, people mix yeast with bread dough. The yeast cells break down the sugars in the dough, and a gas is given off. The gas bubbles cause the dough to rise. You can see the spaces left by the gas in a slice of bread.

budding (bud′ing), a type of reproduction in which a tiny cell grows out and breaks away from another cell.

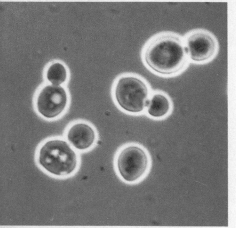

Budding yeast cells

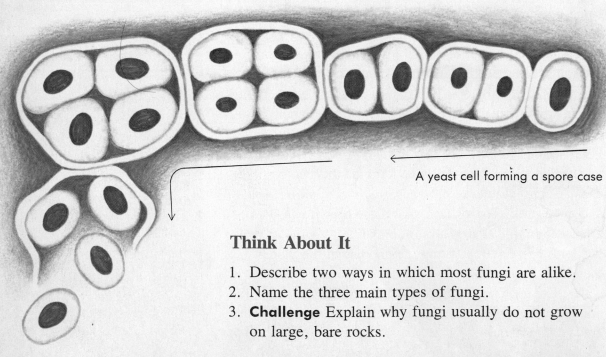

A yeast cell forming a spore case

Think About It

1. Describe two ways in which most fungi are alike.
2. Name the three main types of fungi.
3. **Challenge** Explain why fungi usually do not grow on large, bare rocks.

Activity

Observing Yeast Activity

Purpose
To observe the results after yeast cells have broken down sugar.

You Will Need
• 2 clear bottles
• 2 balloons
• 2 spoonfuls of sugar
• 1 paper cup
• warm water
• 1 package of active yeast
• tape or label card

Directions
1. Label one bottle Y for *yeast* and the other one NY for *no yeast*. Mark the date and time on each bottle.
2. Pour warm—not hot—water into a paper cup, and stir in a spoonful of sugar. Then, pour this sugar water into bottle Y.
3. Refill the cup with warm water, and add another spoonful of sugar to it. Now, pour the sugar water into bottle NY.
4. Add half a package of yeast to bottle Y only.
5. Squeeze the air out of a balloon, and place the balloon on bottle Y, as shown. Place the other balloon on bottle NY in the same way.
6. Set the bottles in a warm, dark place for 24 hours.

Think About It
1. How did the water in the bottles look at the start of the activity?
2. In which bottle did the water change after 24 hours?
3. What might have caused the change in the water?
4. Did anything happen to the balloon in bottle Y?
5. What might have caused a change in the balloon?
6. **Challenge** What could you do to increase the activity in bottle Y?

3 What Is a Protist?

The seaweed and the *Paramecium* (par/ə mē/sē əm) both belong to the protist kingdom. You need a microscope to see most protists. But some, such as the seaweed in the picture, can grow as long as a football field! Protists, both large and small, share three traits.

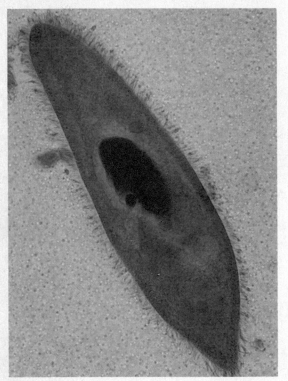

Paramecium

Seaweed

First, all protists live in a wet environment. Some, such as *Paramecium*, live in fresh water. A drop of pond water can hold hundreds of paramecia. Seaweeds and some other protists live in salt water. Still other protists live in wet soil or in the watery parts of other organisms.

nucleus (nü/klē əs), the control center of a cell. [Plural: nuclei (nü/klē ī).]

Second, every protist cell has a **nucleus.** The nucleus is the control center of the cell. You can see the dark, round nucleus in *Paramecium*. Cells of a plant, animal, or fungus also have nuclei.

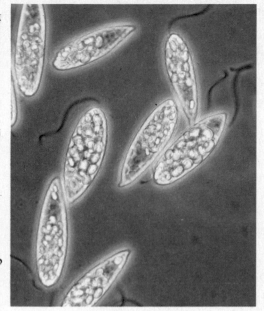

Euglena

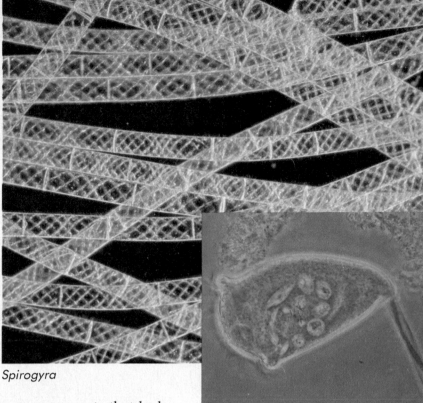

Spirogyra

Vorticella

Third, most protists have one or more parts that look like whips. When these parts are long, they are called **flagella.** When these parts are short, they are called **cilia.** You can see the flagella of *Euglena* (yü glē′nə) in the picture. You can also see the cilia on *Paramecium.* These parts move the protists through water.

Protists are different from one another in many ways. Most protists are made of one cell. *Paramecium, Euglena,* and *Vorticella* (vôr′tə sel′ə) are made of one cell. A few protists, such as *Spirogyra* (spī′rə jī rə), are made of many cells. Most protists that you can see without a hand lens are made of many cells.

Also, protists get food in different ways. Some protists, such as algae (al′jē), can make their own food. *Spirogyra* is an alga (al′gə). Notice the green chlorophyll in its cells. Other protists, such as *Ameba* (ə mē′bə), cannot make food. They must get their food from other organisms. Some organisms, such as *Euglena,* can make food and also get food from other organisms.

flagellum (flə jel′əm), a long, whiplike part that grows out from a cell. [Plural: flagella (flə jel′ə).]

cilium (sil′ē əm), a short, hairlike part that grows out from a cell. [Plural: cilia (sil′ē ə).]

Have You Heard?
 Algae often grow on the sides of fish tanks and make the glass look cloudy or green. Instead of cleaning the glass, many people buy fish called algae-eaters. These fish eat the algae from the sides of the glass and keep the tank clean.

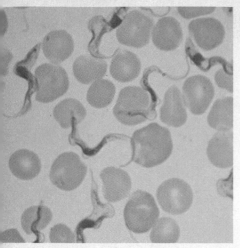
Trypanosomes in blood

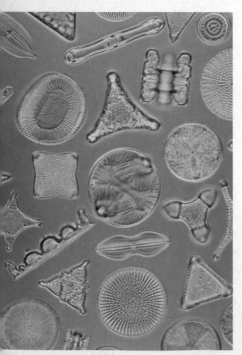
Shells of diatoms

How Are Protists Important to People?

Perhaps you have never seen protists. But these organisms are important to people. Many protists that live in the oceans give off oxygen which people and animals breathe. These protists are also food for small ocean animals. In turn, these small animals are eaten by larger fish. Many people depend upon the larger fish for food.

Some protists can harm animals. The trypanosomes (trip′ə nə sōmz) in this picture cause a sickness in cattle. These protists can enter the blood of a cow through the bite of a fly. The cow becomes sick, and parts of its body swell. Soon, its legs get stiff, and the cow cannot walk. The cow will die if not treated.

Diatoms (dī′ə tomz), another type of protist, form shells such as those shown here. When diatoms die, their hard shells fall to the ocean floor. The shells break apart and form a layer of fine powder. People can dig up these layers and use the powder in metal polish. This powder is even used to make toothpaste!

Think About It

1. In what three ways are all protists alike?
2. What are two ways protists differ?
3. **Challenge** *Euglena* can either make food or get food. When do you think *Euglena* might make food?

Diatoms

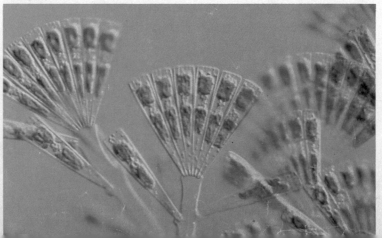

Do You Know?

How Do Algae and Fungi Work Together?

The pictures shown here have one thing in common—few organisms, large or small, can live in these places. Winds are strong. The weather is very cold or very hot. Little rain falls.

Lichens (lī′kənz) are one of the few kinds of organisms that can live in these places. Lichens are the brightly colored patches on the rocks in the pictures. Each lichen is not a single organism, but a pair of organisms that live together. One member of the pair is an alga. The other member is a fungus.

The two organisms survive in harsh environments by helping each other. The alga makes food with the energy of sunlight. Both the alga and the fungus use this food. In return the fungus stores water the alga needs to stay alive.

Teams of algae and fungi work so well that lichens are the only survivors in many harsh environments. Lichens are often the only living organisms in a rocky area on top of a mountain or in the cold Arctic.

An area recently covered with volcanic rock might also first be colonized by lichens. The waste products of these lichens crack the rock into

Lichens on tundra

tiny pieces that become soil. So rock slowly changes into soil with the help of the lichens. When enough soil is present, the seeds of plants can begin to grow.

In some areas, lichens are important food for animals. In fact, in Arctic areas, lichens might be the only food around for animals to eat. Reindeer and musk oxen eat the kind of lichen shown in the picture.

Stories are sometimes told of Arctic explorers surviving on a diet of only lichens. But most lichens have a bitter, unpleasant taste. You would probably not eat lichens unless you had no other choice.

Lichens on mountain

4 What Are Monerans?

A spiral moneran

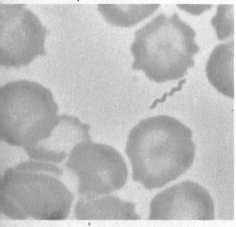

Sometimes you can get a sore throat after playing in the snow. The coldness and wetness can chill your body and make it tired and weak. But the chill does not cause a sore throat. Instead, a tiny organism can reach your throat and begin to feed and grow in number. This organism belongs to yet another kingdom of living things.

The smallest and simplest organisms make up the moneran kingdom. Many monerans are bacteria. And all monerans share two traits. First, a moneran cell lacks a nucleus and many other cell parts. Second, a moneran is much smaller than other cells. The red blood cells, shown on the left, look like giants next to the spiral moneran.

Scientists often classify monerans, such as bacteria, by their shapes. Bacteria are shaped like beads, bars, or spirals. Some monerans live as single cells. Others live in chains or bunches like those in the pictures below.

Chains of monerans

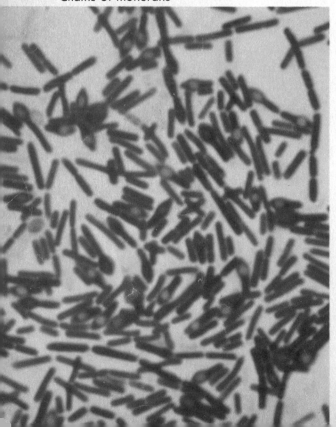

Bunches of monerans

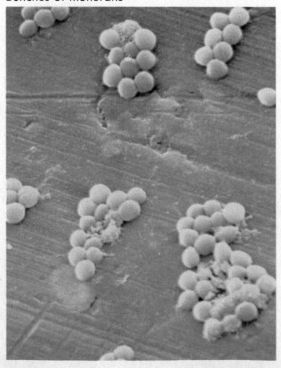

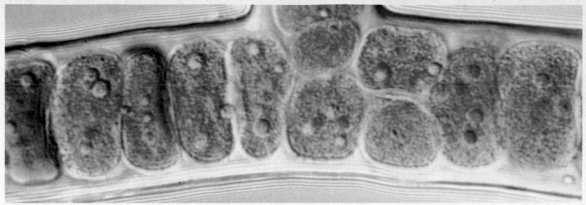

Food-making monerans

You can find monerans everywhere! Millions live in soil, oceans, lakes, rivers, and even in ice. Many monerans live on and in plants and animals. Just a square centimeter of your skin holds more than one million bacteria.

Many monerans are helpful. Some monerans, such as those shown above, live in water and make food. Notice the green chlorophyll inside these cells. Other monerans live in the soil and break down organic matter. Some even break down matter inside other organisms. Such monerans live inside your intestines. These monerans help break down the foods that you eat.

Some monerans are harmful. They can make poisons that cause illnesses in living things. In plants the poisons can cause the stems to swell, as shown in the picture. The swellings can squeeze the transport tubes shut. The tubes will not be able to carry water and food in the plant. In animals the poisons can cause high fevers, sores, or cramps. These poisons build up as the monerans grow in number.

To reproduce, a moneran divides into two smaller monerans. Each new moneran grows in size. Then, each moneran splits to make two more monerans. Now, there are four monerans. The monerans soon split again, and now there are eight monerans. Many monerans can split every twenty minutes! In a short time, there are thousands of monerans.

Have You Heard?
Some kinds of monerans are used to make cheese, yogurt, buttermilk, and even pickles!

Swellings on a plant stem

What Are Viruses?

Scientists can classify living things by the ways those things behave. But scientists do not agree on how to classify a **virus**—a tiny bit in a cell.

Inside a cell, viruses act like living things. They use energy from the cell to make substances and to reproduce. Certain viruses can cause illnesses, such as colds, mumps, and measles. But viruses do not show any of these signs outside a cell.

Viruses do not enter all cells. Some viruses enter only monerans. Other viruses enter only plant cells. And still others enter only animal cells. The pictures show two kinds of viruses.

Many scientists think that viruses are parts that broke away from cells. This might explain why viruses enter and live only in certain cells. Scientists will classify viruses once they learn more about them.

virus (vī′rəs), a tiny bit that has some traits of a living thing when inside a living cell.

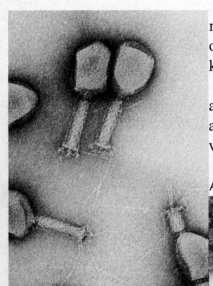

A moneran virus

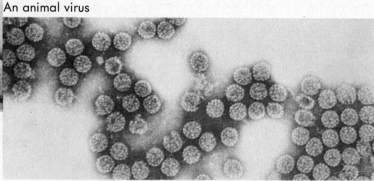

An animal virus

Think About It

1. Name two traits that all monerans share.
2. Describe two ways in which monerans differ from one another.
3. When do viruses seem like living things?
4. **Challenge** A moneran splits every twenty minutes. How many monerans will form from one moneran in two hours?

Tie It Together

Sum It Up

Imagine that you are a scientist trying to classify three unknown organisms. Read the first trait of the organism. On a sheet of paper, write the three letters of the kingdoms that fit that trait. Read the next trait, and write the letters of the two kingdoms that fit that trait. By the time you reach the last trait, only one kingdom will fit the trait. The unknown organism belongs to this final kingdom.

Kingdoms

F   Fungi
P   Protist
M   Moneran

Unknown Organism I
• cannot make its own food ▦▦ ▦▦ ▦▦
• its cells have nuclei ▦▦ ▦▦
• it has cilia ▦▦

Unknown Organism II
• it can only be seen with a microscope ▦▦ ▦▦ ▦▦
• it can make its own food ▦▦ ▦▦
• its cells do not have nuclei ▦▦

Unknown Organism III
• it cannot make its own food ▦▦ ▦▦ ▦▦
• its cells have nuclei ▦▦ ▦▦
• it reproduces with spores ▦▦

Challenge!

1. Describe the differences between fungi and plants.

2. Explain how a mushroom gets food from organic matter.

3. What might happen if some protists lost their flagella or cilia?

4. How would your life be different without monerans?

5. How is a virus like a living thing? How is it different from a living thing?

Science Words

absorb

budding

cilium

flagellum

nucleus

organic matter

virus

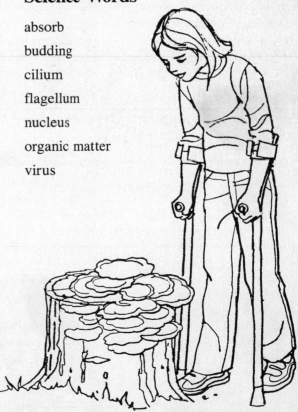

Laboratory

Identifying Woodpeckers

Purpose
To use a key to identify woodpeckers.

You Will Need
• paper and pencil

Stating the Problem
Imagine that you are walking through a forest. You hear a sharp tapping high above you in the branches of a tree. The tapping stops. You see a flash of color as the woodpecker flies away. You see another kind of woodpecker tapping on the trunk of a tree. Still another kind of woodpecker flies across your path and disappears among the leaves of a distant tree. How can you identify these different kinds of woodpeckers? You can use a key to identify the different kinds of woodpeckers shown in the pictures.

Investigating the Problem
Write the letters *A-F* on your paper. Look at the woodpecker labeled *A*. Read the first statement in the key. Only 1 of the 2 statements will be true about woodpecker *A*. Decide which of the 2 statements is true about that woodpecker. Follow the directions to the right of that statement. When you reach the statement that tells you the bird's name, you have identified the woodpecker. Write the name of the woodpecker next to its letter on your paper. Use the key to identify the rest of the woodpeckers in the pictures. Write their names on your paper.

Making Conclusions
1. Did you have trouble identifying any of the woodpeckers in the picture? What made it harder to identify some birds?
2. What kinds of traits are most helpful when you are trying to identify a bird by using a key? What kinds of traits would be most helpful if you were trying to identify any organism by using a key?
3. Suppose you wanted to make a key to help you identify kinds of dogs. What traits might you use in your key?

Key to Kinds of Woodpeckers

1. Head is mostly all one color. Head is more than one color.	go to 2 go to 3
2. Head is red. Head is white.	red-headed woodpecker white-headed woodpecker
3. Head has crest of feathers. Head has no crest of feathers.	pileated woodpecker go to 4
4. Belly is speckled. Belly is a solid color.	yellow-shafted flicker go to 5
5. Belly is yellow. Belly is white.	yellow-bellied sapsucker downy woodpecker

63

Careers

Entomologist

Clarence has always been interested in animals and collecting things. But collecting wasps and beetles may seem like an unusual way of making a living. "Actually, collecting insects is part of one of the most interesting fields in science," says Clarence.

Clarence is an entomologist—a person who studies and classifies insects. "I want to see the insects in their natural surroundings, so I do a lot of traveling. Much of my work is done in Central America. After collecting samples of insects, I try to identify the exact species and genus. It is interesting to see how animals differ from each other even if they look alike."

For the past forty years, Clarence has been teaching his skills to college students. But most of his summers are spent studying insects in faraway places, such as Africa or Asia.

"What really makes this job exciting is knowing you may discover a totally new species of insect.

"Students interested in classifying organisms may have already gotten started by keeping plant or insect collections. Insect-collecting is a popular hobby. Many museums look for young people to help increase and maintain museum collections."

Entomologists graduate from college with a good backround in biology. In high school and college, they sharpen their skills of observing, sorting out, and interpreting information.

Almost everyone, at one time or another, classifies things. You might sort—or classify—your clothes by putting all shirts in one drawer and socks in another drawer. You might classify baseball cards by team.

Most jobs involve some kind of classification. A teacher might write students' names in a record book in alphabetical order. The teacher classifies the students according to the alphabet. In some careers, classifying things is a big part of the job.

At a museum, the **registrar** keeps track of all things in the museum's collections. The registrar makes a list of all the items and classifies them according to the kind of item.

A **research assistant** in botany identifies plants. Research assistants sometimes accompany scientists on trips to other countries to collect a variety of plants.

An **archaeologist** (är′kē ol′ə jist) is interested in finding items, such as tools and weapons, used by ancient civilizations. After digging up the items, the archaeologist classifies them.

Recording clerks at kennel clubs classify dogs according to the breed. If you have a dog, it might be classified as a collie, poodle, or German shepherd.

People wanting to be research assistants, registrars, or archaeologists go to college for two to seven years. Recording clerks need a high-school education. They also get a lot of on-the-job training where they sharpen their classifying skills.

Recording clerk

Archaeologist

On Your Own

Picture Clue

Even though this animal has a bill and webbed feet and lays eggs like a duck, it has hair and gives milk to its young. What type of animal is it? Look on page 22 for its name.

Projects

1. Get some brine shrimp eggs from a pet store. Find out if they are living things by placing them in water and observing them with a hand lens.

2. Visit a zoo, greenhouse, or botanical garden. See how the organisms are named and grouped. Discover which organisms are in the same genus, and find out the meanings of their scientific names.

3. Grow a mold garden inside a large glass jar. Cover the bottom of the jar with a layer of wet sand, and place a few pieces of bread and fruit in the jar. Tightly cover the jar, and observe the growing mold over the next two weeks.

Books About Science

Creatures Great and Small by Michael H. Gabb. Lerner Publications Company, 1980. Animals, from sponges to the largest mammals, are discussed in a question-and-answer format.

Discover the Trees by Jerry Cowle. Sterling Publishing Company, 1977. This reference guide, packed with unusual bits of information, shows how to identify trees.

The Science of Classification by Martin J. Gutnik. Franklin Watts, Inc., 1980. Classification, the process of placing related objects or organisms into groups, is discussed.

Viruses: Life's Smallest Enemies by David C. Knight. Wm. Morrow and Company, 1981. This book contains information about viruses, including how scientists study, describe, and experiment with them.

Unit Test

Complete the Sentences

Number your paper from 1–5. Read each clue. Next to each number, write the missing word or words that complete the sentence.

1. All living things grow, reproduce, respond, are made of cells, and ⬚⬚⬚ .

2. Members of this kingdom have many cells and cannot make their own food. Most of them can move. They are ⬚⬚⬚ .

3. One way to classify a plant is by whether its ⬚⬚⬚ are made in fruits or cones.

4. Most organisms of the ⬚⬚⬚ kingdom grow threads that absorb food from organic matter.

5. A moneran cell does not have a ⬚⬚⬚ that acts as the control center for the cell.

Multiple Choice

Number your paper from 6–10. Next to each number, write the letter of the word or words that best complete the statement.

6. A scientific name is made up of
   a. the kingdom name.
   b. the genus and species names.
   c. the species and common names.
   d. the kingdom and species names.

7. One way an organism is classified is by whether it has one or many
   a. names.
   b. traits.
   c. cells.
   d. species.

8. The ⬚⬚⬚ make up one of the two main groups of animals. This group includes about nine-tenths of the kinds of animals on earth.
   a. protists
   b. invertebrates
   c. mammals
   d. insects

9. This kingdom includes organisms that can make their own food. They are made of many cells that have cell walls. They are ⬚⬚⬚ .
   a. plants.
   b. viruses.
   c. animals.
   d. monerans.

10. Organisms of the ⬚⬚⬚ kingdom live in a wet environment.
    a. fungi
    b. animal
    c. plant
    d. protist

UNIT TWO
THE CELL

Wonderful, wonderful,
  soft and furry.
One eye amber,
  one eye blue.
Ears pointing up,
  tail pointing down.
When you're happy,
  I'm happy too!

Sara Mirza age 9

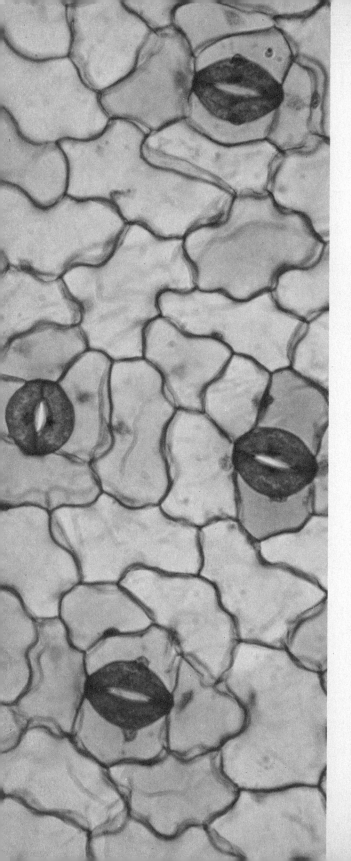

Chapter 5
The Living
Cell

This picture looks like a puzzle. But unlike most puzzles, the puzzle in this picture is alive. The living pieces of this puzzle join to form the bottom layer of a leaf. Scientists study pieces like these to learn more about the puzzle of life.

The lessons in this chapter describe the tiny pieces that make up all living things. Learning about these pieces will help you understand how your body forms and grows.

1 Observing Onion Skin

2 What Is a Cell?

3 What Are the Parts of Cells?

4 How Do Cells Work Together?

1 Observing Onion Skin

Many objects around you look as if they are made from one piece of material. But they look very different up close.

Use a hand lens to look at the boy's shirt in the picture. Hundreds of colored dots make up each color of the shirt. Now, look at the whole picture with the hand lens. This picture is made of thousands of dots.

Thousands of tiny pieces also join to form one large piece of onion skin. Get a large piece of dried onion skin. Do not tear or wrinkle it. With two fingers, gently hold it toward a light or bright window. Carefully look at the skin with the hand lens. If you look closely, you can see the tiny pieces.

Think About It

1. Draw the shapes of the pieces that make up the onion skin. Can you see these pieces without a hand lens?
2. Do you see the tiny pieces more clearly in the light or dark places of the onion skin?
3. **Challenge** If the onion skin is made of thousands of pieces, what can you infer about a whole onion?

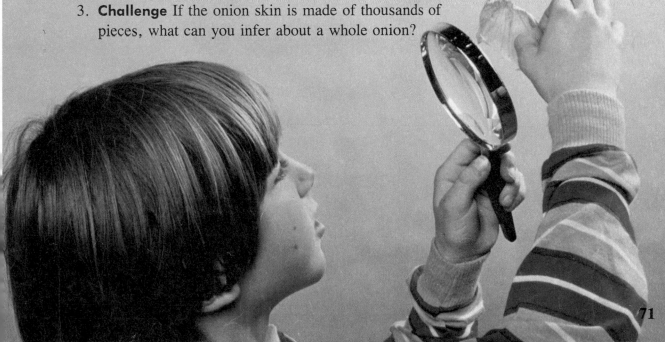

2 What Is a Cell?

You cannot see each brick of your school building from far away. But up close you can see how each brick fits into place. In the same way, your body is made of many tiny pieces that fit into place. These pieces—or cells—are so tiny that you need a microscope to see them. Dandruff and peeled skin are really bunches of dead skin cells. These dead cells fall off, and living cells take their place. In all, more than a trillion cells make up your body!

Cells are the building blocks of all organisms. Many of the smallest organisms—monerans—are made of one cell. Some protists are also made of one cell, while others are made of many cells. The number of cells gets larger as organisms grow. This picture shows the many cells that make up a small piece of onion.

A cell is the smallest living part of an organism. A tiny cell on the tip of your nose carries on the same life activities as your whole body. Cells get energy from food. They use this energy to grow and to respond to their surroundings. Cells also reproduce—or make more cells of the same kind.

Many kinds of cells make up your body. You have skin cells, muscle cells, nerve cells, and bone cells. Your stomach, heart, lungs, and brain are made of cells. The picture shows that even your blood is made of cells.

Skin cells of an onion

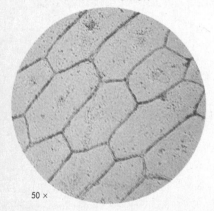

50 ×

Blood cells

6130 ×

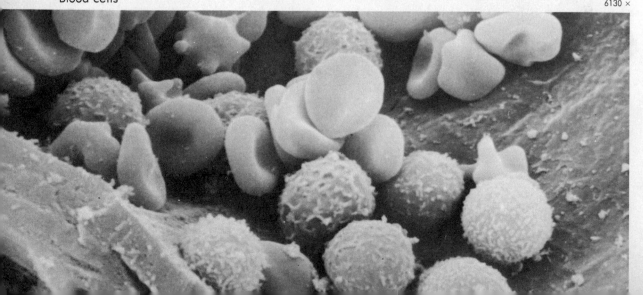

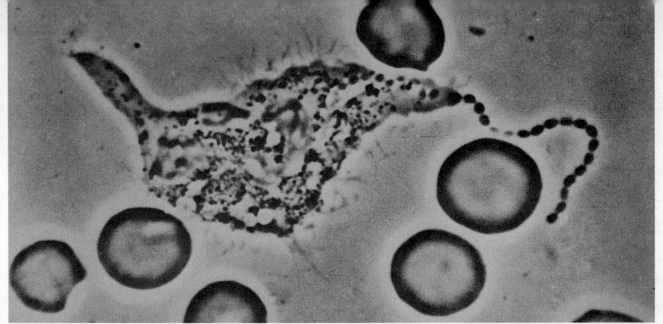

A blood cell attacking bacteria   10,000 ×

Cells help organisms grow. A puppy does not grow just because its cells get bigger. Instead, muscle cells produce more cells to make longer and stronger muscles. Also, skin cells produce more skin cells to make the skin larger. The number of cells becomes larger as the puppy gets older. The number of cells stops getting larger once the puppy becomes an adult dog.

Cells also help repair the body of an organism. For example, blood cells rush to a cut. Some blood cells form a scab to keep out bacteria and dirt. Other blood cells, such as the ones shown here, destroy any bacteria that entered through the cut. Underneath the scab, healthy cells produce new cells that take the place of the damaged ones. The scab falls off after the new cells are in place. Cells usually take a few days to repair a cut.

Have You Heard?

Sometimes a tadpole loses its tail while escaping from a fish or turtle. When this happens, the cells of the tadpole can reproduce and form a new tail!

Think About It

1. What is a cell?
2. Explain two ways in which cells help organisms.
3. **Challenge** What might happen to you if your cells did not reproduce?

3 What Are the Parts of Cells?

membrane (mem′brān), a thin lining that holds the cell together.

cytoplasm (sī′tə plaz′əm), the part of the cell that is inside the membrane but outside the nucleus.

In a way, your classroom is like a cell of your body. Walls, a floor, and a ceiling surround your classroom. This space holds many parts that make up your classroom: desks, books, pencils, blackboard, pupils, and a teacher. This space would not be a classroom without these parts.

Cells would not be cells without their important parts too. Compare the picture with the drawing of the animal cell. First, a thin **membrane** surrounds the cell and holds it together. The membrane also allows only certain substances to enter or leave the cell. Second, the dark nucleus acts as the control center of the cell. The nucleus directs the activities of the cell. The nucleus also sends messages to other cell parts. Finally, all other cell parts float in the **cytoplasm.** Many activities that keep the cell alive take place in the cytoplasm.

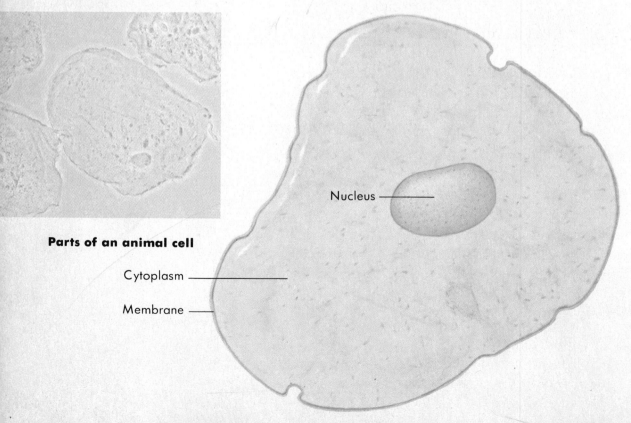

Parts of an animal cell

Cytoplasm ————

Membrane ——

Nucleus ————

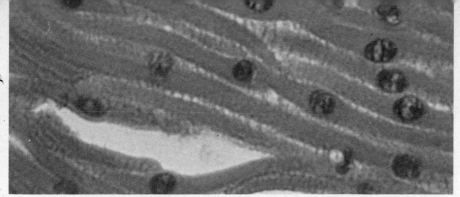

Long muscle cells

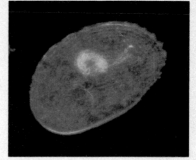

A protist made of one cell

Find the membrane of each cell shown on this page. Food and water must pass through the membrane to reach the cell. The membrane also keeps dangerous substances from entering the cell.

Find the nucleus of each cell. Stringy parts are inside the nucleus. These strings—or **chromosomes**—store directions that the cell uses to carry on its activities. A cell will soon die if its nucleus is taken out. The cell would no longer have directions to carry on its activities.

The cytoplasm covers all the space inside the membrane but outside the nucleus. You can see other cell parts in the cytoplasm. Some parts break down food and get energy for the cell. Other parts make new substances for the cell. Still other parts carry messages to the rest of the cell.

chromosome (krō′mə sōm), a stringlike part in the nucleus that stores the directions for the activities of the cell.

Have You Heard?

You have 46 chromosomes in each of your body cells. But the number of chromosomes in a body cell differs among most organisms. A housefly has 12 chromosomes in each body cell. A cat has 38 chromosomes, a potato plant has 48, a dog has 78, and a crayfish has 200!

A nerve cell

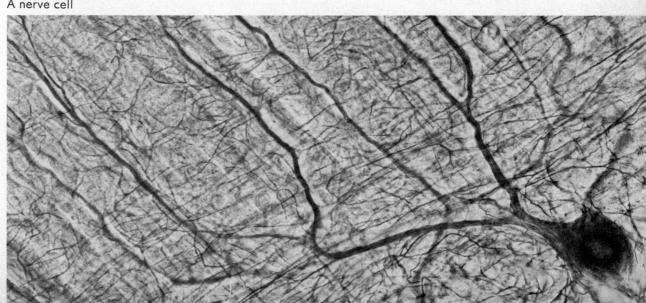

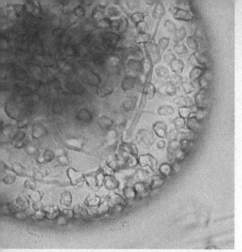

Green chloroplasts in an alga

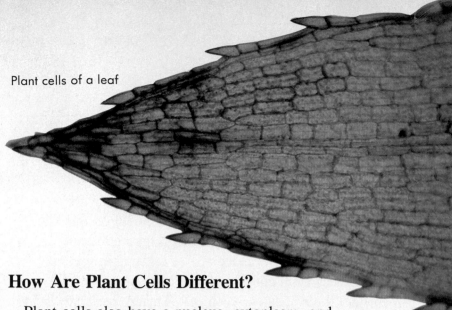

Plant cells of a leaf

How Are Plant Cells Different?

Plant cells also have a nucleus, cytoplasm, and membrane. But many plant cells also have green, egg-shaped parts like the ones in these plant cells. The **chloroplasts** store green chlorophyll that traps energy from the sun. The plant cells use this energy to make food. Protists, such as this alga, also have chloroplasts for making food.

Notice the stiff cell wall that covers the membrane of each plant cell. The wall makes a sticky substance that cements it to nearby cell walls. The walls make the plant firm and help it stand up.

A plant cell often has a large bag—or **vacuole**—that holds water. When full, the vacuole pushes the cytoplasm against the membrane. The plant cell then becomes stiffer. When empty, the vacuole folds in, and the cytoplasm moves away from the membrane. The plant cell becomes less stiff. Plants wilt when their cells do not have enough water in their vacuoles.

chloroplast (klôr′ə plast), an egg-shaped cell structure that holds chlorophyll.

vacuole (vak′yü ōl), a baglike cell structure that often holds water.

Think About It

1. Describe three parts found in most cells.
2. Name three parts found mainly in plant cells.
3. **Challenge** How would your body change if your cells suddenly had walls?

Do You Know?

How Can People Look at Cells?

Cell part magnified under electron microscope

People used to believe that many diseases were caused by magic or bad luck. The organisms that were the real cause of some diseases were too small to be seen. Many of these organisms were made of only one cell.

After the microscope was invented, people were able to see some of the one-celled organisms that cause sickness. They also saw the cells that make up all living things.

Cell magnified under light microscope

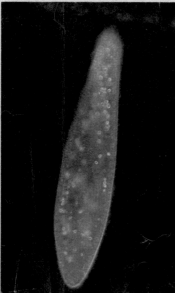

A microscope can make a cell look thousands of times larger than it really is. The kind of microscope that you might use in science class is called a light microscope. It uses light and glass lenses.

The object to be studied, such as a thin piece of plant tissue, is placed on the viewing stage. A beam of light shines through the tissue. The glass lenses magnify the tissue. Notice that the picture shows a cell that has been magnified 266 times.

Some cells or cell parts are too small to be seen with a light microscope. When greater magnifying power is needed, scientists might use an electron microscope. This kind of microscope uses small particles called electrons. A beam of electrons passes through an object under an electron microscope similarly to the way that a beam of light passes through an object under a light microscope. The picture shows a cell magnified 10,450 times.

A scanning electron microscope is used to see the surface of objects. In this microscope electrons do not pass through an object. Instead electrons bounce off the surface of the cell. Notice how different the cell looks when seen with a scanning electron microscope.

Cell magnified under scanning electron microscope

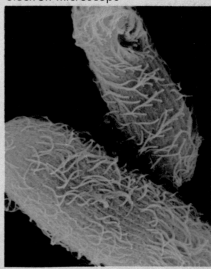

4 How Do Cells Work Together?

tissue (tish/ü), a group of the same type of cells that are working together to do the same job.

The cell layers of a hydra

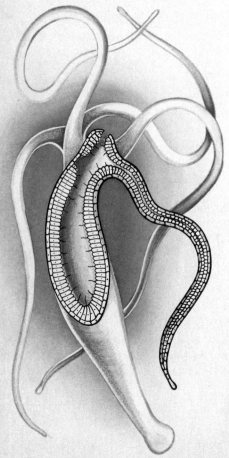

The picture shows an animal found in many ponds. The hydra looks like a pipe with arms. But in the drawing, you can see that the hydra is made of different cell layers. The outside layer protects the hydra. The inside layer absorbs food that the hydra catches and pulls through its opening.

Like the hydra, your body has groups of cells that work together. Five kinds of cell groups—or **tissues**—make up your body. Skin tissues cover your body. Connecting tissues, such as bone tissue, connect and hold up parts of your body. Muscle tissues allow you to move. Nerve tissues send and receive messages throughout your body. Finally, blood tissues carry food, water, and oxygen to cells.

Feel the inside of your cheeks with your tongue. Food passes easily along this smooth skin tissue when you swallow. However, this tissue ends at your lips. Here, rougher skin tissue begins. This tissue protects your face and other body parts. Even the skin tissue on your palms is different. This tissue has ridges that help you grab objects. All these skin tissues work together to form your skin.

A hydra after eating a water flea

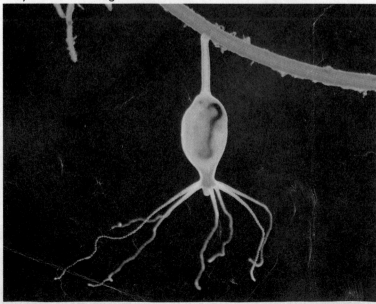

Different tissues that work together form an **organ.**
Your skin is made of tissues other than skin tissues.
Nerve tissues in your skin help make a burn hurt. Blood
tissues appear when you cut yourself. Muscle tissues
give you "goose flesh" on cold days. The drawing
shows skin tissues, which make up the body's largest
organ.

Vertebrates have many organs. Your heart, lungs,
stomach, intestines, brain, and eyes are organs. Most
organs are made of muscle, nerve, and blood tissues.

Many organs can work together to form a **system.**
Your stomach, liver, and intestines form part of your
digestive system. Your stomach breaks down food. Your
liver makes a digestive juice that also breaks down
food. Your intestines absorb the food and pass it to your
blood.

Tissues can work with different systems. Your
muscles work with your bones to help you jump, run, or
sit. Also, your muscles work with your lungs. Notice in
the picture the large muscle beneath your lungs. When
you breathe in, this muscle pulls down to draw air into
your lungs. When you breathe out, the muscle moves up
and pushes out air.

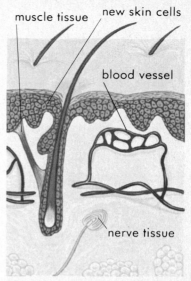

Skin is made of tissues

organ (ôr′gən), a group of
different tissues working
together.

system (sis′təm), a group of
organs working together.

Find Out

What systems make up your
body?

Muscle pulls down

Muscle pushes up

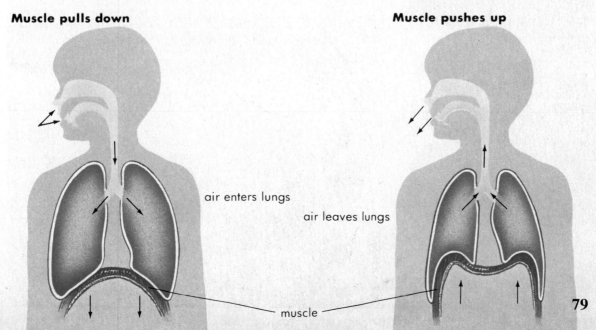

air enters lungs

air leaves lungs

muscle

Tissues of a moss plant

How Do Cells Form Organisms?

Many monerans and protists are each made of a single cell. These organisms do not have tissues. Instead, different cell parts carry on the life activities of these organisms.

A fungus is made of different tissues. For example, the fuzzy threads of a mushroom are tissues that absorb food from organic matter. The stalk tissue holds up the cap. The cap tissue makes spores. A mushroom needs all these tissues to live.

Some plants only have tissues. The picture shows the different tissues of a moss. Some tissues hold the plant in the soil and take in water. Other tissues make food. Still other tissues form spores.

Many invertebrates have organs and systems. Notice the drawing of the earthworm. An earthworm has a stomach and an intestine that form part of its digestive system. The earthworm also has a system of vessels that carry blood throughout its body. The earthworm even has a system of nerves and a tiny brain!

All vertebrates have systems. A fish has a system of muscles that helps it swim. A system of bones holds the muscles together and gives the fish its shape. Gills belong to another system that gets oxygen for the fish. A fish even has a nervous system that allows it to smell and taste things underwater!

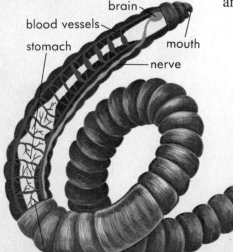

brain

blood vessels

stomach

mouth

nerve

intestine

Organs and tissues of an earthworm

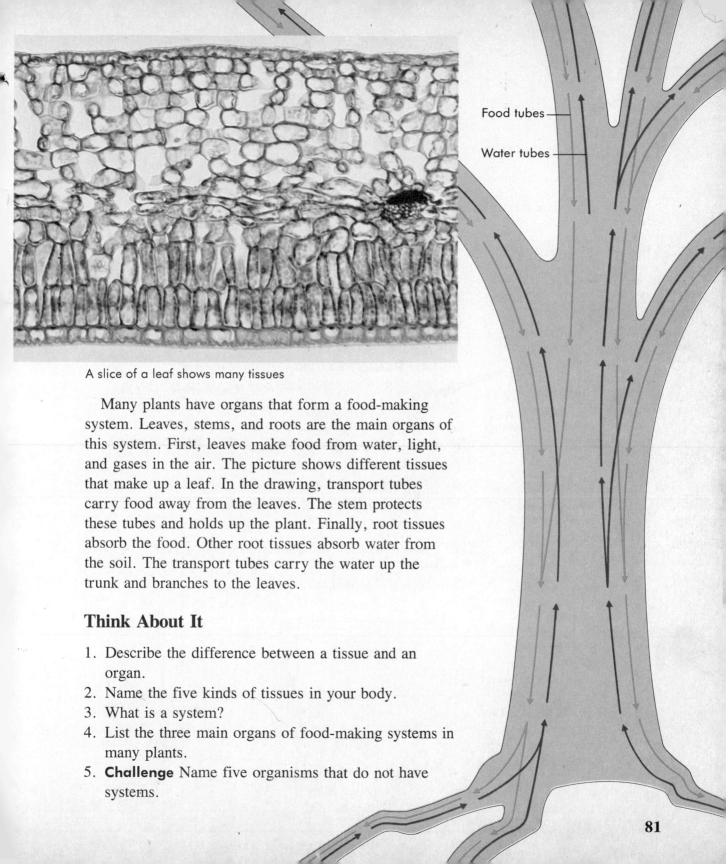

A slice of a leaf shows many tissues

Food tubes

Water tubes

Many plants have organs that form a food-making system. Leaves, stems, and roots are the main organs of this system. First, leaves make food from water, light, and gases in the air. The picture shows different tissues that make up a leaf. In the drawing, transport tubes carry food away from the leaves. The stem protects these tubes and holds up the plant. Finally, root tissues absorb the food. Other root tissues absorb water from the soil. The transport tubes carry the water up the trunk and branches to the leaves.

Think About It

1. Describe the difference between a tissue and an organ.
2. Name the five kinds of tissues in your body.
3. What is a system?
4. List the three main organs of food-making systems in many plants.
5. **Challenge** Name five organisms that do not have systems.

Activity

Building a Limb

Purpose
To build a model of a vertebrate leg, and to observe its parts at work.

You Will Need
- 2 paper-towel tubes
- 1 toilet-tissue tube
- 2 rubber bands
- scissors
- masking tape
- metric ruler
- red and green colored pencils or crayons

Directions
1. Mark one long tube *A* and the other one *B*. Mark the short tube *C*.
2. Mark a line 2 cm from the end of tube *A*. Then, carefully flatten the end of the tube. Next, draw a red line across the tube as shown in the drawing. Make a red dot at the end of this line.
3. Notice how the green line in the drawing connects the red dot to the corner of tube *A*. Draw a green line on the tube as shown in the drawing.
4. Measure, mark, and draw the colored lines as shown for tubes *B* and *C*. Notice that tube *B* has 2 ends to be drawn.
5. Flatten each tube end, and cut the tube only along the green lines.
6. Tape the tubes as shown in the next drawing.
7. Cut a rubber band, and tape an end to tube *A*. Stretch it, and tape the other end to tube *B*.
8. Tape short pieces of rubber band to tubes *B* and *C* as shown.
9. Compare the movement of your model to the movement of your leg.

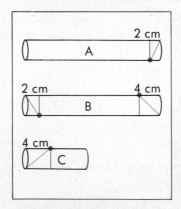

Think About It
1. Name the kind of tissue that the tubes stand for.
2. What kind of tissue does the tape stand for?
3. What kind of tissue do the rubber bands stand for?
4. Describe how the rubber bands work with the tubes as you move the parts of the model.
5. **Challenge** Describe how the muscles, bones, and knee of your leg might work together as you walk.

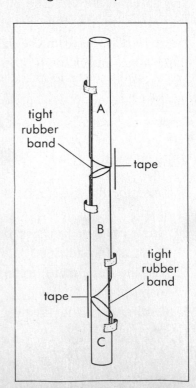

Tie It Together

Sum It Up

nucleus

chromosomes

membrane

cell wall

cytoplasm

vacuole

chloroplasts

1. Decide which cell parts in this list belong in an animal cell. Then, draw a picture of an animal cell, using the parts you picked.

2. Decide which cell parts belong in a plant cell. Then, draw a picture of a plant cell, and use the parts that you picked.

3. Listed here are four important parts of many organisms. All the vowels of each word are in the right place. First, copy the spaces and letters on a sheet of paper. Then, fill in the rest of the letters for each word. Put the parts in order from the smallest to the largest.

    o _ _ a _

    _ e _ _

    _ y _ _ e _

    _ i _ _ u e

Challenge!

1. Explain how a tiny cell inside a mold spore can form thread tissues on a slice of bread.

2. An unknown organism has a cell wall, chloroplasts, but no nucleus. Into what kingdom would you classify this organism?

3. Are your fingernails a tissue, organ, or system?

4. The tail of a dog is part of several systems. Name two of these systems.

Science Words

chloroplast

chromosome

cytoplasm

membrane

organ

system

tissue

vacuole

Chapter 6
Activity in Cells

All organisms need energy. A shark uses energy to swim and to catch fish. Grasses use energy to grow. You use energy to play and even to breathe.

The hummingbird in the picture beats its wings over fifty times a second! This organism needs great amounts of energy. The cells of the hummingbird provide it with energy. Cells are the important energy centers of all organisms.

The lessons in this chapter describe how the cells of an organism get and use the energy they need.

1 Observing the Movement of Water

Water is all around you. It floats in the sky as clouds. It falls to the earth as rain and snow. Water seeps through the soil. Water also passes into cells of organisms.

Get several carrot slices that have been left out overnight. Carefully describe how each slice bends back and forth. Then, place the slices in a cup of water. Take out the slices after one hour, and describe any changes in the slices. Compare these slices to some that were not placed in water.

Think About It

1. How flexible were the slices before they were soaked in water?
2. How flexible were the slices after they had soaked?
3. What might have caused this change?
4. **Challenge** Describe what might happen if you were to put a raisin in a cupful of water.

2 How Do Cells Get Food and Water?

particle (pär′tə kəl), a very tiny bit of a substance.

Have You Heard?

Blood also carries oxygen to your cells. When you inhale, oxygen particles pass through your lung cells and into your blood.

At this moment you might feel thirsty or hungry. But you do not drink water or eat food just to fill an empty stomach. You drink and you eat because your cells need water and food.

All organisms need water and food for their cells. The water and food must be in tiny bits—or **particles**—to enter a cell.

Water particles easily pass into cells. A carrot slice becomes stiff after soaking in a cupful of water. Billions of water particles pass through the membranes of the carrot cells and into their vacuoles. The carrot cells then hold more water particles.

Many water particles reach your blood when you drink a glass of water or juice. The water particles pass from your stomach and into the cells of your intestines. Blood vessels lie next to these cells. The water particles pass from the cells of the intestines into the blood.

How body cells get food and water

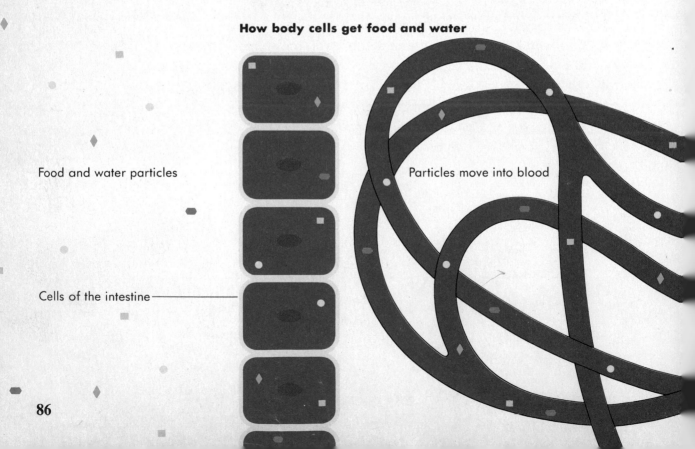

Food and water particles

Particles move into blood

Cells of the intestine

Food must be broken down into particles before it can reach your blood. First, your teeth grind food into small pieces. Second, your stomach and intestines work to break the pieces into particles. Then, the particles move into the cells of the intestines. Finally, the food particles move from these cells into your blood.

Soon after eating, your blood has many **nutrients**—or food and water particles that your body needs. The cells of your body need nutrients to carry on their activities. Blood carries these nutrients to all your body cells.

Nutrients move from the blood into the cells. Water and some food particles can pass through the membranes of the cells. Cells also use energy to pull in other food particles. The drawings show how nutrients in your intestines reach your body cells.

When nutrients move into the cells, the blood becomes low in nutrients. Your brain receives a signal from parts of your body. In turn, your brain makes you feel hungry and thirsty again.

Think About It

1. What are nutrients?
2. How does blood help your cells get nutrients?
3. **Challenge** Explain how a hamburger provides nutrients for the cells of your feet.

Blood carries particles to body cells

Have You Heard?

Insects, such as flies and grasshoppers, also have blood in their bodies. However, insect blood can be green, yellow, or even colorless!

nutrient (nü′trē ənt), a food or water particle that organisms need in order to grow and to stay alive.

Cells

87

Activity

Making a Cell Model

Purpose
To observe the passing of particles through the membrane of a cell model.

You Will Need
- 1 plastic sandwich bag
- 12 cm of string
- 1 marble
- a pint-size container
- a cupful of starch and water mixture
- 5 mL of iodine and water mixture

Directions
1. Fill the container halfway with water.
2. Place the marble in the plastic bag.
3. Carefully pour half the starch and water mixture into the bag.
4. Tie the top of the bag with the string.
5. Dry off any starch and water mixture that might have dripped onto the sides of the bag. If the bag leaks, use another bag.
6. Imagine that the bag of mixture is a model of a cell. Name the parts of the model that stand for the nucleus, cytoplasm, and membrane.
7. Place the bag in the container of water. The water level should be the same as the level of starch and water mixture inside the bag.
8. Carefully pour the iodine and water mixture into the water, as shown in the picture.
9. Observe any changes that take place.
10. Add 1 drop of iodine and water mixture to the rest of the starch and water mixture in the cup. Notice the color change. Compare this color change with any that you see in your cell model.

Think About It
1. Did the starch inside the bag change color?
2. Did the iodine particles pass into the bag, or did the starch particles pass out of the bag?
3. **Challenge** What might happen if you placed a bag of iodine in a container of starch and water mixture?

Do You Know?

Food Gives You Energy

Labels on food packages give information about nutrients in the food. Notice all the different nutrients listed under "nutrition information" in the picture. Some nutrients help cells make repairs. Other nutrients can give the body energy. Different foods give you different amounts of energy.

People can measure the amount of energy that they get from foods. The unit of measurement for food energy is the Calorie (kal′ər ē). One serving of the food in the package supplies 90 Calories of energy.

You might notice that doing certain activities sometimes makes you feel hungry. When you do these activities, you use a lot of energy. You can measure the amount of energy you use in Calories.

If you sit in a chair for an hour, you will use 125 Calories. A 25-minute walk uses about the same amount of energy. Bicycling, working in a garden, and playing baseball all use the same amounts of energy.

Other activities use even more energy. The runners in the picture use about 600 Calories in one hour. A swimmer can also use about this much energy in one hour. An hour of mountain climbing uses 600 Calories too.

The chart shows other activities which you might do. You can use this chart to help find out how many Calories of energy you use in one day.

Activity chart

Activity	Calories/hour
Basketball	450
Dancing	500
Football	400
Piano playing	175
Skipping rope	500
Sleeping	70
Tennis	480

Running uses energy

Food label

NUTRITION INFORMATION PER SERVING

	1 OZ.	WITH ½ CUP WHOLE MILK
SERVING SIZE	1 OZ. (1 CUP)	
SERVINGS PER CONTAINER:	9	
CALORIES	90	170
PROTEIN, GRAMS	3	7
CARBOHYDRATE, GRAMS	25	31
FAT, GRAMS	0	5

PERCENTAGE OF U.S. RECOMMENDED DAILY ALLOWANCE (U.S. RDA)

PROTEIN	3	12
VITAMIN A	100	100
VITAMIN C	100	100
THIAMINE	100	100
RIBOFLAVIN	100	100
NIACIN	100	100

3 How Do Cells Get Energy?

cell respiration (sel res′pə rā′shən), the cell process that uses energy and oxygen to break down nutrients and to gain energy.

What do walking, talking, thinking, and sleeping have in common? You must use energy to do these activities! Every activity uses energy. People, like other organisms, must build up their energy supply. Energy comes from food.

An organism depends on its cells to get energy from food. **Cell respiration** takes place inside cells. During cell respiration, a cell uses energy and oxygen to break down nutrients. Energy escapes as the nutrients split apart. Notice in the picture how the cell gains energy during cell respiration.

Blow your breath onto your hand. You can feel the heat from your body. The heat is energy given off by your cells.

Cells use energy in several ways. A cell uses energy to pull certain nutrients through its membrane. A cell also uses energy to break down nutrients and to gain more energy. Some cells, such as muscle cells, use energy to move parts of your body.

Cell respiration releases energy from food

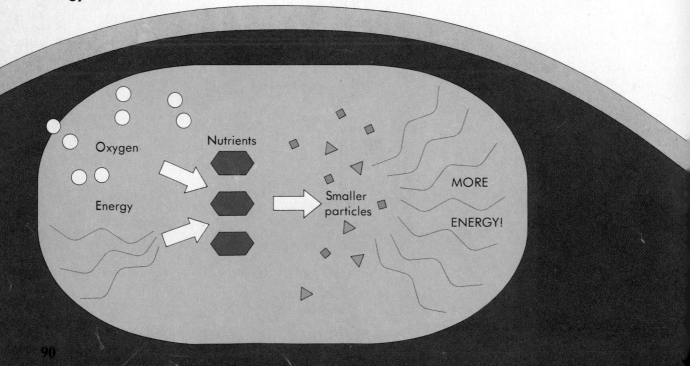

Oxygen

Energy

Nutrients

Smaller particles

MORE

ENERGY!

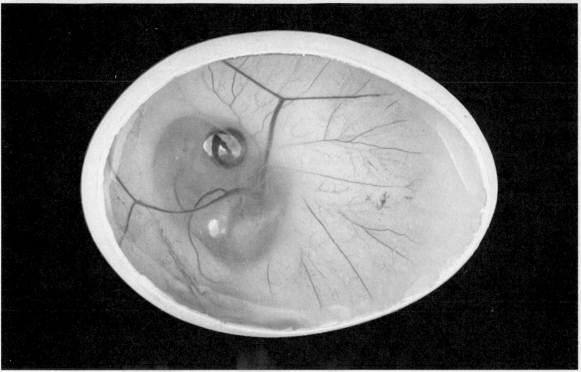

A chick developing in an egg

The inside of a bone

A cell also uses energy to make new substances from nutrients. For example, certain chicken cells made the yolk and the white of the egg in this picture. Other chicken cells made the hard substance of the shell.

Your cells also use energy and nutrients to make substances. Notice the picture of a bone cut into halves. The blood vessels look like large holes. The rings around the holes are substances made by the bone cells. The bone cells are not easy to find. They look like small, dark spiders around some of the rings.

Think About It

1. Explain how a cell gets energy through cell respiration.
2. Name two ways in which a cell uses energy.
3. **Challenge** What might happen if chicken cells did not get enough nutrients?

4 How Do Cells Grow and Reproduce?

There is much activity in most cells. The cells get energy from nutrients. They use energy to make substances. Cells also use energy to grow and to reproduce.

To grow, a cell uses energy to make new substances. The cell uses these substances to build up parts in its cytoplasm and membrane. The cell grows as the cytoplasm and membrane become larger.

Sometimes a cell stops growing when its membrane pushes against other cells. The cell cannot get larger. Also, chromosomes can direct a cell to stop growing. Other times, substances from nearby cells can signal a cell to stop growing.

Some cells die after growing. Feel your skin with your fingers. The surface you touch is made of dead skin cells. New skin cells push dead skin cells to the surface. The dead cells form a layer that protects the new cells from scrapes and scratches.

Compare one of your fingernails with your skin surface. Both are made of dead cells. But the fingernail cells store a hard substance—keratin (ker′ə tən). Living cells make keratin, which collects in the cells when they die. Animal claws and even the tortoise shell in this picture are made from dead cells that store keratin.

Cells make the hard substance of shells

When a cell stops growing, it often reproduces. These pictures show how a cell reproduces. First, the chromosomes double in number. Second, the cell uses energy to stretch and pull apart the chromosomes and cytoplasm. Finally, the cell divides into two smaller **offspring cells.** These cells have the same parts and chromosomes as the first—or parent—cell. In **cell division** each parent cell produces two offspring cells.

Like the parent cell, offspring cells grow and reproduce. Each cell grows and divides into offspring cells. These new cells also grow and divide. The number of cells gets larger as cell division goes on.

The picture shows a tissue that formed from some cells. The cells grew and divided many times. Cell division can produce thousands of cells in a short time.

Think About It

1. How do cells use energy to grow?
2. How do cells use energy in cell division?
3. **Challenge** There are 32 cells in a certain bunch. If each cell divides once, how many cells will the bunch have?

Tissue formed by cell division

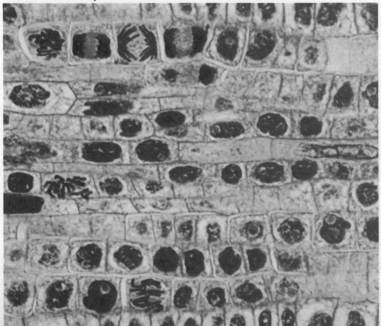

offspring cells (ôf′spring′ selz), the cells that result from cell reproduction.

cell division (sel də vizh′ən), cell reproduction in which a parent cell divides into two offspring cells.

A dividing cell

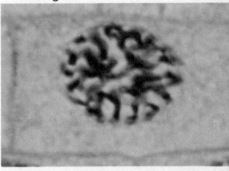

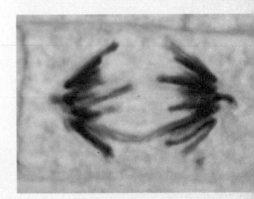

5 How Do Organisms Use Energy?

At this moment you are using energy. Cells give you energy that moves your eyes across this page. Your heart uses this energy to pump blood. And your stomach uses energy to break down the food you ate for breakfast or lunch.

A cow uses energy to change grass into milk. First, the different stomachs of a cow break the grass into nutrients. The nutrients move into the blood and then into the body cells of the cow. Certain body cells use energy to make milk from the nutrients.

Some living things can even make a substance that gives off light! Fireflies break down food to free energy. Certain cells use the energy and nutrients to make the substance. Since this light does not give off much heat, people call it cold light. Fireflies use cold light to find other fireflies in the dark.

The fish in this picture uses cold light to catch smaller fish. Notice the strip of tissue that looks like a shining worm. Cells in this strip make the cold light. The bright "worm" attracts small fish. As the small fish swim closer, the angler fish swallows them in a swift gulp.

Have You Heard?

The cells of an octopus make a dark, inky liquid. When attacked by a predator, the octopus releases the ink into the water, and the water becomes cloudy. The predator cannot see the octopus, and the octopus can escape.

A glowing angler fish

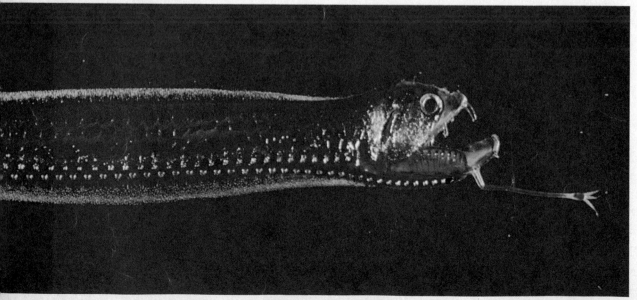

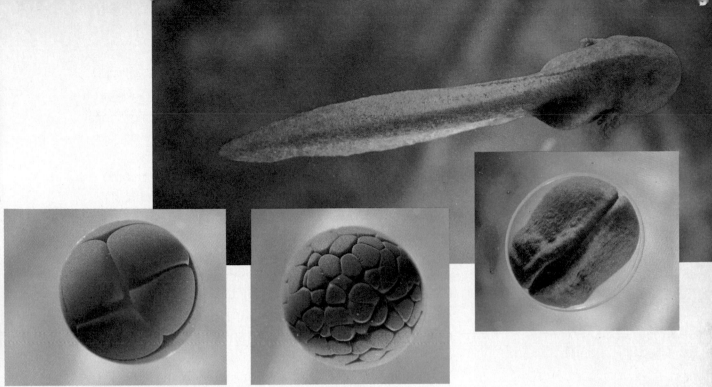

Tadpole developing from an egg

Living things also use energy to develop. These pictures show how a tadpole forms from a frog egg. First, the egg cell divides into offspring cells. Second, cell division goes on until the bunch of cells looks like a popcorn ball. Finally, cells keep dividing and begin to form different tissues. Plans in the chromosomes direct the tissues to form the tail and body of a tadpole.

Most bees can change plant sugar into honey. The bees gather sugar from certain flowers. The cells of bees break down the sugar into nutrients. Special cells use energy to make honey from the nutrients. The bees store the honey in combs. Young bees—or larvae—eat the stored honey.

A spider can use energy to make silk. The spider makes the silk in small organs near its rear tip. These organs are made of cells that change nutrients into silk. The spider uses this silk to spin webs and to wrap up trapped insects. Other spiders line their homes or tunnels with this silk.

Find Out

Find pictures that show how a human develops from a few cells into a baby. Use an encyclopedia, science book, or health book to find the pictures.

What Is Metabolism?

Every activity, from thinking to running, uses energy. Some activities break down substances. Other activities make new substances. All these activities make up the **metabolism** of an organism.

This chart shows the rates of metabolism for some common mammals. Each organism uses a certain amount of energy to keep alive.

Some organisms must eat often because they quickly use up energy. These organisms have a high rate of metabolism. The shrew in this picture has a very high rate of metabolism. It spends its whole life sniffing, scratching, and digging for food. If you ate like a shrew, you would need to eat 180 hamburgers every day!

An elephant has a low rate of metabolism. The elephant does not eat often because it slowly uses energy. If you ate like an elephant, you would need to eat about four hamburgers a day.

Think About It

1. Name three ways in which an organism uses energy.
2. What is metabolism? Explain why some animals must eat large amounts of food.
3. **Challenge** How do cells keep an organism alive?

metabolism
(mə tab/ə liz/əm), all the activities of an organism that either break down substances or make new substances.

high metabolism
Shrew

House Mouse

Rat

Rabbit

Cat

Dog

Sheep

Human

Horse

Elephant
low metabolism

Metabolisms of Common Mammals

A shrew spends most of its life hunting

Tie It Together

Sum It Up

Unscramble the letters of the words in these sentences.

1. Nutrients are particles of <u>odof</u> and <u>rawet</u> that your body needs.

2. <u>Lobod</u> carries nutrients to the cells of your body.

3. A cell gets energy from food by the process of <u>clel pirateisron</u>.

4. <u>Lecl nivoisid</u> allows an organism to change from one cell into millions of cells.

5. Your metabolism includes all your activities that <u>kreab nowd</u> nutrients and <u>keam</u> new substances.

Challenge!

1. What might happen to an organism if a cell did not break down nutrients?

2. When does your blood become low in nutrients?

3. Explain how cell division allows an apple seed to grow into an apple tree.

4. Which organism do you think has a lower rate of metabolism—a tortoise or a hare? Explain your answer.

Science Words

cell division

cell respiration

metabolism

nutrient

offspring cells

particle

Chapter 7
Heredity

Imagine walking through a woods and spotting these organisms near a stream. You would have no trouble recognizing them. The deer has brown fur, four legs, a long neck, and large ears. The myna bird has black feathers, two scaly legs, wings, and an orange bill. The grass plant is green and has long, thin leaves. But how did these organisms get their special traits?

The lessons in this chapter tell about the traits of organisms and the reasons you are different from everyone else in the world.

1 Observing Common Traits

Think of some brothers and sisters you know. You might notice common traits that they share. Some brothers and sisters are about the same height. They might have the same hair or eye color. A few brothers or sisters have freckles. Others have the same-shaped nose or chin. Brothers and sisters might even share the same sound of voice. You can also find many of the same traits in their parents.

The people in the picture share traits. The girl and the boy are sister and brother. Two of the adults are their parents. First, find common traits between the sister and brother. Then, carefully compare the children with the adults. Pick the two adults you think are the parents of the girl and boy.

Think About It

1. What traits do the brother and sister have in common?
2. Which two adults did you pick as the parents, and what traits did you look for?
3. **Challenge** Name three ways in which a puppy might look like its parents.

99

2 Where Do Organisms Get Their Traits?

A pig with her piglets

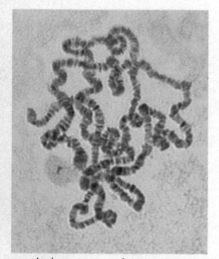
A chromosome from a cell

This pig recently gave birth to piglets. The young pigs look like their parents. They have the same broad bodies and kind of tails. The piglets run about on pig hoofs, instead of paws or feet. You would not mistake a piglet's snout for the snout of a dog or horse.

Parents pass on their traits to their offspring. A stork cannot lay eggs that hatch into ducks or swans. It can only pass on stork traits to its offspring. The young storks will grow long, sharp bills and thin, curved necks. They can only show the traits of storks that their parents passed on to them.

Cells carry the directions for the traits of an organism. Each nucleus has a set of chromosomes. The picture shows that each chromosome looks like a tape with bands. The directions—or **genes**—for traits lie along these bands. The chromosomes come in pairs. So a gene on one chromosome matches a gene on the partner chromosome.

gene (jēn), a direction for a trait. Genes are found along the bands of a chromosome.

Many pairs of genes work together to form the traits of a living thing. In pigs, many gene pairs can direct the growth of a snout like the one shown here. Several gene pairs might have directions for the size of the snout. Other gene pairs might have directions for a round, flat end. Different genes might direct skin tissue to grow over the snout. Still more gene pairs might direct hairs to grow from the skin.

Heredity is the passing of genes from parents to offspring. In cells, heredity takes place the moment a cell divides. The chromosomes and genes double. Now, there are two sets of genes. The cell then divides into two offspring cells. Each cell receives—or **inherits**—a set of genes.

Imagine a maple tree that grew from a seed one hundred years ago. The picture shows how the leaves and fruits might have looked. Each seed carried the genes of the maple tree. The seeds fell to the ground and grew into young maple trees. These trees had the same kind of bark, leaves, and seeds as their parents. Soon, seeds formed on these trees and fell to the ground. They grew into new maple trees. In time the new maple trees formed more seeds that fell and grew into more maple trees. The maple trees that you see today are much like those which grew from seeds one hundred years ago.

Pig snout

heredity (hə red′ə tē), the passing of genes from parent to offspring.

inherit (in her′it), to receive a set of genes from 1 or 2 parents.

Maple leaves and fruits

What Makes Organisms Different from One Another?

Have You Heard?
The antelope jack rabbit is the largest hare, and it has the most powerful hind legs of all hares. The antelope jack rabbit can cover 4 m in a single hop and can travel 64 km per hour!

How would you find a hare that was in a group of cats? You might look for the size and shape of its ears. You might also look for the kind of legs and paws of a hare. You might look for differences in the tail too.

Different organisms have different genes for the same trait. A hare has gene pairs for long, thin ears. A cat has gene pairs for short, cone-shaped ears. A hare has genes for large paws and powerful hind legs. But a cat has genes for smaller paws and shorter hind legs. For tail size, a hare has genes for a short, fluffy tail. Most cats have genes for long, smooth tails.

Both the lynx and the house cat are types of cats. But, as the pictures show, they have different genes for the same traits. A lynx has many gene pairs that cause a short tail and pointed, black ear tips to form. The house cat has different gene pairs for a long tail and rounded ear tips. Both cats are different from each other because they inherited different genes.

House cat

Lynx

102

Himalayan cat

Tortoise-shell cat

Rex cat

Even organisms of the same species can have different genes for a trait. The house cats pictured here have genes for cat fur. But each cat has different genes for the color and length of fur. The Himalayan cat has dark markings on its long, thick fur. The curly whiskers of the Rex cat match its curly fur. And the tortoise-shell cat has a patched coat. These house cats show differences in the same trait—or **variations**—for fur. Variations are caused by different genes.

People show many variations of traits. For example, **melanin** is the substance that gives your skin its color. One gene pair directs your skin cells to make melanin. But many other gene pairs have directions for the amount of melanin that the cells can make. Eight or more genes might work together to make the many variations of skin color. You might find over ten variations of skin color just in your class!

Melanin also gives your eyes their color. Some gene pairs cause the eye cells to make very little melanin. People with these genes have blue eyes. Other gene pairs cause the cells to make more melanin. People with these genes have green eyes. Variations in eye color depend on the amount of melanin made by the eye cells. Dark-brown eyes have the most melanin.

variations (ver′ē ā′shənz), differences in a trait among organisms of a species. Genes cause variations.

melanin (mel′ə nən), the chemical that gives skin, eyes, and hair their colors.

103

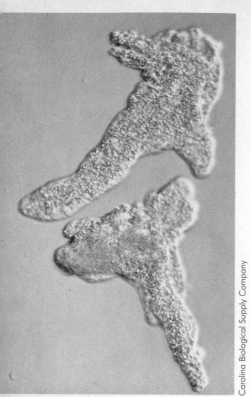

Ameba proteus
and offspring

How Does Heredity Affect Variations?

Ameba proteus (prō′tē əs) has only one parent. It inherits all its genes from the one parent. You cannot tell which is the parent and which is the offspring shown here. Some other organisms that reproduce by splitting show few variations. These organisms change very little over time.

Organisms made of many cells usually have two parents. The offspring inherits half its genes from each parent. The genes from both parents will shape the way this offspring looks and behaves.

Organisms with two parents inherit different genes from each parent. This mixing of genes causes many variations among members of the same species. Some offspring might look more like one parent. Some might look like both parents. And some offspring might not look like either parent. These guinea pigs show many variations from their parents even though they inherited genes from both parents.

Think About It

1. What is a gene?
2. What is heredity?
3. What causes differences among organisms?
4. **Challenge** Make a list of all the variations of human hair that you see in your classroom.

Offspring can differ from parents

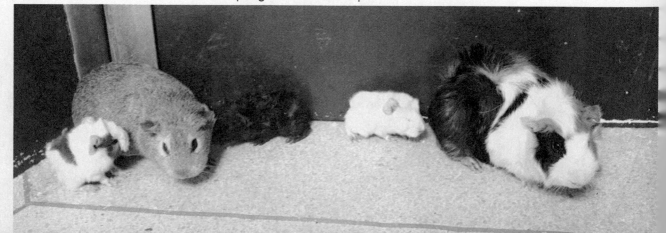

Activity

Recording Variations of a Human Trait

Purpose
To learn which eye color is found in most classmates.

You Will Need
• 1 sheet of lined paper
• colored pencils
• 1 ruler

Directions
1. Use the ruler to make a chart like the one in the picture. You can make this chart by drawing only 2 lines.
2. Write *blue* beneath the first row of boxes. Write *green* beneath the next row and *brown* beneath the last row.
3. Number the boxes 1 to 25, going up the sheet, as shown.
4. Now, count all your classmates who have blue eyes. Color a box for each student with blue eyes. If 5 students have blue eyes, then 5 boxes should be colored above the word *blue*.
5. Next, count your classmates who have green eyes. Color a box for each student with green eyes.
6. Finally, count your classmates who have brown eyes, and color the boxes.
7. Remember to color only 1 box for each student. Do not forget to count your teacher and yourself!

Think About It
1. Name the variations of eye color.
2. Which variation do most classmates have?
3. Which variation do the fewest classmates have?
4. **Challenge** What eye color do you think most students in your school have? How could you find out?

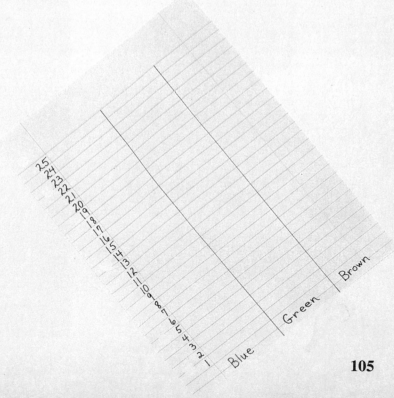

3 How Do Genes Affect Traits?

Plant growers often mix the traits of the same kind of flowers to make new variations. A grower can gather pollen from a red flower of a four-o'clock plant. This pollen carries genes for a red flower. Then, the grower brushes the pollen onto the pistil of a white four-o'clock flower. The pistil holds egg cells that carry the genes for a white flower. Each new seed will inherit a gene for red and a gene for white flower color. Soon, the seeds grow into pink four-o'clocks. The colors of both parents blend together in the offspring plants.

But most traits do not appear at the same time. Instead, one trait appears while the other trait stays hidden. One gene has the directions for the trait that appears. This is the **dominant gene.** The other gene in the pair has the directions for the hidden trait. This is the **recessive gene.** Usually, a hidden trait does not appear unless both genes in the pair are recessive genes.

Some traits appear mixed

parent plants

pollen

pistil

Flower of offspring plant

Notice the puppies and their parents in the picture. One parent has two genes for long fur. The other has two genes for short fur. Each puppy inherited one gene for long fur and one gene for short fur. But all the puppies have short fur. The gene for short fur is the dominant gene for fur length. The gene for long fur is the recessive gene.

Have You Heard?

A dominant gene causes dogs to bark. But some dogs inherit 2 recessive genes for the barking trait. These dogs cannot bark! Some hunters like to use these basenji (bə sen′jē) dogs to track prey.

Pups with their parents

A dominant gene causes dark fur in rabbits. Notice the family of rabbits in this picture. Both parents have one gene for dark fur and one gene for white fur. Three of the young rabbits have dark fur. They inherited at least one dominant gene from their parents. But one young rabbit has white fur. This offspring inherited two recessive genes for fur color, one from each parent. The white rabbit can only pass a white-fur gene to its offspring.

A rabbit with her young

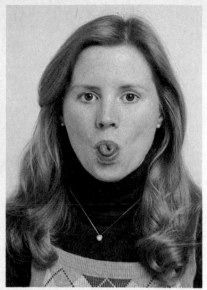
Tongue curling

What Are Some Dominant Traits in Humans?

Try to curl your tongue as the person in the picture is doing. If you can, then you have at least one dominant gene for this trait. People who cannot curl their tongues do not have a dominant gene for this trait.

Compare the ears in the pictures with those of your classmates. A dominant gene causes a person to have free earlobes. Each classmate with this trait inherited at least one dominant gene. But pupils with attached earlobes inherited two recessive genes. These pupils inherited one recessive gene from each parent.

Freckles form when melanin gathers in places on a person's skin. Another dominant gene causes this trait. People with freckles also have other genes that cause variations. Some genes cause different numbers of freckles. Other genes cause different sizes of freckles.

Think About It

1. What is a dominant gene?
2. What is a recessive gene?
3. **Challenge** Two black rabbits can produce white rabbits. But two white rabbits cannot produce black rabbits. Explain.

Free earlobe

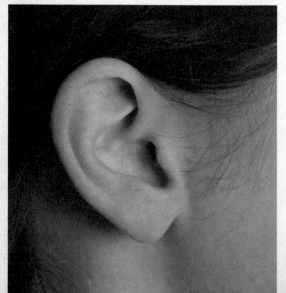

Attached earlobe

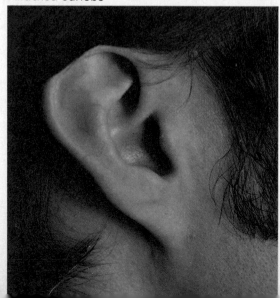

Do You Know?

There Are Many Different Dog Breeds

Dogs have helped people do work for thousands of years. In earlier times, people needed dogs to help them hunt and to give them protection. So the dogs they kept around their homes or camps were hunters and watchdogs. In later times, people needed dogs that could act as shepherds. So breeds, or kinds, of dogs that would protect other animals were developed.

Today, dogs are used in the ways mentioned and in other ways as well. Dogs guide the blind, pull sleds through the snow, rescue people who are lost, and often provide friendship.

Scientists think that, a long time ago, all dog breeds looked very much like wolves. Some modern dog breeds look more like their wild ancestors than other breeds do. Notice how much the

Malamute looks like wolf

malamute in the picture looks like a wolf.

Some breeds of dogs have developed naturally. Dogs whose ancestors lived in cold climates for many years grow thick coats of fur. The dingo, whose ancestors hunted the speedy kangaroo, has long legs for running. But most of the breeds of dogs have been developed by people.

When people needed a fast, fearless hunter, they chose dogs with those traits. Only the fastest and bravest dogs were bred. The best puppies were then raised and mated, and so on. When people needed dogs with short legs to hunt animals that live in holes in the

ground, the dogs with the shortest legs were raised and mated.

Physical traits, such as leg length and coat color, and some kinds of behavior, are controlled by genes. Dog breeders know which genes are dominant. Barking is dominant over silence. Foxhounds bark loudly while tracking their prey. Irish setters, bred for the recessive trait, track without barking.

Developing new breeds or making changes in a breed of dogs takes a long time. Many generations of puppies must be born and bred before the traits of the new breed are established.

4 What Can Happen to Genes?

mutation (myü tā′shən), a change in the directions for a trait that produces a new trait which can be inherited.

Many organisms grow from two cells that come together. Each cell carries a set of genes from a parent. The genes match up, and cell division begins. Every gene pair can affect one or more traits as the cells form tissues. The cells use the directions of the genes to build the organism.

Sometimes the directions for a trait can change. The trait also changes. Such a change in the directions is a **mutation.**

Notice the leaves of the white plants in the picture. These plants inherited a trait caused by a mutation. Usually, leaf cells inherit the directions to make green chlorophyll. But the cells of these plants inherited directions that changed. The new directions do not allow the cells to make chlorophyll. These plants will die because they need chlorophyll to make food.

Plants with colorless leaves

Sheep with mutation for short legs

Mutations often harm a living thing that inherits them. The sheep in the picture grew short legs because of a mutation. These sheep cannot run fast or jump very high. Mountain lions and wolves can easily catch them in the wild. Some ranchers like to raise these sheep because they cannot jump over fences and run away!

The flies in the pictures inherited short or curly wings that were caused by mutations. They cannot fly to food or fly away from danger. If left alone, the flies will die before they can pass their wing traits to any offspring.

Suppose the fly with short wings lives long enough to become a parent. Its offspring might inherit the gene for short wings. But the offspring will also inherit a gene for normal wings from the other parent. The gene for normal wings is the dominant gene, so the offspring will have normal wings. An offspring must inherit two genes for short wings in order to have short wings. A recessive trait may take many years to appear.

Wing mutations of fruit flies

Think About It

1. What is a mutation?
2. How can a mutation affect an organism?
3. **Challenge** A mutation caused an orange tree to form seedless oranges. Explain how this mutation can be either harmful or helpful.

5 Can People Influence Traits They Inherit?

How many of your classmates wear glasses? Many people inherit a dominant gene that causes poor sight. The first picture shows the shape of a normal eye. The second picture shows how this gene causes the eye to grow longer than usual. A person with this trait can see nearby things, but faraway things look fuzzy. Notice in the third picture how the glasses correct this trait.

Medicine can give you substances that genes fail to give. People can inherit two recessive genes that cause diabetes (dī′ə bē′tēz). A person with diabetes cannot make enough **insulin,** a substance that helps sugar enter body cells. Without enough insulin the cells will not get the energy they need from sugar. But people with diabetes can take shots of insulin. They can also learn what foods they should eat to help control the amount of sugar their cells get.

insulin (in′sə lən), a substance made in the body that helps sugar enter cells.

Find Out

When did people begin to wear eyeglasses to correct their sight? Find the answer in a library book about eyeglasses or spectacles.

Eyeglasses correct vision

Object appears clear

Object appears fuzzy

eyeglass

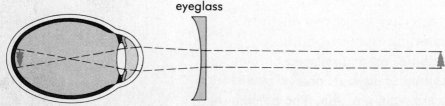

Object appears clear again

112

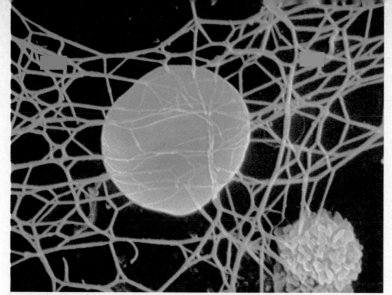

Trapped blood cells

Another recessive gene pair causes hemophilia (hē′mə fil′ē ə). When cut, a person with this blood illness keeps bleeding for a very long time. The blood cannot form a scab. A person with hemophilia can die from a loss of blood.

In the past many people with this disease died from simple cuts. But now a special substance can be placed on a cut. This substance forms a net and traps blood cells, as shown. Also, a person can learn ways to slow the bleeding from simple cuts. In this way they do not lose much blood on the way to the hospital. Once in the hospital, the person is given more blood.

A different recessive gene pair causes another blood illness. In sickle cell anemia (sik′əl sel ə nē′mē ə) the blood cells change shape when the blood loses oxygen. This usually happens when the body does heavy work. These boat-shaped cells, as shown, block the blood vessels. A person with this illness often feels weak. When the cells change shape, the person might feel strong pain in the knees, elbows, or shoulders.

Someone with sickle cell anemia must rest often while working or playing. If the cells change shape, medicine can be taken to stop the pain. The person might also go to the hospital and be given more blood.

Have You Heard?

Scientists think that the sickle-cell gene began as a mutation. People who inherited just 1 gene for this mutation did not suffer from sickle cell anemia. The trait also protected them from a dangerous disease—malaria. The protist that causes malaria became trapped and died when blood cells changed shape. Since malaria can kill people, those people with 1 sickle-cell gene lived to pass the gene to their children.

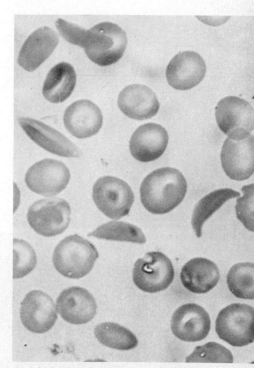

Sickled blood cells

How Can Habits Influence Traits?

Traits can be influenced by the ways people live. Many people inherit genes for healthy teeth but do not brush their teeth. Bacteria can mix with sugar from foods and make holes in their teeth.

The man in the picture has genes for small muscles. But he built up his muscles through careful eating and by lifting weights.

Sometimes people with genes for a healthy body might not get enough food to eat. Their body cells cannot get enough nutrients to grow and to divide as usual. In turn, their muscles and bones might become weak. Such people might lose too much weight and become too tired. Their bodies would not be very healthy anymore.

Genes store the directions for your traits. Your cells use these directions to build tissues, organs, and systems. Usually, your body grows by these directions. But mutations can change the directions. Medicine, habits, and ways of living can also influence traits.

Think About It

1. Describe three inherited illnesses.
2. How can some inherited illnesses be treated?
3. **Challenge** Name three habits that can influence your weight.

Exercise can influence body traits

Tie It Together

Sum It Up

A farmer mates two prize chickens. The traits of these chickens are listed below.

Rooster

- normal feathers
- no feathers on his legs
- a tall, thin, red comb on top of his head

Hen

- silky feathers
- feathers on her legs
- a short, wide, red comb on top of her head

The eggs hatch, and the chicks grow up to become roosters or hens. The traits of these offspring are:

- all offspring have normal feathers
- all offspring have feathers on their legs
- one offspring has no comb
- all offspring with combs have tall, thin, red combs

Decide if the following traits are caused by a dominant gene, a recessive gene, or a mutation.

1. silky feathers
2. feathers on the legs
3. short, wide, red comb
4. no comb

Name a few things the farmer can do to make sure the chickens stay healthy.

Challenge!

1. How does a tiger get its stripes?

2. A bull has black-and-white spots, and a cow is solid black. All their offspring have solid-black coats. Does a dominant or a recessive gene cause solid-black fur in cattle?

3. The gene for blonde hair is recessive. A mother and father have blonde hair. Both parents color their hair dark brown. What kind of hair will their offspring have?

4. Besides hemophilia and sickle cell anemia, what are two inherited illnesses that scientists are trying to treat?

5. A mouse gives birth to ten baby mice. But one baby mouse is born with no tail. Explain two ways this might have happened.

Science Words

dominant gene

gene

heredity

inherit

insulin

melanin

mutation

recessive gene

variations

Laboratory

Comparing Movement of a Liquid Through Different Materials

a

b

Purpose
To compare the rates at which a liquid moves through several different materials.

You Will Need
- newspaper
- assorted cans or glass jars
- masking tape
- marking pen
- small plastic bag
- unwaxed paper cup
- 3 waxed paper cups
- plastic-foam cup
- balloon
- starch-and-water mixture
- water
- iodine
- medicine dropper
- clock with a second hand

Stating the Problem
Many organisms have different kinds of cells. Some cells allow certain particles to pass through their membranes easily. Other cells do not allow such particles to move in and out easily. For example, a plant's root cells allow water and other particles to pass quickly in and out of the cell. Some leaf cells, however, do not allow water and other particles to pass through their membranes easily. You can compare the rates of movement of a liquid through a variety of materials.

Investigating the Problem
1. Cover your desk with sheets of newspaper. Label a set of cans or jars A, B, C, and so on. Place a material to be tested, such as a plastic bag or paper cup, in each can, as shown in picture a.
2. Predict each material's ability to let a liquid pass through it. Make an ordered list of the materials to be tested. At the top of the list, write the name of the material you predict

c

will let liquid pass through most quickly. At the bottom of the list, write the material that you predict will let liquid pass through least quickly or not at all.

3. Ask your teacher for a mixture of starch and water. Pour 50 mL of this mixture into each material to be tested, as shown in picture *b*. Pour carefully so that the starch-and-water mixture does not get on the outside of the material to be tested. Tie off the balloon and the plastic bag.

4. Pour water into each can or jar so that the water level is even with the level of the starch-and-water mixture in the bag, cup, or balloon.

5. Fill a waxed paper cup half full of starch-and-water mixture. Fill another

waxed paper cup 1/4 full of water. Put 1 or 2 drops of iodine in the water. Add 3 drops of the iodine-and-water mixture to the starch-and-water mixture in the cup. Note the change in color of the liquid. Set this paper cup aside. *CAUTION: Do not allow the iodine to touch your skin or clothes.*

6. Add 10 drops of iodine to the water surrounding each material to be tested.

7. Start timing the experiment. Observe

and record how long it takes for the starch-and-water mixture in each material to begin to change color. See picture *c*.

8. Make a bar graph as shown in picture *d*. Use your results to fill in the graph.

Making Conclusions

1. What caused the starch mixture to change color? How do you know this?

2. How do the results of your experiment compare with the predictions that you made?

3. Did the starch-and-water mixture move through the materials? Explain how you know.

4. Which material acts most like a plant's root cells? How is this material like root cells? Which material acts more like a plant's leaf cells? How is this material like leaf cells?

d

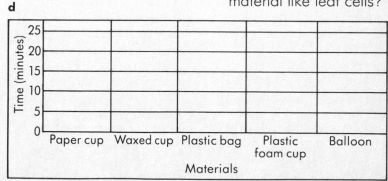

117

Careers

Medical Technologist

When people think of a career in medicine, they usually think of being nurses or doctors. But Anita knows that her job as a medical technologist is extremely important in making people healthy.

"A big part of my job," says Anita, "is looking at blood cells under a microscope. When a doctor or nurse takes a blood sample from a patient, it is sent to a technologist. By looking at the blood cells and performing tests, I can tell if the blood is healthy or diseased. If something looks wrong in the blood, I have to figure out what is wrong. When I report my findings to the doctor, he or she can decide how to treat the patient.

"I enjoy the variety of things I do. Besides studying blood samples myself, I teach my skills to medical students and doctors. Sometimes I go to meetings to learn new things about blood cells and blood diseases. Other times I meet with the doctors to check on certain patients. I even visit schools to talk with children."

Anita went to college for four years to become

a medical technologist. She spent another year working to become an expert on blood cells. But technicians, who help technologists in the lab, only need one or two years of training after high school. "Most hospitals have their labs open 24 hours a day.

That means people are needed to work at all times. Many people work here only in the evenings so they can go to school during the day.

"No matter what job you have, the field of medicine will be an exciting and challenging area."

A lot of people work together in hospitals to make patients well. Every time you go to the doctor, your condition and treatment is written in a medical record. The **medical records technician** keeps track of these records. The technician files, types, and reviews the accuracy of the records. The doctor depends on accurate, up-to-date records to treat the patient in the best way.

High-school graduates can become medical records technicians with some on-the-job training.

Many workers in hospitals and laboratories are technologists with at least two years of training in college.

A **cytotechnologist** examines tissue cells under a microscope. This person looks closely at the color, size, and shape of the cell for signs of disease. The technologist reports his or her findings to the patient's doctor.

A **serology** (si rol′ə jē) **technologist** helps make medicines to treat diseases. Many of these medicines come from plants or animal organs. The technologist also helps to find out how much of the medicine the patient should take.

Blood bank technologists collect, test, and store blood. They classify the blood according to type. Patients that need blood depend on the work of these technologists.

Many technologists of all kinds are working in research centers. They are trying to find cures for cancer and other diseases.

Blood bank technologist

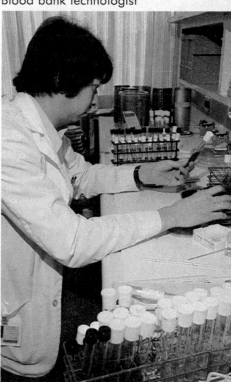

Medical records technician

On Your Own

Picture Clue

Turn to page 110 to learn how traits can change. Such a change caused the cat to have one brown and one blue eye.

Projects

1. You can find out if sunlight and darkness affect a trait. Plant a few uncooked beans in two potfuls of soil. Cover each pot with a large bag. Check the soil every day, and add water to keep it moist. Keep the pots covered until the plants are 5 centimeters tall. Then, remove the bag from one pot, but keep the other pot covered. Observe the plants every day, and look for changes in the leaf colors.

2. Find a picture of a simple skeleton. Make a model of it by using straws, pipe cleaners or thin wire, tape, and rubber bands. Cut the straws to match the bones in the picture. Run the pipe cleaners through the straws, and bend the straws into the shape of the skeleton. Use tape to connect the straws. You might also tape rubber bands to the straws to show where the muscles can be found.

3. Tear a small leaf from the tip of a plant in a fish tank. Place the leaf on a glass slide, add a drop of water, and cover the leaf with a thin cover slip. Observe the slide under a microscope, and look for the chloroplasts inside the leaf cells.

Books About Science

Small Worlds Close Up by Lisa Grillone and Joseph Gennaro. Crown Publishers, Inc., 1978. This book is full of unusual pictures that were taken with a special microscope which allows you to see parts of plants, animals, and minerals.

Your Skin Holds You In by Helen Doss. Julian Messner, 1978. This book has many wonderful secrets about your largest organ—your skin.

Living Light: Exploring Bioluminescence by Peg Horsburgh. Julian Messner, 1978. Many plants, animals, and fungi that produce cold light are discussed in this book.

Inside An Egg by Sylvia A. Johnson and Kiyoshi Shimizu. Lerner Publications Co., 1982. This book shows the way a chicken develops inside an egg, from a few cells to a chick.

There's Only One You: The Story of Heredity by Velma Ford Morrison. Julian Messner, 1978. The secret code of genes and the way heredity results in certain traits are some of the things covered by this book.

Unit Test

Matching

Number your paper from 1–5. Read the description in Column I. Next to each number, write the letter of the word or words from Column II that best match the description in Column I.

Column I

1. the building blocks of an organism

2. the direction for the trait of an organism

3. a change in the directions for a trait

4. a group of different organs working together

5. a group of different tissues working together

Column II

a. organ

b. system

c. cells

d. cell division

e. gene

f. mutation

Multiple Choice

Number your paper from 6–10. Next to each number, write the letter of the word or words that best complete the statement.

6. Organisms get energy from nutrients through
   a. genes.
   b. metabolism.
   c. cell respiration.
   d. mutations.

7. The sum of an organism's activities makes up its
   a. cell division.
   b. energy.
   c. system.
   d. metabolism.

8. Genes are passed on from parent to offspring by the process of
   a. cell division.
   b. cell respiration.
   c. heredity.
   d. metabolism.

9. An organism grows by
   a. cell division.
   b. mutations.
   c. genes.
   d. cell respiration.

10. Plants are usually green and stiff because their cells have
    a. a nucleus and cytoplasm.
    b. chloroplasts and vacuoles.
    c. chloroplasts and membranes.
    d. cytoplasm and vacuoles.

UNIT THREE
CHANGES
THROUGH TIME

Can you climb the mountains
    that are beneath the clouds?
Or do you live in the desert
    like I do?
Maybe we will meet someday.
Will we be scared of each other?

Dennis Manuel *age 10*

Chapter 8
Adaptation
for Survival

Balanced on its long legs, the great blue heron in the picture waits for food. When it sees a fish or a frog, it moves quietly through the water. When it is close enough, the heron uses its long bill to catch its food. The heron's long legs and sharp bill make the bird a good hunter in wetlands.

The lessons in this chapter will describe how organisms have traits that help them live in their environments.

1 Identifying Special Traits

2 What Is an Adaptation?

3 How Do Species Change?

4 What Happens to Species That Cannot Adapt?

1 Identifying Special Traits

Some dogs make good pets because they are friendly and easily trained. People depend on other dogs to do certain jobs. The huskies in the picture have strong muscles and thick hair. They can pull heavy loads and can live in a very cold climate. Other dogs, such as the bloodhound, have an extremely good sense of smell. Bloodhounds can find people who are lost in the woods.

People help develop different types of dogs. A person who raises bloodhounds tries to raise dogs that have a very good sense of smell. When two dogs that have a good sense of smell mate, they often produce offspring with a good sense of smell. There are many different types of dogs that people have raised. Each type has its own special traits.

Look at the dogs in the pictures. Their bodies look very different. Make a list of the traits in these dogs, and show how the dogs differ. Then, tell what jobs you think each dog can do.

Think About It

1. Name some traits that are similar in all dogs.
2. **Challenge** Name another animal that is raised for a special purpose.

Huskies

Dachshund

Chesapeake Bay retriever

2 What Is an Adaptation?

adaptation (ad′ap tā′shən), a trait that makes an organism well suited to its environment.

Walkingstick

Have You Heard?

Key deer are adapted to live in the Florida Keys because they can drink the salty water that is found there.

The long bill of a heron and the thick fur of a husky dog help those organisms live in their habitats. A trait that makes an organism well suited to its surroundings is an **adaptation.**

Look carefully at the first picture. What looks like a twig is really an insect called a walking stick. Hungry birds who eat insects have a hard time seeing the walking stick. Looking like a twig can help the walking stick avoid being eaten by predators. The second picture seems to show thorns on a stem. But what look like thorns are really little insects called treehoppers. Like the walking stick, they might avoid being eaten by hungry birds because they look like parts of the plant. The ways a treehopper and a walking stick look helps them stay alive—or survive.

Treehoppers

Special body traits are not the only kinds of adaptations. Sometimes the way a species behaves helps the species survive. Notice how the large, hairy musk oxen in the picture form a circle around their young. By acting in this way, the oxen protect their young from wolves and bears. Young musk oxen protected by their parents are more likely to grow up and reproduce. The way the musk oxen behave helps the species survive.

Think About It

1. Define adaptation, and give an example.
2. Describe a way that musk oxen have adapted to their environment.
3. **Challenge** Think of two ways in which a plant could be adapted to live in a dry habitat.

Musk oxen protecting young

3 How Do Species Change?

Adaptations help organisms survive. The spotted fur on this fawn makes the fawn hard to see among the trees. If the fawn is not easily seen by its predators, it might live long enough to become an adult deer that can reproduce. The adult deer will pass on the genes for spotted fawn fur to its offspring.

If a fawn had solid-colored fur, it would be seen more easily by predators. The solid-colored fawn might not live long enough to reproduce. Spotted fawns would have a better chance to survive. As time went on and more spotted fawns lived to reproduce, there would be more genes passed on for spotted fur than for solid-colored fur.

A spotted fawn is hard for predators to see

Galapagos tortoise

Cactus ground finch on prickly pear cactus

A person who raises dogs often selects the traits of the dogs that will be raised. In the wild it is not people but the environment that causes certain traits to be selected. If an organism has a trait that will help it survive in its environment, it might live long enough to pass on that trait. **Natural selection** takes place when organisms of a species survive and reproduce because they are well suited to their environment. It usually takes a long time for change to happen through natural selection.

Charles Darwin was one of the first people to form the idea of natural selection. More than 150 years ago Darwin sailed around the world. On his trip he collected organisms and studied how adaptations can help organisms survive. He started to form ideas about how species change. Two of the organisms he studied are shown in the pictures.

natural selection, process by which organisms of a species are able to survive and reproduce because they are adapted to their environment.

Frogs produce many eggs

How Does Natural Selection Work?

Darwin noticed that most species produce many more offspring than can live in the environment. Look at the frog eggs in the picture. Not all of these eggs will survive to become adult frogs.

Darwin also saw differences—or variations—among the organisms in a species. Look at all the plants in the picture. At first glance they might all look alike. But if you look closer, you will notice that each plant is a little different from the others. One might have more leaves than the others. Another might have larger flowers. In a species you can almost always find variations among the organisms, even if the variations are small. These variations come from changes in the genes of the organisms.

Variations among
African violets

Darwin thought that, because only some organisms in a species survive, the environment must affect different organisms in different ways. Variations among the organisms in a species give some organisms a better chance for surviving in the environment. If one organism has a better chance of surviving, its traits will be passed on to the next group of offspring. Variations in a species are needed for change in the species to take place.

Cold weather did not cause the fox in the picture to grow a heavy fur coat. But a fox that has a heavy fur coat has a better chance of surviving in cold weather. This fox will probably have offspring with heavy coats. Over a long time, through natural selection, most foxes in the species will have heavy coats.

A heavy fur coat helps the arctic fox survive

Florida pine forest

When Does Natural Selection Occur?

Changes in a species do not happen overnight. Most changes take many, many years. But sometimes we can actually see natural selection work. These pine trees look the same on the outside. But the drawings below show that some trees have thin bark and others have thick bark. During a long dry spell, forest fires are common. Then, bark thickness can mean life or death to a pine tree.

When a fire does start, the pine trees with thin bark are often killed by the fire. But the trees with the thick bark are better protected from the flames. More pine trees with thick bark survive the fire and produce seeds. The forest will have more trees with thick bark in the years after the fire. The type of pine tree that survives is the type most suited to the conditions around it.

Think About It

1. What were two things that Darwin noticed?
2. Explain why variations in a species are necessary for changes in a species to occur.
3. Describe how natural selection might occur, using a fawn as an example.
4. **Challenge** How did the giraffe get its long neck?

Thin bark

Thick bark

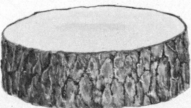

Activity

Measuring Variations

Purpose
To observe and measure variations in a group of peanuts.

You Will Need
• 20 peanuts in the shell
• centimeter ruler

Directions
1. Measure the length of each of 20 peanut shells to the nearest tenth of a centimeter. Record each length on your paper.
2. Find the average length of a peanut shell by adding all the length measurements. Divide by 20, which is the number of peanuts you measured.
3. Copy the graph on a separate sheet of paper. On your graph, show how many peanuts you have of each length by coloring in the correct number of squares for each length measurement.

Think About It
1. Were you surprised at the differences in lengths in your group of peanuts? What was the range from shortest to longest?
2. State a possible advantage and disadvantage to the peanut plant in making small peanuts. Do the same for large peanuts.
3. **Challenge** If you were a peanut farmer, which traits would you select in growing peanut plants?

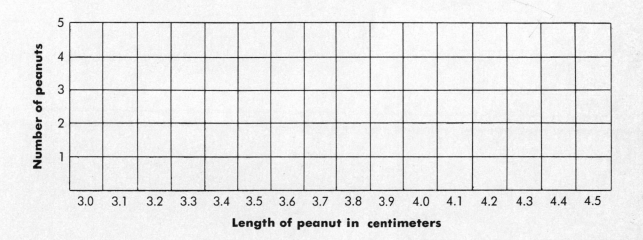

4 What Happens to Species That Cannot Adapt?

Species change when they adapt to their environments. But, over a length of time, environments also change. Less rain might fall each year, or the climate might get colder. If a species cannot adapt to the new environment, every member of that species may die. When every member of a species has died, that species is **extinct.** It will never be seen alive again.

Extinction has happened many times in the history of life on earth. Many scientists think that, for every species alive today, one thousand species have become extinct. The drawings show two species that have become extinct.

extinct (ek stingkt′), no longer existing.

Brontotherium

Dodo bird

Restoration of a woolly mammoth

The woolly mammoth is one extinct species. Notice how this animal looks like elephants of today. From studying the remains of mammoths, most scientists think that these animals lived thousands of years ago. The climate then was very cold. But with its long, woolly coat, the mammoth was well adapted to the cold environment. The mammoth lived in the grasslands and ate the plants there.

The mammoth became extinct ten to twelve thousand years ago. Around that time the climate where the mammoths lived became warmer. As the climate warmed, the grassland habitat needed by the mammoth changed to a boggy habitat. Some scientists think that the mammoth became extinct because it could not adapt to the new conditions.

Find Out

Endangered species are species that may become extinct unless they are protected by people. Find out about endangered species of plants and animals in your area.

The dodo bird lived on a small island in the Indian Ocean. It was a large, slow-moving bird, unable to fly. Birds of this species, first seen by Portuguese sailors in 1507, were hunted and killed until the dodo became extinct in the late 1600s.

Can People Cause Extinctions?

Less than 150 years ago, billions of passenger pigeons lived in North America. People sometimes saw the sky grow dark when great clouds of these birds passed overhead. But as people cut down the forests where the pigeons lived, the pigeons' habitats were destroyed. Pigeons were hunted for food, and many pigeons were also shot as pests. The last passenger pigeon, Martha, shown in the picture, died in the Cincinnati Zoo in 1914.

"Martha": the last passenger pigeon

Sometimes habitats that have remained the same for hundreds of years change rapidly when people build houses, farms, and factories. Swamps may be drained, or forests may be cleared. When species cannot adapt to new conditions, they are in danger of becoming extinct.

Manatee in Florida river

The shy, slow-moving animal in the picture is a manatee. This species is in danger of becoming extinct. Manatees live in rivers and warm waters near coasts. They help keep the waterways clear by eating water hyacinths that clog the waterways. Their habitats are being destroyed as the rivers fill with mud that runs off from farms. Also, many manatees are killed every year by powerboats that speed up and down the waterways. Now, laws protect the manatees by preserving areas where they live. Also, powerboats are not allowed in some places where manatees live.

Extinction has happened many times when environments have changed naturally and species could not adapt. But when people change the environment, extinction can happen very quickly. A species that becomes extinct is lost forever. By taking care of the environment, we can help save species that are important to people and other organisms.

Think About It

1. Define extinction, and give an example.
2. What could cause the manatee to become extinct?
3. **Challenge** How might mice be affected if their predator, the barn owl, became extinct? What might happen to species that mice eat?

137

Do You Know?

People Are Trying to Save Endangered Species

Whooping cranes

To people in Japan, the crane is a symbol of happiness. But the crane species pictured, the whooping crane, which lives in North America, might soon become extinct. Some people are working hard to save this rare bird.

The whooping crane is nearly 150 centimeters tall, about the height of an eleven-year-old. The crane's wingspan is over 2 meters. Its trumpetlike call, which can be heard from a great distance, gives the whooper its name.

In 1941, the whooping crane almost became extinct. Less than 20 cranes arrived at the species' wintering site. Only 2 or 3 of the cranes laid eggs that season. People realized that the whooping crane would die out unless steps were taken to save the bird.

The first and most important step was to protect the marshy land where the cranes live. No building is allowed on these plots of land. The land is left wild, and people are not allowed to disturb the birds.

Another way scientists are trying to save the whooping crane is by putting its eggs in the nests of sandhill cranes. This idea sounds strange, but there is good reason for trying it. Whooping cranes almost always lay 2 eggs each year. But only 1 baby crane usually survives. Scientists hope that sandhill cranes will act as foster parents to the young whooping cranes. Then, 2 young whooping cranes will survive instead of only 1.

The number of whooping cranes alive is still quite small. People might have to work for many years to save this bird from extinction.

People all over the world are trying to save many plants and animals from extinction for many reasons. A variety of animals and plants is needed to preserve different habitats. Plant and animal species are dependent on one another for their survival. Some endangered organisms might even provide food or medicines for people someday. The beauty of a plant or animal, such as the whooping crane, is only one reason that people try to save living things from extinction.

Tie It Together

Sum It Up

Write two or three sentences to describe each picture below. Use the words above the pictures in your sentences.

natural selection
variation
predators

adapt
environment
extinct

Challenge!

1. Describe the habitat of a bird that you know. List the adaptations that allow the bird to live there.

2. Explain what might happen to species in your state if another ice age occurred and the climate became very cold.

3. Describe the variations in hair color that you might find among humans.

4. Why is it important to save species from extinction?

5. One way to try to save species from extinction is to keep some members of the species in a zoo. What is an advantage and a disadvantage to this method?

Science Words

adaptation   natural selection
extinct

Chapter 9
The Fossil Record

This is the skeleton of a dinosaur that weighed more than the largest elephant. It stood tall enough to look into the top windows of a two-story house. A tooth of this animal was as long as a new pencil.

The name of this meat-eating animal is *Tyrannosaurus* (ti ran′ ə sôr′əs), which means "tyrant lizard." No one ever saw a living *Tyrannosaurus*. The last of the dinosaurs became extinct about 63 million years ago. The reason they became extinct is still a mystery.

The lessons in this chapter describe some organisms that once lived on earth. You will see how scientists have learned about these organisms.

1 Comparing the Sizes of a Dinosaur and a Person
2 What Were Dinosaurs Like?
3 What Are Fossils?
4 What Is the Fossil Record?

1 Comparing the Sizes of a Dinosaur and a Person

Tyrannosaurus was a large dinosaur, but some dinosaurs were even larger. This dinosaur, called *Brachiosaurus* (brāk ē ō sôr′əs), weighed about 45,000 kilograms—as much as 8 large elephants. This dinosaur's head rose 12 meters above the ground—taller than a three-story building. *Brachiosaurus* was about 23 meters long—almost as long as the distance from home plate to first base on a baseball diamond. Imagine the size of this animal standing next to you!

Let 1 centimeter equal 1 meter, and make a drawing of yourself. Then, make a drawing of *Brachiosaurus* next to you. Compare your height to the height of *Brachiosaurus*.

Think About It

1. How many times taller than you was *Brachiosaurus?*
2. **Challenge** Scientists estimate that *Brachiosaurus* was a slow animal which moved at a speed of 3 kilometers an hour. How would large size be helpful to such a slow animal?

Brachiosaurus

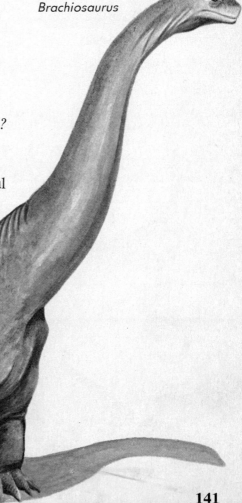

2 What Were Dinosaurs Like?

Many years ago, scientists found the buried bones of a very large animal. The bones did not look like those of any animal living on earth today. Scientists inferred from these bones that a different kind of animal once lived on earth but was now extinct. They called this animal a dinosaur, which means "terrible lizard."

No one has ever seen a living dinosaur. Scientists study bones and other traces left by dinosaurs, such as footprints and preserved eggs. From this study scientists think dinosaurs were not really lizards. But, like lizards, dinosaurs were reptiles.

Scientists have found traces of many different kinds of dinosaurs. Some dinosaurs were as small as chickens. Other dinosaurs were huge like *Brachiosaurus*. By studying the traces left by the dinosaurs, scientists have inferred that the dinosaurs were adapted to many different habitats and ways of living.

One type of dinosaur, called *Struthiomimus* (strüth′ē ō mī′mus), ran on two legs. The drawing of *Struthiomimus* is based on the traces that scientists studied. This dinosaur grew about as large as an adult human. Scientists infer that large eyes gave this dinosaur keen eyesight and long legs gave it great speed. These adaptations probably allowed *Struthiomimus* to escape from enemies and to catch the small animals that it ate.

Preserved dinosaur eggs

Struthiomimus

Diplodocus and *Allosaurus*

Another type of dinosaur, *Diplodocus* (di plod′ə kəs), walked on four legs. As you can see from the drawing, *Diplodocus* had a very long neck and a very long tail. Its length from head to tail was about 27 meters—longer than two school buses. This giant dinosaur had short, blunt teeth. Scientists think that these teeth were good for pulling leaves off tree branches. They inferred that the long neck and blunt teeth of *Diplodocus* were adaptations which allowed *Diplodocus* to eat leaves from the tops of the tallest trees.

Allosaurus (al ō sôr′əs) was a dinosaur that walked on two legs. It stood almost 5 meters tall—taller than a one-story house. Scientists think that it used its heavy tail for balance. The drawing shows that *Allosaurus* had a huge mouth with long, sharp teeth. Scientists have found the bones of another kind of dinosaur with *Allosaurus* teeth marks on them. *Allosaurus* probably ate all kinds of meat—perhaps even *Diplodocus!*

Have You Heard?

Iguanodon (i gwä′nə don′), which means "teeth of the iguana," was so named because its teeth resembled the teeth of the iguana, a tropical lizard. The teeth of the *Iguanodon*, a large, plant-eating dinosaur, grew in several rows. As old teeth on the outside row fell out, they were replaced by new ones from the inside row.

Find Out

Use library books to find out about the discovery of a dinosaur called "Supersaurus." One of its neck bones is as big as a kitchen table!

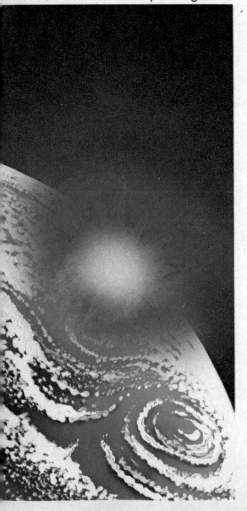

Perhaps an asteroid hit the earth 63 million years ago

How Did the Dinosaurs Become Extinct?

About 63 million years ago, dinosaurs and many kinds of plants, animals, and sea life became extinct. No one really knows how so many species disappeared about the same time. Many scientists think a change in the earth's climate caused the extinctions. But how might the climate change have come about?

In Italy and Denmark, scientists found large amounts of a substance that is rare on the earth's surface. This substance is also found in large amounts in asteroids. The finding led scientists to think that an asteroid hit the earth 63 million years ago. The asteroid would have smashed into dust when it hit, as the drawing shows. Large amounts of dust in the air might have blocked out some of the sunlight. With less sunlight the climate would have become colder. Dinosaurs and other species might not have been able to adapt to the new conditions.

Not all scientists agree that an asteroid caused the changes in climate. Scientists know that the dinosaurs became extinct, but the reason is still a mystery.

Think About It

1. Which adaptations allowed *Diplodocus* to eat leaves on tall trees?
2. What made scientists infer that *Allosaurus* was a meat eater?
3. **Challenge** Some scientists think that small mammals may have eaten many dinosaur eggs. How could this have helped cause the dinosaurs to become extinct?

Activity

Drawing a Dinosaur in Its Habitat

Purpose
To infer how a dinosaur might appear in its habitat.

You Will Need
• drawing paper
• colored pencils or crayons

Directions
1. Scientists found the remains of a dinosaur in the mountains of California. From the bones, they observed that the dinosaur had a long neck, large eyes, 4 paddlelike legs, and a short, fat tail. The length of the dinosaur was about 12 meters. From remains found inside the stomach area of the dinosaur, scientists infer that it ate fish.
2. Imagine that you have been hired by a museum to make a drawing of this dinosaur in its habitat.

From the information given, make a drawing of what you think the dinosaur looked like. Draw the dinosaur in the habitat where you think it would have lived.

Think About It

1. In what kind of habitat did you place your dinosaur? Explain how you inferred that it lived in this kind of habitat.
2. What kind of teeth did you draw on your dinosaur? How could you infer the kind of teeth that it probably had?
3. **Challenge** How would you make your drawing different if scientists inferred that the dinosaur ate plants?

145

3 What Are Fossils?

Imagine that you are walking along a beach. Something on the sand catches your eye. You notice a triangular shaped object like the one in the picture, and you reach down to pick it up. You have found a trace of an animal that was once alive.

A **fossil** is the remains or traces of an organism that was once alive. When most organisms die, they decay without leaving a trace. But sometimes an organism or part of an organism is preserved as a fossil.

Usually, an organism's hard parts, such as bones, teeth, and shells, are the only body parts that become fossils. In some cases a whole organism becomes a fossil. The picture shows a fossil insect trapped in hardened tree sap.

Footprints and outlines of leaves in soft mud can become fossils. If the mud hardens and changes to rock, the print of the organism remains. The fossil footprints in the picture were made by a dinosaur.

Fossil shark tooth

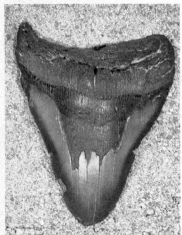

Dinosaur footprints

Fossil insect in hardened sap

Trilobite mold and cast

Dead organism sinks to bottom

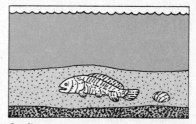

Sediment covers organism

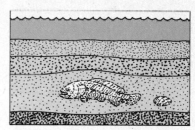

Organism becomes a fossil

Most fossils form when organisms die and sink to the bottom of a stream, ocean, or swamp, as the picture shows. There, the organisms are covered by mud, sand, or clay that settles to the bottom of the water. The matter that settles is called **sediment.** Over many years thick layers of sediment build up. The weight of the upper layers of sediment changes the layers beneath them into rock. The remains of organisms in the rock layers are fossils.

If the trapped organism decays and leaves a hollow space in the rock, it forms a fossil known as a **mold.** Sometimes molds fill with soft sediment that hardens to form a **cast.** A cast is shaped like the organism that was trapped. The picture shows a mold and cast of an extinct animal called a trilobite (trī′lə bīt). The mold is on the left, and the cast is shown on the right.

sediment (sed′ə mənt), matter that settles to the bottom in a liquid.

mold, a hollow shape left when an organism decays.

cast, a fossil that forms when a mold fills with sediment.

Have You Heard?

Animals such as clams live buried in the mud of lakes or seas. When they die, they are already buried. For this reason they are a very common kind of fossil.

147

What Can Fossils Tell Us?

The location of fossils can tell scientists how the earth's surface has changed. The sea animals in the picture were found in rock layers on dry land. Scientists inferred that the rock layers were once covered with water. The rocks and fossils most likely formed beneath a sea. Later, they were pushed up as the earth's crust shifted.

Fossils help us learn about many kinds of organisms that are now extinct. Scientists study the fossils of extinct organisms to learn what the organisms looked like and how they lived.

Think About It

1. What is a fossil?
2. Explain one way fossils are formed.
3. **Challenge** Scientists have discovered fossil fish in rocks that were found in the desert. What might the scientists infer?

Fossil sea animals

Discover!

A Surprising Fossil Find

Strange as it may seem, the tiny fossil in the picture can tell us how continents might have moved!

The fossil is a jawbone of a small squirrellike mammal, which scientists think lived 50 million years ago. Scientists have found many similar fossil jawbones in South America and some in Australia. But this fossil was found on the continent of Antarctica!

The fossil is the first clue that mammals once lived on Antarctica. No mammals live on the icy continent today. From this fossil, scientists have inferred that Antarctica once had a warmer climate than it now has. Icy Antarctica might once have been covered with swamps, grasslands, or forests!

The fossil jawbone gives evidence for a more dramatic surprise. Usually, species of animals develop in one area and spread to other areas. But how could land-dwelling mammals cross the thousand kilometers of ocean that separate South America and Australia?

One possible answer is that the two continents once were connected by the land of Antarctica. Then, animals might easily have crossed from South America to Australia.

The fossil jawbone from Antarctica gives evidence that South America, Antarctica, Australia, and the other continents were once joined as one super-continent, shown in the picture. Then, the super-continent began to break apart. The pieces have moved away from one another to become

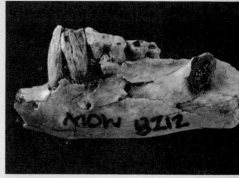

Fossil jawbone

the separate continents seen today.

The discovery of the fossil jawbone gives us evidence about life from the past. This tiny fossil is also an important clue in piecing together the jigsaw puzzle of the moving continents.

Super-continent that broke apart

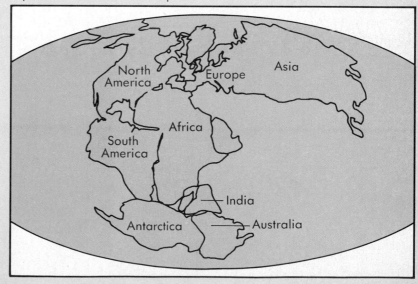

149

4 What Is the Fossil Record?

Fossils in stone fence post

Sometimes you can see fossils such as these in stone used for building. The stone for these walls comes from the **sedimentary rock** layers of the earth. Most fossils are found in this kind of rock. Sedimentary rock forms when many layers of sediment build up and turn to rock. If sedimentary rock layers are not moved by the shifting of the earth's crust, the oldest fossils are found in the lowest rock layers. Newer fossils are usually in layers closer to the earth's surface.

Thick layers of sedimentary rock lie under the ground's surface in much of the southwestern United States. In Arizona the Colorado River has cut through these layers to form the Grand Canyon. The picture shows the many different layers of sedimentary rock in the walls of the canyon.

A variety of fossils are in the layers of the Grand Canyon's walls. The very old layers at the bottom often contain only simple sea organism fossils. Fossils of more complicated sea life, such as fish, are usually found higher in the canyon's walls.

Rock layers of Grand Canyon

Scientists study sedimentary rock layers from all over the world. They have been able to prepare a record of these rock layers and their fossils, called the fossil record. This chart shows some of the types of organisms whose fossils scientists have studied. It also shows the time period during which most scientists think these organisms lived. The fossil record suggests that organisms have changed over long periods of time. As more fossils are discovered, scientists will be able to draw a clearer picture of the past.

The Fossil Record

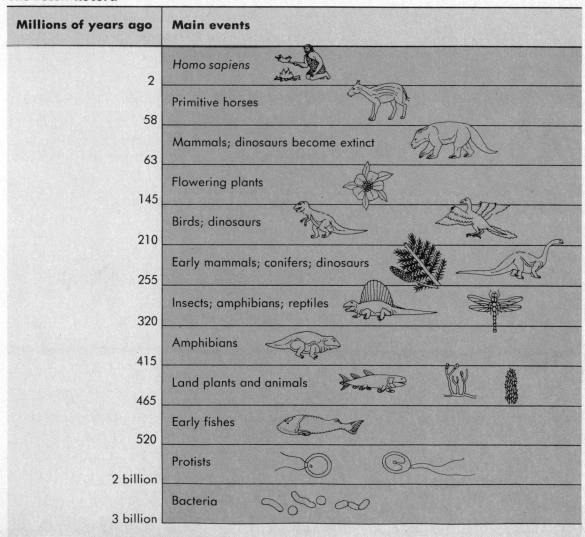

Millions of years ago	Main events
	Homo sapiens
2	
	Primitive horses
58	
	Mammals; dinosaurs become extinct
63	
	Flowering plants
145	
	Birds; dinosaurs
210	
	Early mammals; conifers; dinosaurs
255	
	Insects; amphibians; reptiles
320	
	Amphibians
415	
	Land plants and animals
465	
	Early fishes
520	
	Protists
2 billion	
	Bacteria
3 billion	

What Can Scientists Infer from the Fossil Record?

Sometimes scientists find many fossils of one type of organism. Fossils of an organism and its ancestors give scientists a picture of how the organisms have changed. The drawings show how most scientists think horses have changed through time.

The first horse that appeared in the fossil record was about the size of a large cat. From fossils of its teeth, scientists infer that the horse ate leaves. This little horse, named *Eohippus* (ē′ō hip′əs), had four toes on each front foot and three toes on each hind foot. Scientists think that this horse lived in a marshy habitat.

Mesohippus (mes′ō hip′əs), another type of horse, was found later in the fossil record. It was the size of a collie dog, and it had three toes on each front and hind foot. Scientists infer that this horse lived on plains and ate grass.

Merychippus (me′rē kip′əs), a horse the size of a pony, appeared later in the fossil record. It had three toes on each foot. But only the large, center toe touched the ground when it walked. *Merychippus* also ate grass and lived on plains.

Equus (ek′wəs) appeared most recently in the fossil record, around one million years ago. This large horse is the kind that is living today. It has hoofs that are well adapted to running on the hard ground of the plains. *Equus* also eats grass.

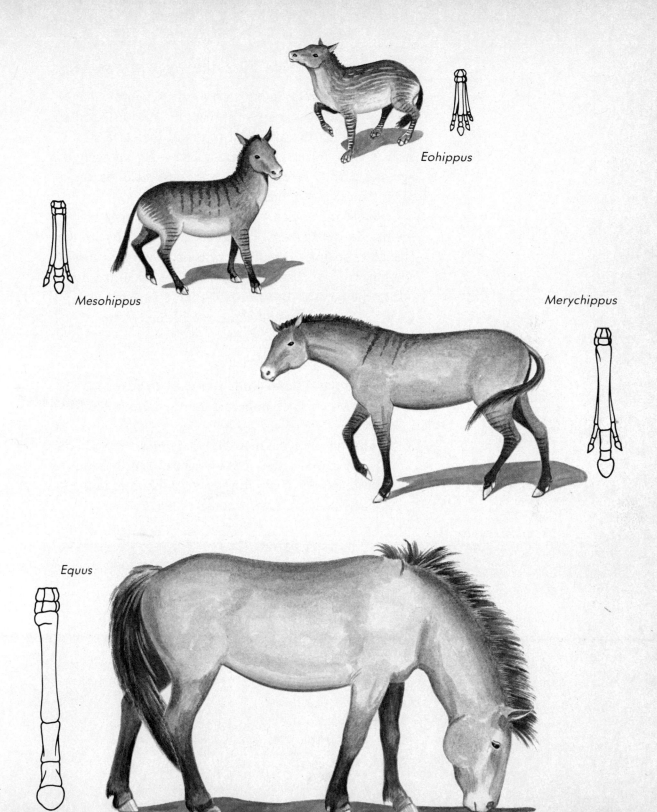

Eohippus

Mesohippus

Merychippus

Equus

153

How Can Scientists Find the Ages of Fossils?

The layer of rock in which a fossil is found sometimes helps scientists estimate the age of the fossil. Scientists think that different layers of the earth's surface were formed at different times. By knowing the age of a certain layer, scientists can estimate the age of the fossils found in that layer.

Scientists use other ways to estimate the ages of fossils. Every organism contains certain substances that change over time. Scientists measure how much these substances have changed by using a machine like the one in the picture. By measuring these substances in fossils, scientists can infer the age of the fossils.

Think About It

1. What is the fossil record, and what does it suggest?
2. What two changes in horses can be seen in the fossil record?
3. **Challenge** Imagine that the whole fossil record could be compressed into one 24-hour day and that each hour equaled 125 million years. What time in the day would dinosaurs have become extinct?

Estimating the age of fossils

Tie It Together

Sum It Up

Write a story about the picture below. Use the Science Words in your story.

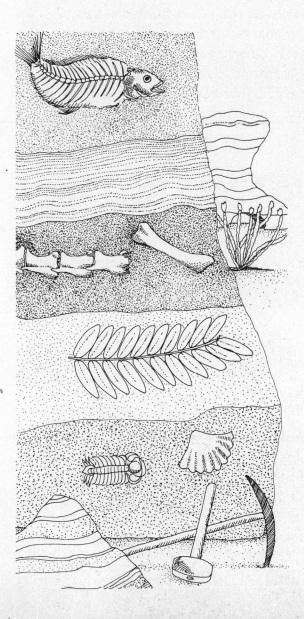

Challenge!

1. Name some adaptations found in dinosaurs, and explain how they made the dinosaurs adapted to their surroundings.

2. What are two different things that might happen to a fish which died and sank to the bottom of a lake?

3. Why would a fossil found in the upper layers of the earth's surface probably be younger than one found near the bottom layers of a deep canyon?

Science Words

cast

fossil

mold

sediment

sedimentary rock

Laboratory

Making Models of Fossils

a

Purpose
To make models that demonstrate how different types of fossils form.

You Will Need
- waxed paper
- tape
- clay
- seashell or other small object
- petroleum jelly
- small milk carton
- scissors
- water
- spoon
- plaster of Paris

Stating the Problem
Imagine that you are a scientist looking for fossils. One kind of fossil that you might find shows the shape of an object, such as a shell. You find another kind of fossil that has the same solid form as the original object but is made of a different material than the original object. How could these different types of fossils form?

Investigating the Problem
1. Tape a piece of wax paper to your desk. Roll a layer of clay 2-4 cm thick onto the wax paper. Press the outside of a shell or another small object into the clay, as shown in picture a. Remove the object.
2. Without showing your classmate the original object, ask him or her to study the shape in the clay and to identify the object that left that shape.
3. Coat the inside of the shape with a thin layer of petroleum jelly.
4. Cut off the top of a small milk carton. Clean out the milk carton. Read the directions on the package of the plaster of Paris. Study picture b. Mix the plaster of Paris in the milk carton,

b

Making Conclusions

1. Which kind of fossil model did you make in step 1? Explain how you recognized the type of fossil.
2. Which kind of fossil model did you make in step 5? Explain your answer.
3. Tell how the way you made each of your fossil models is similar to the way different types of fossils form on earth.
4. How did your classmate identify the objects that you used for your models? Can scientists identify their fossils in the same way? Explain your answer.

following the directions on the package.

5. Pour the plaster into the shape that your object made in the clay. See picture c. Throw away the milk carton. Let the plaster harden overnight.
6. Carefully remove the plaster shape from the clay. Ask a classmate to identify the object that made the shape.

c

Careers

Research Assistant

Just back from a trip to Alaska, Christine takes a moment to relax. What was she doing in Alaska? "You might say I was treasure hunting."

Christine is a research assistant at a museum. Her main job is searching for fossils and identifying them. "Every now and then, we go on a trip to Canada or Alaska to collect fossils. Sometimes we find a new kind of fossil no one has ever seen before! *That* is what I call a treasure!"

As a research assistant, Christine works with paleontologists—scientists who study fossils. "I like my career because I do a little of everything. Besides searching for fossils, I identify the rocks in which we find the fossils. I also make simple maps of the area and keep records in a notebook. On this trip to Alaska, the scientists asked me to take pictures of each fossil."

Christine's work is not always outside. In the laboratory, she must measure and record the size of each fossil. She also spends some time doing research in the library.

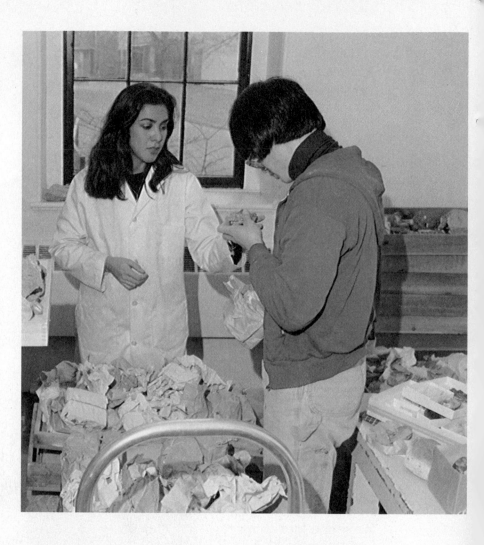

Research assistants go to college. In fact, some college students work as research assistants while they continue their studies.

"Almost every kind of scientist needs research assistants. I am interested in fossils. But research assistants also work with minerals, plants, animals, chemicals and electronic equipment.

"There is a lot that we do not know about the world. A research assistant uses his or her knowledge to help make new discoveries."

A lot of different jobs offer people the chance to work with fossils.

A **paleontologist** (pā′lē on tol′ə jist) studies fossils to trace the history of life on earth. This expert spends a lot of time outside. He or she oversees a dig site, where buried fossils are uncovered. They may have one or more assistants who help find the fossils. In the laboratory, the paleontologist determines the age of the fossils.

People who want to be paleontologists go to college for four to seven years.

In a museum, a **preparator** works on the fossils. This person prepares the fossils so they can be shown or studied. The preparator uses chisels, small knives, brushes, and other tools to remove rock from the fossil. This person must be very careful. A wrong hit with a chisel could crack the fossil instead of the rock. The preparator also puts together dinosaur skeletons at museums. The bones are connected and supported by metal rods.

The **collection manager** keeps track of all the fossils in a museum. The manager keeps a record of each fossil. This person is also in charge of loaning fossils to other museums and universities around the world.

Senior citizens, college students, and high-school students often work as volunteers to help collection managers.

A **fine arts packer** packs fossils to be transported. This person knows that some fossils are very delicate. The packer treats the fossils like treasures.

Working with fossils is very interesting. But the workers must have a lot of knowledge about this science. People who want to be preparators and collection managers go to college for at least four years.

Paleontologist

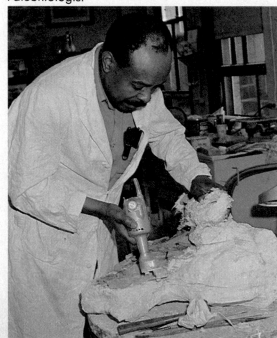

Preparator

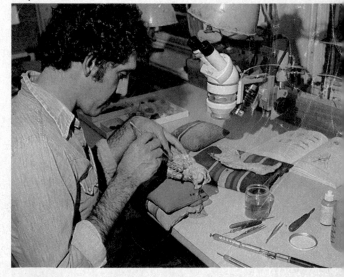

159

On Your Own

Picture Clue

The animal on page 122 might look like a dinosaur, but it is an animal that exists today. It is a kind of tropical lizard. Read the *Have You Heard* on page 143 to find out its name.

Projects

1. Observe variations in a group of plants or animals.

2. Visit a museum, and report to the class on the fossils that are on display.

3. Use a book, such as *How to Make a Dinosaur* by Sigmund Kalina, to learn how to make models of different kinds of dinosaurs.

Books About Science

Dinosaurs in Your Backyard by William Mannetti. Atheneum Publishers, 1982. Some scientists think that dinosaurs were not reptiles but were warm-blooded animals.

The Smallest Dinosaurs by Seymour Simon. Crown Publishers, Inc., 1982. Not all dinosaurs were big. Read about seven of the smallest ones.

Then There Were None by Charles E. Roth. Addison-Wesley Publishing Company, Inc., 1977. Describes how people have reduced the chances for survival of many wildlife species.

Unit Test

Matching

Number your paper from 1–5. Read the description in Column I. Next to each number, write the letter of the word from Column II that best matches the description in Column I.

Column I

1. no longer existing
2. a fossil that forms when a mold fills with sediment
3. matter that settles to the bottom of a liquid
4. a trait that helps an organism survive
5. remains or traces of past life

Column II

a. adaptation
b. fossil
c. variation
d. cast
e. sediment
f. extinct

True or False

Number your paper from 6–10. Next to each number, write *true* if the sentence is correct and *false* if the sentence is incorrect. Make each false statement true by changing the underlined word or words and writing the correct word or words on your paper.

6. A hollow shape left when an organism decays is a cast.

7. Sedimentary rock is made of layers of pressed sediment.

8. Variations in a species help the species become extinct.

9. Natural selection happens when organisms of a species survive and reproduce because they are adapted to their environment.

10. People can help save species from extinction by protecting the species' habitats.

UNIT FOUR
MATTER

Glowing, pulsating
With the life
    of heat and warmth
Shooting, sparkling flare.

Ryan Jones *age 10*

Chapter 10
Properties of Matter

When you see salt, it is usually in a saltshaker. You might not pay much attention to each little grain of salt. You could learn more about salt grains if you looked at them under a microscope. Notice the shape of each grain in the picture. You would learn even more about salt if you could see the tiniest particles that make up each grain.

The lessons in this chapter describe the particles that make up everything around you. You can find out how salt, air, water, and even your desk are alike.

1 Identifying Unknown Substances

The picture shows four bottles. Each bottle has a white substance in it. In front of the bottles are four labels. Each label has the name of one of the substances on it. But how do you know which label goes on which bottle? By learning something about each substance, you could put the correct label on each bottle.

You will get some salt and some sugar from your teacher. But you will not know which substance is which. Your job is to decide which is salt and which is sugar. To find out, you may use any of your senses *except taste*. *Never taste any substance, even if you think you know what it is.* You may examine samples of salt and sugar that are correctly labeled. You may also use the clues below.

Clue 1 Observe the shapes of the unknown grains with a hand lens. Compare them with the grains in the labeled jars.

Clue 2 Wet the substances with a few drops of water, and compare them by touching them.

Clue 3 Mix small amounts of the substances in water, and observe how the mixtures change. Compare them with labeled substances mixed in water.

Think About It

1. How did you find out which substance was which?
2. **Challenge** How could you tell the difference between baking soda and starch?

2 What Is Matter?

volume (vol′yəm), the amount of space that an object takes up.

Suppose you decided to build a tree house. You would gather wood and nails and start to build.

The finished house takes up space. The air inside the house takes up space. When you sit in the house, you take up some of the space. The amount of space that each object takes up is its size—or **volume.** Each object has a volume which you can measure.

The house, the air, and your body also have **mass**—the amount of material in an object. You can measure the mass of an object on a balance. The boy in the picture is measuring the mass of the wood block.

The idea to build the house does not take up any space. The idea is not made of any material, so it does not have any mass.

Anything that takes up space and has mass is **matter.** Houses, air, and people are all matter. Matter includes every object you can think of. To decide if something is matter, you must ask, Does it have mass? Does it take up space? If you answer yes to both questions, then that object is matter. Since an idea does not have mass or take up space, an idea is not matter.

Measuring mass

mass (mas), the amount of material in a substance.

matter, anything that has mass and takes up space.

What Are the States of Matter?

Matter comes in different forms and sizes. It can be a solid, a liquid, or a gas. These three forms are called the **states of matter.**

A solid is one state of matter. Solids have a definite shape and a definite volume. Wood, nails, pencils, coins, and ice are solids. The iceberg in the picture shows that a solid has a definite shape and a definite volume.

A liquid is another state of matter. Water, milk, vinegar, and vegetable oil are liquids. Liquids do not have a definite shape. The picture shows that, if you pour orange juice from a bottle into a glass, the juice will take the shape of the glass. But liquids do have a definite volume. Fifty milliliters of orange juice will take up fifty milliliters of space whether you pour it into a glass or spill it onto the floor.

state of matter, 1 of 3 forms of matter: solid, liquid, or gas.

Find Out

The fourth state of matter is called plasma. Look in library books to find out about this state of matter.

A liquid takes the shape of its container

A solid has a definite shape

168

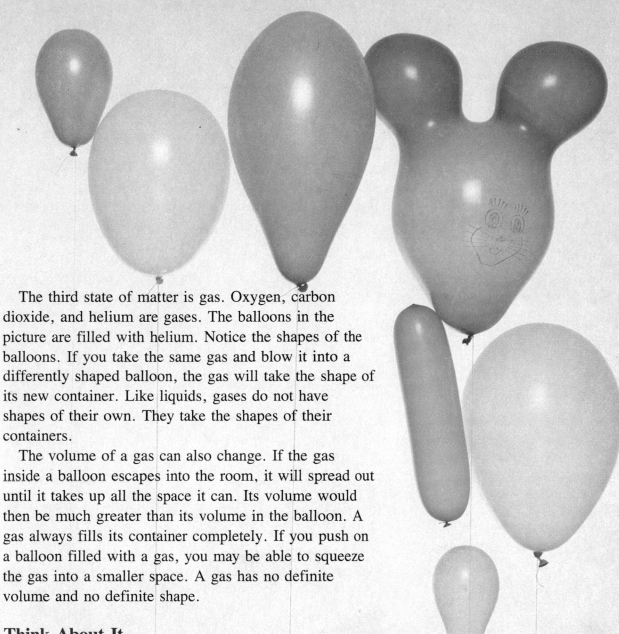

The third state of matter is gas. Oxygen, carbon dioxide, and helium are gases. The balloons in the picture are filled with helium. Notice the shapes of the balloons. If you take the same gas and blow it into a differently shaped balloon, the gas will take the shape of its new container. Like liquids, gases do not have shapes of their own. They take the shapes of their containers.

The volume of a gas can also change. If the gas inside a balloon escapes into the room, it will spread out until it takes up all the space it can. Its volume would then be much greater than its volume in the balloon. A gas always fills its container completely. If you push on a balloon filled with a gas, you may be able to squeeze the gas into a smaller space. A gas has no definite volume and no definite shape.

Think About It

1. What is matter?
2. Name and describe three states of matter.
3. **Challenge** If you change the shape of a lump of clay, is it still a solid? Explain.

A gas always fills its container completely

169

3 What Are Properties of Matter?

The onion in the picture is a purple-and-white solid. It has a strong smell. It can bring tears to your eyes. The onion also has a strong taste. Each of these statements describes the onion. When you describe an object, you tell what its properties are.

A property tells exactly what the substance is like. Some properties of lemon juice are its yellow color, its liquid state, and its sour taste.

Properties of matter can be divided into two kinds. **Physical properties** are the first kind. Some physical properties are state, color, shape, hardness, taste, and odor. Physical properties can be measured and observed without changing the identity of the substance.

physical properties (fiz′ə kəl prop′ər tēz), properties that can be seen or measured without changing the identity of a substance.

The properties of the onion describe it

Gasoline is a liquid that has a slightly yellow color and a strong smell. Its liquid state, color, and odor are physical properties. Iron is a solid, hard metal that is attracted by a magnet. Iron's solid state, hardness, and magnetic attraction are some of its physical properties.

Chemical properties of a substance tell how the substance will act in the presence of other substances. Wood can burn when oxygen is present. Rust forms when oxygen joins with iron. The abilities of wood to burn and of iron to rust are examples of chemical properties.

The pictures show wood and iron before and after they join with oxygen.

Think About It

1. What do properties tell about matter?
2. What are some examples of physical properties?
3. What do chemical properties tell you about matter?
4. **Challenge** A dark car gets hot when the sun shines on it. Is this a physical or chemical property? Explain.

chemical properties (kem′ə kəl prop′ər tēz), properties that tell how a substance will act in the presence of another kind of matter.

Iron nails will rust

Wood joins with oxygen when it burns

4 What Makes Up All Matter?

atom (at′əm), a particle that is the building block of matter.

The black material inside your pencil is a form of carbon. Imagine chipping a tiny piece off your pencil point. Then, divide the piece into two. Divide one of the halves into two again. If you did this ten more times, you would then need a microscope to see this tiny piece of carbon. Imagine that you keep dividing the piece into halves until you get the smallest possible piece of carbon. It would be much smaller than the broken pencil point in the picture. This tiniest bit of carbon that is possible is an **atom.** Your pencil point contains millions of carbon atoms.

All matter is made of atoms. Atoms are the building blocks of matter. Atoms are so small that you cannot see them. In fact, atoms are so small that the period at the end of this sentence contains more atoms than there are people in the world.

Even though scientists cannot see atoms, they can infer what atoms are like. They make different models to show how the atom might look if people could see it. Scientists base their models on how atoms act in experiments.

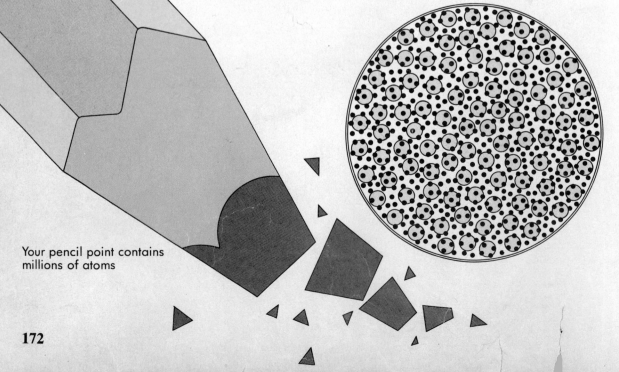

Your pencil point contains millions of atoms

Scientists have found that most of the mass of the atom is in its center. This central part of the atom is called the **nucleus.** The nucleus is made of small particles. One of the particles that makes up the nucleus is the **proton.** A proton has a small charge of positive electricity. The other kind of particle that makes up the nucleus is the **neutron.** The neutron has no charge of electricity. Atoms of different substances have different numbers of protons.

The **electron** is the third kind of particle that makes up an atom. An electron has a small negative charge of electricity. In an atom the number of electrons is the same as the number of protons. Their electrical charges balance, so the atom is neutral—or has no charge.

The size of the nucleus is very tiny compared with the size of the whole atom. If an atom were the size of your classroom, the nucleus might be no bigger than a speck of dust. Most of the area around the nucleus is empty space. Electrons move about in this space.

Scientists used to think electrons revolved around the nucleus as planets revolve around the sun. Today, scientists know electrons move quickly throughout the atom. The model used today is called the electron cloud model, shown in the picture. The electrons are somewhere in that cloud. Exactly where the electrons are at any second is not known. The darker parts of the cloud are the places where the electrons are most likely to be found.

nucleus (nü′klē əs), the central part of an atom. [Plural: nuclei (nü′klē ī).]

proton (prō′ton), a particle with a positive charge of electricity that is part of the nucleus of an atom.

neutron (nü′tron), a particle with no charge of electricity that is part of the nucleus of an atom.

electron (i lek′tron), a part of an atom with a negative charge of electricity that moves about in the space an atom occupies.

Electron cloud model

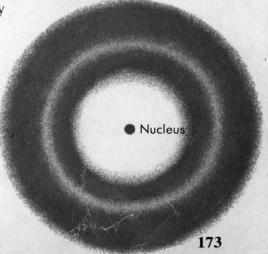

● Nucleus

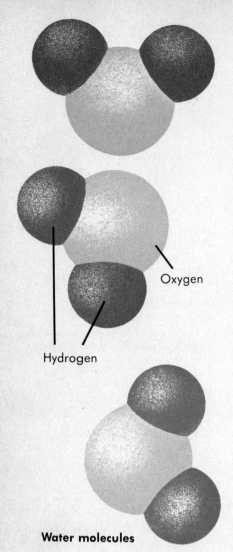

Oxygen

Hydrogen

Water molecules

molecule (mol′ə kyül), a combination of two or more atoms.

Have You Heard?

Atoms are so small that if the atoms in a tennis ball were as big as grains of sand, the tennis ball would be more than 100 kilometers high.

How Can You Tell Atoms Apart?

Not all atoms have the same number of protons, neutrons, and electrons. Over one hundred different kinds of atoms have been discovered. Each different kind of atom has a different number of particles.

Atoms are identified by the number of protons in the nucleus of each atom. Hydrogen is the simplest atom. All hydrogen atoms have one proton, and most have no neutrons. A hydrogen atom has one electron. Any atom that has just one proton is hydrogen.

All carbon atoms have six protons and most have six neutrons in their nuclei. Six electrons move around the nucleus of each carbon atom.

One of the heaviest atoms is uranium. It has 92 protons and usually 146 neutrons in its nucleus. The uranium atom has 92 electrons. A special kind of uranium is used as a source of nuclear energy. It has 143 neutrons in its nucleus.

Atoms can join with other atoms. When two or more atoms join, they form a **molecule.** Some molecules are made of only a few atoms. In the picture you can see that a water molecule is made of two hydrogen atoms and one oxygen atom. Other molecules are much larger. Some of the molecules in your body are made of hundreds of atoms.

Think About It

1. Describe the nucleus and the two parts that make up the nucleus of an atom.
2. What is an electron?
3. **Challenge** A neutral iron atom has 26 protons and, usually, 30 neutrons. How many electrons does it have?

Activity

Making Models of Molecules

a

b

c

Purpose
To make models of molecules with 2 or more atoms.

You Will Need
• 8 toothpicks
• 3 different colors of clay
• newspaper

Directions
1. Cover your desk with newspaper.
2. Use 1 color of clay to make 6 small spheres. These spheres will be your hydrogen-atom models.
3. Make 3 small spheres from a second color of clay. These spheres will be your oxygen-atom models.
4. Use the third color of clay to make 2 small spheres. These spheres will be your carbon-atom models.
5. Join 2 hydrogen atoms and 1 oxygen atom with toothpicks as shown in picture *a* to form a water molecule.
6. Join 2 oxygen atoms and 1 carbon atom as shown in picture *b* to form a molecule of carbon dioxide.
7. Use picture *c* to find out how to connect the atoms you have left. This model is a molecule of methane, a gas formed when plants rot.

Think About It
1. How many atoms are in a water molecule? In a carbon dioxide molecule?
2. How many atoms are in the methane molecule?
3. **Challenge** The drawing below shows a model of a molecule of sugar. How many atoms of each kind are in the molecule?

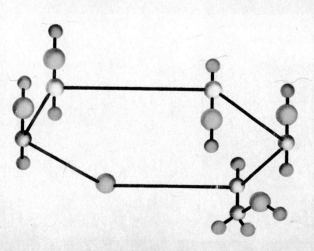

175

5 What Are Elements and Compounds?

element (el′ə mənt), a substance that cannot be broken down into a simpler substance by ordinary means.

symbol (sim′bəl), a shorthand way of writing the name of an element.

Silver is an element

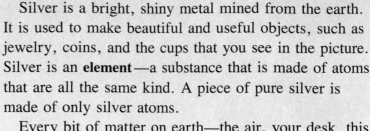

Silver is a bright, shiny metal mined from the earth. It is used to make beautiful and useful objects, such as jewelry, coins, and the cups that you see in the picture. Silver is an **element**—a substance that is made of atoms that are all the same kind. A piece of pure silver is made of only silver atoms.

Every bit of matter on earth—the air, your desk, this book—is made of one or more elements. Hydrogen is the lightest element. It is a gas that will burn. Mercury is a heavy, metal element. It is a liquid that is so heavy that a small bottle full of it would weigh as much as a brick.

Symbols are an easy way to write the names of elements. Scientists have given each element a symbol. Some symbols are the first letter or two of the element's name. Other elements were named using a language other than English. Their symbols do not seem to fit their names. The symbol for silver is Ag, from the Latin word for silver—*argentum*. The chart shows you some of the names and symbols of other elements.

Names and symbols of elements

Element	Symbol
Hydrogen	H
Oxygen	O
Carbon	C
Iron	Fe
Mercury	Hg
Nitrogen	N
Sulfur	S
Chlorine	Cl
Sodium	Na
Copper	Cu

Names and Formulas of Compounds

Compound	Formula
Carbon dioxide	CO_2
Salt	$NaCl$
Sugar	$C_{12}H_{22}O_{11}$
Hydrogen peroxide	H_2O_2
Sulfuric acid	H_2SO_4

Salt is a compound

Compounds are substances that are made of atoms of more than one element. Water is a compound made of hydrogen and oxygen atoms. Table salt is another compound. Salt, shown in the picture, is made of two elements, sodium and chlorine. In a compound the atoms of elements join in special ways that hold them tightly together. It is often difficult to separate the atoms of a compound.

The easy way of writing symbols of elements is also used in writing the names of compounds. The shortened way of writing the name of a compound is its **formula.** Because two atoms of hydrogen (H) combine with one atom of oxygen (O), the formula for water is H_2O. The 2 in the formula tells you how many hydrogen atoms there are. The chart shows the formulas of some other compounds.

compound (kom′pound), a substance made of two or more elements that are chemically joined.

formula (fôr′myə lə), a group of symbols that is used to write the name of a compound.

Think About It

1. How is an element different from a compound?
2. What is the difference between a symbol and a formula?
3. **Challenge** One gas that you breathe out is called carbon dioxide, CO_2. How many atoms of carbon are in one molecule of carbon dioxide? How many atoms of oxygen?

Have You Heard?
Two poisons, sodium and chlorine, join chemically to form a new, nonpoisonous substance—table salt.

Find Out
What is the most abundant element on earth?

Do You Know?

What Are Elements Like?

From the wonderful variety of elements come all other substances that make up the world. Most elements are metals. Perhaps you have seen iron, tin, copper, or aluminum. They are bright, shiny metals that are tough and strong.

But metals are not all alike. Some, such as gold, silver, and platinum, are beautiful to look at. People have used them for centuries in jewelry. Other metals, such as calcium and lead, look dull.

Some metals, such as osmium and iridium, are among the hardest substances in the world. Others, such as sodium, are very soft. One metal, mercury, is actually a liquid. And another metal, gallium, would melt if you held it in your hand.

Not all elements are metals. Some of the nonmetals are brightly colored like the yellow sulfur shown in the picture. Bromine is a dark, red liquid. It might be pretty to look at, but you should not get close to it. Bromine has a terrible

Diamonds on graphite

odor and can make you quite ill! Another nonmetal, iodine, is a steel-gray solid. But when it is heated, iodine turns into a deep-purple gas, as shown.

In some ways carbon is the most unusual of all elements. Sometimes it occurs as the very soft graphite from which "lead" in pencils is made. Or, strange as it sounds, carbon can occur in the crystal-clear form of diamond—the hardest natural substance in the world.

Sulfur

Iodine

Tie It Together

Sum It Up

The boys sat around the campfire, drinking hot chocolate. Tom held the metal cup to warm his hands. Smoke from the fire rose into the cold night air. The logs snapped and hissed as they burned. You could tell from the smell that they were pine logs. The heat from the fire felt good. Erik pushed a marshmallow onto a stick and held it over the fire. The marshmallow soon turned golden and gooey. Erik plopped the marshmallow into his mouth.

1. List the substances in the story that are matter.

2. Describe as many physical properties of each substance as you can.

3. List as many chemical properties of each substance as you can.

4. Which things have a definite shape and a definite volume?

5. Which things have a definite volume but no definite shape?

6. Which things have no definite shape and no definite volume?

7. Name and describe the three particles in atoms.

8. Is water an element or a compound? Explain.

Challenge!

1. It is round and flat. It is red and shiny. It can fit into your hand. Do these properties describe an apple, a button, a quarter, or a cookie?

2. A container of liquid can be half full. A container of gas is always completely full. Explain.

3. Describe the physical properties of honey.

4. The smallest particle that has the properties of an element is an atom, but the smallest particle that has the properties of a compound is a molecule. Explain.

5. Laughing gas is a sweet-smelling compound of nitrogen and oxygen that is sometimes used by dentists. Another compound of nitrogen and oxygen is a very poisonous gas. How can both of these compounds be made from the same elements?

Science Words

atom	molecule
chemical properties	neutron
compound	nucleus
electron	physical properties
element	proton
formula	state of matter
mass	symbol
matter	volume

Chapter 11
Matter and Heat

Skiing can be a pleasant way to spend a cold, crisp winter afternoon. Gathering around a blazing fire is just the thing to warm you when you get cold. But even though the air is very cold, you might have to back away from the fire because of the heat.

The lessons in this chapter will help you learn about heat and how it affects matter.

1 Predicting Melting Speed
2 What Is Heat?
3 How Does Heat Affect Matter?
4 How Does Matter Become Heated?

1 Predicting Melting Speed

People might wish to have the ice in the picture melt soon. The ice will melt if the weather gets warm. The sun will warm the air. The ice will receive heat from the air and the sun.

Think of as many ways as you can to melt an ice cube. You may use materials in your classroom or those supplied by your teacher. Choose three ways to melt an ice cube. *Check with your teacher to make sure the methods you have chosen are safe to try.* Predict which of the three ways will melt an ice cube the fastest. Try the three methods you have chosen. Record how long it takes for each ice cube to melt.

Think About It

1. Which ice cube melted fastest? Was your prediction correct?
2. What made the ice melt fastest?
3. **Challenge** Could any of your methods be used to melt ice on streets in the winter? Explain how.

Heat will melt the ice

2 What Is Heat?

Perhaps you have felt as hot in the summer as the people in the picture seem to feel. Sometimes the sun seems to be baking the earth. Describing where heat comes from is easy. Heat comes from the sun, from fires, or from other hot objects. Defining heat is more difficult.

Heat is a flow of energy from warmer objects to cooler ones. If you place your hand on an ice cube, your hand will begin to feel cold. Also the ice cube will begin to melt. Heat flows from your hand to the ice cube. Imagine placing the ice cube in a very cold freezer. If the air in the freezer is colder than the ice cube, heat will flow from the ice cube to the air. Heat flows out of the ice cube until the ice cube has the same temperature as the air in the freezer.

Baseball fans on a hot, summer day

Molecules in hot water move rapidly

The water in the pan is made of molecules that are always moving. If you add heat to the water, the molecules will move faster. The hotter you make the water, the faster the molecules will move.

Temperature is related to how fast the molecules of a substance are moving. Temperature is measured with a thermometer. When molecules move slowly, the temperature is lower. The water is cold. When molecules move rapidly, the temperature is higher. The water is hot.

Heat and temperature are not the same thing. Imagine that you have a cup and a bathtub, each filled with warm water. The mass of the water in the bathtub is greater than the mass of the water in the cup. The temperature of the water in the cup and in the bathtub is the same. But the bathtub holds a greater mass of water, so the bathtub contains more heat.

temperature (tem′pər ə chər), a measurement, shown as a reading on a thermometer, that is determined by the speed at which particles of matter are moving.

Find Out

Find out the difference between the Celsius and the Fahrenheit temperature scales.

Think About It

1. What is the difference between heat and temperature?
2. What do you use to measure temperature?
3. **Challenge** Does an ice cube have any heat? Explain.

3 How Does Heat Affect Matter?

The bridge in the picture was built with spaces in it. Notice the toothlike seams across the bridge. In summer the teeth are close together. But in winter the spaces between the teeth are wide.

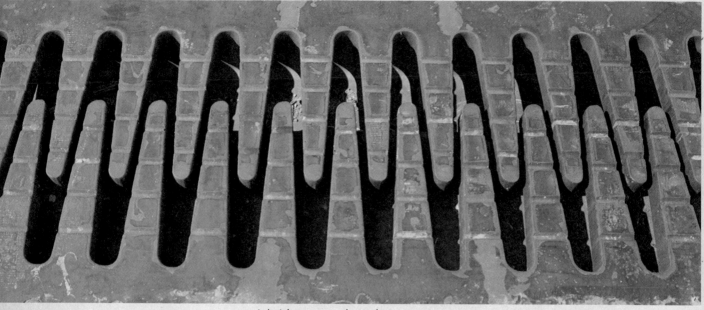

A bridge expands and contracts

expand (ek spand′), to become larger in size; to take up more space.

contract (kən trakt′), to become smaller in size; to take up less space.

Alcohol expands and contracts

Heat causes objects to increase in size—or to **expand.** The solid bridge expands during hot weather. Spaces must be placed in the bridge to give the concrete and steel room to expand.

When most objects cool, they decrease in size—or **contract.** The spaces in the bridge become wider when the bridge cools and contracts.

Heat also causes liquids and gases to expand. The red liquid in the thermometer is colored alcohol. When the alcohol becomes heated, it expands. It moves higher in the glass tube. You can read the temperature by looking at the numbers and marks on the thermometer.

When the alcohol in the thermometer cools, it contracts. The alcohol moves lower in the glass tube, showing a lower temperature.

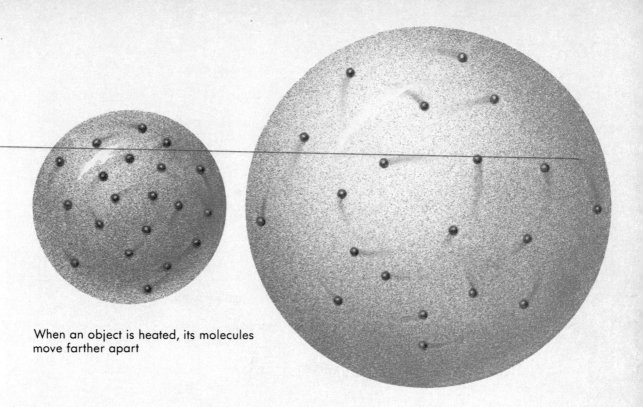

When an object is heated, its molecules
move farther apart

An object expands when its molecules move farther
apart. An object contracts when its molecules move
closer together. The red dots in the drawing represent
molecules. When a flame heats an object, the molecules
of the object move faster. They bump against other
molecules and push each other farther apart. As the
molecules move farther apart, the object expands.
Notice that the number of molecules in the two drawings
is the same. But the size of the object has become larger
because the spaces between the molecules are larger.

Have You Heard?

Very cold weather can snap
electrical wires. The wires
become so tight as they
contract that they break.

Think About It

1. Define expand and contract.
2. What happens to molecules in an object when the
   object expands?
3. **Challenge** Many highways have spaces in them
   every several meters. What might happen to a
   highway if there were no spaces in it?

Activity

Observing Expansion and Contraction

Purpose
To infer, based on observations, that gases expand when heated and contract when cooled.

You Will Need
• bottle with small opening
• balloon
• container of hot water
• container of cold water

Directions
1. Carefully stretch the opening of the balloon around the opening of the bottle, as the picture shows.
2. Place the bottle in the container of hot water. If you cannot push the bottle underwater, roll it around gently in the water, as shown, until it is wet. Allow the bottle to become hot. Observe any change in the balloon.

3. Remove the bottle from the container of hot water, and place it in the container of cold water. Allow the bottle to become cold. Observe any changes in the balloon.
4. Remove the bottle from the water, and dry it. Watch the balloon as the bottle returns to room temperature.

Think About It
1. What happened to the balloon as the bottle was heated? When the bottle was cooled?
2. What caused any changes in the balloon?
3. **Challenge** Which do you think will expand the most when heated—a solid, a liquid, or a gas?

Do You Know?

What Is a Bimetallic Strip?

The way metals change when they are heated is one example of their different properties. Suppose you heat a copper bar and a steel bar by exactly the same amount. The copper bar will expand more than the steel bar.

This property is used in a device called a bimetallic strip. The word *bimetallic* tells you that two metals are joined together. What do you think will happen when this kind of bar is heated? The copper part will expand more than the steel part, and the bar will bend.

Now, what happens if the strip is cooled? Just the opposite change takes place. The copper part contracts more than the steel part, and the bar

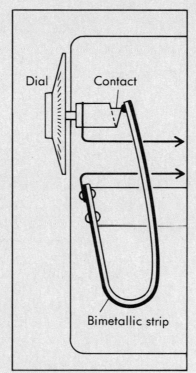

The furnace turns on

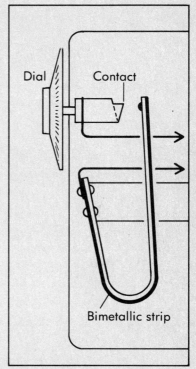

The furnace turns off

bends in the other direction.

You might have a bimetallic strip in your home. The *thermostat* that controls the operation of your furnace contains a bimetallic strip. The diagram shows how one kind of thermostat works.

The bimetallic strip is bent into a **J**-shape. As the room cools, the strip bends. When the strip bends far enough, it touches an electrical contact and turns the furnace on. As the room warms up, the strip moves away from the contact, and the furnace turns off.

4 How Does Matter Become Heated?

conduction (kən duk/shən), the flow of heat due to the transfer of energy from one particle striking another.

The girl in the picture is roasting a hot dog over a campfire. The handle of the long fork is very hot, even though it is not in the fire. Heat flows from the prongs of the fork to the handle. Notice that only the prongs of the fork are in the flames. The molecules in this part of the fork move back and forth very rapidly. These fast-moving molecules bump into nearby molecules and cause them to move faster. Energy passes from molecule to molecule along the fork. Soon, molecules at the other end of the fork are moving faster. In this way, heat flows from one end of the fork to the other. This kind of heat flow is **conduction.**

If you watch a burning fire, you may notice that smoke, sparks, and hot air rise from the fire. When hot air rises, you see another way in which heat moves. **Convection** is the flow of heat from one place to another by moving matter. Convection takes place in liquids and gases.

The air above the wood stove in the picture is heated in the same way as the air above the fire. When the air is heated, the molecules of air move faster. As the molecules move faster, they bump into nearby molecules. These collisions force the molecules farther apart. As the molecules move apart, fewer molecules are in a given volume of air. The molecules are not as closely packed. The air is less dense.

The warm, less-dense air rises, and colder, denser air takes its place. As more warm air rises, some of the air is forced downward. This air is heated again. The picture shows that a circular movement of air forms. Gradually, all the air in the room becomes warmer.

convection (kən vek/shən), the flow of heat due to the flow of hotter material in a liquid or gas.

Have You Heard?

The Gulf Stream, which warms the climate of western Europe, is a giant convection current in the ocean.

Find Out

How does a hot-air balloon work?

Convection currents around a wood-burning stove

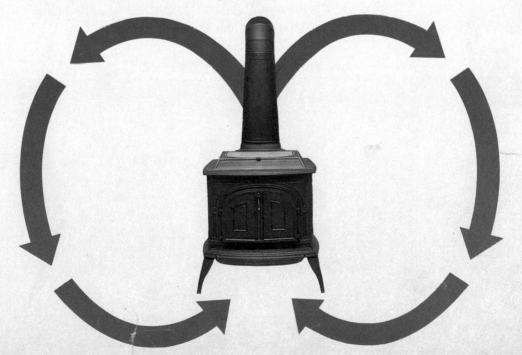

How Is Matter Heated by Radiant Energy?

The people in the picture are enjoying a warm day at the beach. They are experiencing a third way in which matter can be heated.

There are few molecules in space between the sun and the earth. The sun's energy cannot reach earth by conduction or convection. Energy from the sun travels through space as **radiant energy.** When radiant energy strikes an object, the energy is changed into heat.

All hot objects give off radiant energy. When this energy strikes your skin, the energy is absorbed and changed into heat. You feel this heat when you stand near a fire. Only the side of you that is facing the fire becomes warmed.

radiant (rā′dē ənt) **energy,** energy that flows through space, even in the absence of matter.

Think About It

1. Name and describe three ways in which matter can be heated.
2. Explain how heat travels from one end of a metal fork to the other.
3. **Challenge** Explain why the air is hotter above a toaster than along the side of the toaster.

Radiant energy travels through space

Tie It Together

Sum It Up

Write a story about the picture below. Use the science words in your story to explain what is happening.

Challenge!

1. Think of a way to keep an ice cube from melting in a warm room.

2. Metal lids on jars can often be loosened by running hot water over them. Explain why this works.

3. A potato will bake faster if a large nail is pushed into it. Explain.

4. A metal ball will just fit through a metal ring. What happens if the ball is heated? Explain.

5. Which contains more heat—a cup of boiling water or Lake Michigan? Explain.

Science Words

conduction

contract

convection

expand

heat

radiant energy

temperature

Chapter 12
Changing Matter

Changes happen around us every day. The car in the picture might travel easily on the road one day. The next day the road might be nearly blocked with snow. The sun might come out during the day and melt the snow, turning it to liquid water. When night comes, the temperature could drop and cause the water to freeze again.

Some changes affect the appearance of matter. Other changes affect how matter is put together.

The lessons in this chapter will help you understand changes in matter that occur in the world around you.

1 Observing Changes
2 What Are Physical Changes?
3 How Does Matter Change State?
4 What Are Chemical Changes?

1 Observing Changes

Matter can change in many ways. Matter changes because of the conditions that surround it or because of the substances it contacts. You would be surprised if your soup did not cool once you took it off the stove. You expect crackers you put into the soup to get soft. You can find out about some of the ways matter can change.

Get a small cup or jar from your teacher. Fill the cup half full with water. Add one of the following materials to your cup: a seltzer tablet, salt, small pieces of tissue paper, soil, bits of chalk, a tea bag, steel wool, oil, soap, or dried beans. Stir the contents of your cup, and record your results. If possible, let your cup sit overnight and observe any changes the next day.

Think About It

1. What changes did you and your classmates observe?
2. What changes did you observe the next day?
3. **Challenge** Would any of the changes have taken place without adding water? Explain.

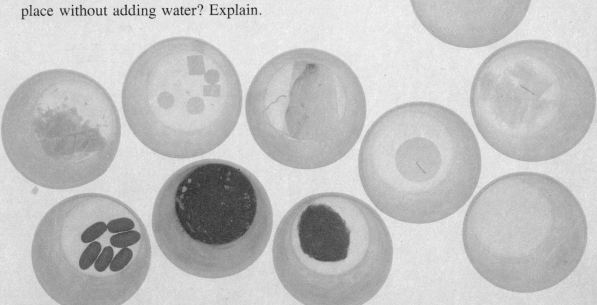

2 What Are Physical Changes?

The wood carver changes the shape of the wood

physical (fiz′ə kəl) change, a change in an object's appearance but not in its composition.

The artist in the picture is carving ducks from wood. As he carves the wood, he changes its shape. The changes he makes in the wood do not change the wood into something else. The wood is still wood.

Changes in the appearance of a substance, but not in what it is made of, are **physical changes.** A block of wood can be sawed into pieces until nothing is left but a pile of sawdust. The block of wood has been changed greatly in shape, but the sawdust is still wood. The wood has gone through a physical change.

A change in shape is one kind of physical change. Change in size is another kind of physical change. A rubber band that stretches when it is pulled changes its size. A bridge that expands when it gets hot changes its size. This expansion is an example of a physical change. Contraction that occurs when an object is cooled is also a physical change. Expansion and contraction change the size of an object but not what makes up the object.

Matter can change from solid to liquid, liquid to gas, and back again. Changing the state of matter is another physical change. When an ice cube is heated, it changes from ice to water. If the water is heated, it will become a gas, **water vapor.** Whether it is ice, water, or water vapor, it is still water. It has just gone through a physical change. Other materials can change state too. Copper will turn to liquid if you make it hot enough, but it is still copper. The picture shows liquid copper being poured into molds. When it cools, the copper will change to a solid.

water vapor (vā′pər), water that is in the form of gas.

Think About It

1. What is a physical change?
2. Give three examples of physical changes.
3. **Challenge** Imagine shaping a piece of aluminum to make aluminum foil. Explain how this is an example of a physical change.

Liquid copper pouring into molds

3 How Does Matter Change State?

Imagine attending a football game with thousands of other people. When the game is over, everyone crowds toward the exits. You can hardly move, because so many people are around you.

Molecules are packed into a solid material in a similar way. Molecules in a solid, such as an ice cube, are not free to move very much. Heat causes the molecules to move. But the molecules are held together in one place, as the drawing shows. At the ball game, you might be able to jump up and down, but other people crowded around you keep you in one place.

When heat energy is added to an ice cube, the ice slowly changes to a liquid. As you add heat to the ice, some molecules escape the holding effect of the nearby molecules. The molecules are still close together, but they can move around each other, as the pictures show. This change of state occurs when ice is heated to its **melting point.** The temperature at which a solid changes to a liquid is its melting point. Ice melts at 0° Celsius. The melting point is the same temperature as the **freezing point.** If water is cooled, it will freeze and become ice at 0° Celsius.

melting point, the temperature at which a substance changes from solid to liquid.

freezing point, the temperature at which a substance changes from liquid to solid; same temperature as the melting point.

Ice slowly changes to a liquid

As more heat is added to water, the molecules move faster and faster, and the temperature rises. Molecules begin to break away from the surface of the liquid and to mix with the air. Finally, the molecules move so fast that molecules within the liquid also escape from nearby molecules. They form bubbles of gas under the surface. The water is **boiling**—or rapidly changing to a gas. In a gas, the molecules move apart. Notice in the pictures that the molecules are no longer close together. They are free to move anywhere. The temperature at which a liquid exposed to the air rapidly changes to a gas is its **boiling point.** Water's boiling point is 100° Celsius. When water vapor cools, it changes back to a liquid.

Every pure substance has definite melting points and boiling points. Copper must be heated to its melting point before it will turn to liquid. The melting point of copper is much higher than the melting point of ice. The melting point and boiling point of a substance are two of its physical properties.

boiling, rapid change of state from liquid to gas that takes place within the liquid as well as at its surface.

boiling point, the temperature at which a substance exposed to the air rapidly changes from liquid to gas.

Water changes from liquid to gas

What Are Evaporation and Condensation?

Suppose you let a pan of water sit outside on a warm, summer day. At the end of the day, the pan might be dry. The water seemed to disappear. The water slowly changed from a liquid to a gas—or **evaporated.** Evaporation can take place at a temperature that is lower than the boiling point. But evaporation involves only molecules at the surface of the liquid. Some molecules at the surface of the liquid have enough energy to break away. Those molecules are then free to move in the air as a gas.

When the air is cold and damp, evaporation takes place slowly. When air is warm and dry, evaporation takes place more quickly. The girl in the picture is using warm air to make the water on her hair evaporate faster.

evaporate (i vap′ə rāt′), slow change from liquid to gas occurring at the surface of a liquid.

Have You Heard?

Rain never falls on parts of the Sahara Desert. Clouds pass over these areas, and raindrops fall. But the desert heat evaporates the water before it hits the ground.

On some mornings the grass is very wet even though it did not rain during the night. Water molecules in the air changed from a gas to a liquid—or **condensed.** Condensation happens when warm, moist air cools. During the day the air around your yard might be warm. At night the air cools. Water vapor in the air condenses on cool surfaces. Water drops, like the ones in the picture, might form on the grass. These drops, called dew, might also form on car windows and roofs.

condense (kən dens'), change from gas to liquid.

Both evaporation and condensation are physical changes, because they are changes in state.

Water vapor in the air condenses as dew

Think About It

1. Explain what happens when ice melts and when water boils.
2. What is evaporation? Condensation?
3. **Challenge** Why does a mirror in your bathroom often steam up when the shower is on?

4 What Are Chemical Changes?

chemical change
(kem/ə kəl), a change
in which one or more new
substances are formed.

When you carve a piece of wood, you cause a physical change. The wood remains wood. You have just changed its shape. But when you burn wood, as in this fireplace, what you have left is not wood. The molecules that make up the wood join with oxygen in the air. You cannot recognize the wood anymore because it has become something different.

The burning of wood is a **chemical change**—a change in which new substances are formed. Here, the new substances formed are ashes, water vapor, and carbon dioxide gas. The ash formed when wood burns is a soft, gray powder. The water vapor and carbon dioxide are colorless, odorless gases. The new substances formed in a chemical change look different and act differently than the original substance.

The pictures show the elements sodium and chlorine. Sodium is a silvery metal that is so soft it could be cut with a knife. Chlorine is a heavy, greenish yellow gas. Both sodium and chlorine are dangerous poisons. If sodium metal is combined with chlorine gas and then heated, there is a flash of light. A chemical change takes place. A new, white substance, sodium chloride, is formed. The compound, sodium chloride, is table salt. It is not a poison. Salt is used to flavor foods. Sodium chloride has very different properties from the elements that form it.

Silver is a shiny metal. Sulfur is a yellow powder. Mustard and egg yolks have sulfur in them. If a silver spoon is used with mustard or eggs, a chemical change takes place. A black coating, called tarnish, forms on the spoon. Tarnish is a compound formed when silver and sulfur join. It has different properties than silver or sulfur. Notice the difference in the two spoons in the picture.

Sodium

Chlorine

The tarnishing of silver is a chemical change

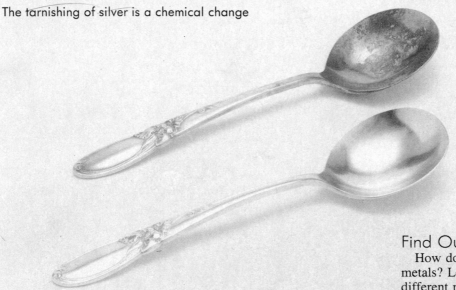

Find Out

How does oxygen affect metals? Leave samples of different metals in air outside for several weeks. Which metals combine with oxygen most readily?

201

Hydrogen gas bubbles form

Carbon forms when sugar is heated

A yellow solid forms

How Do You Recognize Chemical Changes?

When a new substance with new properties forms, you know that a chemical change has taken place. You can be sure that a chemical change is taking place if you see a fire. But sometimes it is hard to tell if a new substance has formed.

Some chemical changes take place very slowly. When iron rusts, it may be weeks before you notice the change.

Sometimes a gas is formed during a chemical change. When magnesium metal is placed in vinegar, hydrogen gas forms. Notice the bubbles of hydrogen in the picture.

A color change is another sign that a chemical change may have taken place. When sugar is heated for a long time, carbon forms. Notice in the picture that carbon is a black solid.

Sometimes two liquids will form a solid when they mix together. The picture shows that, in this chemical change, a yellow solid forms. After a while, the solid will settle in the bottom of the glass.

Think About It

1. What is a chemical change?
2. Give three examples of chemical change.
3. List three signs that tell you a chemical change has occurred.
4. **Challenge** When iron is left in the rain, it rusts. How do you know that a chemical change occurred?

Activity

Testing for Iron

Purpose
To infer, based on observations, which fruit juices contain iron.

You Will Need
- 5 clear-plastic glasses
- strong tea
- samples of 4 different fruit juices
- plastic spoon

Directions
1. Pour a small amount of each juice sample into a different glass, as shown in the picture.
2. Add tea to a depth of about 2 cm to each glass, and stir with a spoon. When tea is added to fruit juice that contains iron, particles of a dark solid will form.
3. Allow the glasses to sit undisturbed for 15 minutes.
4. Look down into each glass. Then, carefully lift each glass. Look up through the bottom of the glass, as the boy in the picture is doing. Notice if dark particles are settling on the bottom of the glass. Record your observations.
5. Allow the glasses to sit undisturbed for 2 more hours. Again, look for dark particles. Record your observations.

Think About It
1. Which of the juices you tested contained iron?
2. What evidence was there in these juices that a chemical change had taken place?
3. **Challenge** How could you tell if some juices contained more iron than others?

203

Do You Know?

You Have Chemical Helpers at Home

Chemical changes happen every day and make your life cleaner, safer, healthier, and more pleasant.

Some chemical changes are easy to notice. Think what happens when you bake bread. After you have mixed the bread dough, you let it rise. The dough puffs up to twice its size because of a chemical change. Yeast in the dough changes sugar into carbon dioxide gas. This gas is trapped in the dough. It forms bubbles of all sizes and makes the mixture swell up. If you look closely at a slice of bread, you can see where the bubbles formed.

Many cleaning products make use of chemical changes. The dull tarnish that builds up on silverware is a compound of the metal. To return the bright, shiny

Removing tarnish from silver

finish to the metal, you must remove the tarnish. Metal cleaner contains a chemical that reacts with the tarnish on the metal. The tarnish is removed, and the metal looks new again, as the picture shows.

People once cleaned tarnished silver by letting it sit in a pan of sour milk overnight. A chemical in the milk reacted with the tarnish. In the morning the tarnish rinsed right off with cold water. Sour milk had done as good a job as an hour of hard scrubbing.

Do you know other ways that chemical changes can help around your house?

Tie It Together

Sum It Up

Tell whether each of the following produces a chemical change or a physical change.

1. water boiling
2. lighting a match
3. ice cream melting
4. adding magnesium to vinegar
5. carving wood
6. a nail rusting
7. tearing a bag open
8. combining tea with pineapple juice
9. cutting paper
10. breaking a window
11. stretching a rubber band
12. sharpening a pencil
13. silver tarnishing
14. gas burning on the stove
15. dew forming on grass

Challenge!

1. How are boiling and evaporation alike? How are they different?

2. What happens to the wax in a candle when the candle burns? What evidence of chemical changes do you observe? What physical changes occur?

3. On cold days the windows in your house sometimes get wet on the inside. How does this happen?

4. A piece of aluminum foil is placed in a blue liquid. After 24 hours, the foil looks copper colored and the liquid is colorless. Has a chemical change occurred? Explain.

Science Words

boiling

boiling point

chemical change

condense

evaporate

freezing point

melting point

physical change

water vapor

Chapter 13
Mixtures and Solutions

The girl in the picture is making a fresh-fruit salad. She has cut pieces of watermelon, strawberries, peaches, grapes, pineapple, and oranges. When she finishes mixing all the fruits in a bowl, she will have a delicious salad. When she tastes the salad, she can still taste the separate fruits. If her little sister loves strawberries, she can easily pick them out. Each kind of fruit can be separated from the others.

The lessons in this chapter describe many mixtures around you. Some of the mixtures are foods, but there are other kinds of mixtures too.

1 Mixing and Separating
2 What Is a Mixture?
3 Which Mixtures Are Solutions?
4 What Are Acids and Bases?

1 Mixing and Separating

At one time you may have eaten a pizza that had sausage, tomatoes, peppers, onions, and cheese on top. Your closet at home may have different clothes mixed together. In both cases, at least two things are mixed together. Each of these mixtures can be taken apart by hand.

To study mixing, you will need sand, salt, water, a spoon, two small jars, and filter paper. Put a spoonful of salt and a spoonful of sand in one of the jars. Add water to the jar until the jar is three-fourths full. Stir the mixture for three or four minutes. Observe what happens as you stir.

Take a round piece of filter paper, and fold it into halves. Now fold it into halves again. Open it up to form a cone like the one in the picture. Rest the cone in the opening of the second jar. Slowly pour the contents of the first jar into the paper cone, and observe what happens. Set the cone and its contents aside.

Pour a few drops of liquid from the jar into a jar lid. Place the lid in a warm place, and let the liquid evaporate. Look carefully at what is left in the lid after the liquid evaporates.

Think About It

1. Which part of the mixture was separated by the filter paper?
2. Which part of the mixture was separated when the liquid evaporated?
3. **Challenge** Think of a way to separate a mixture of powdered iron, sand, and water.

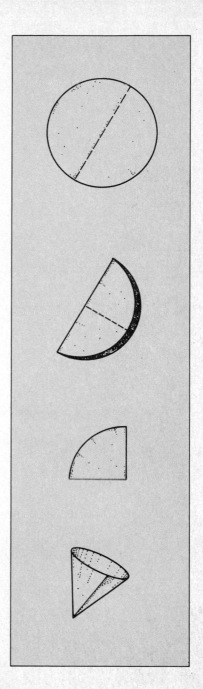

2 What Is a Mixture?

Everywhere you look, you find mixtures. Soil is a mixture of sand, clay, plant and animal matter, and other substances. The water you drink is a mixture of minerals, gases, and pure water.

A **mixture** is two or more substances that are placed together but are not chemically joined. No new substances are formed in a mixture. To make a fruit salad, you can put in any kind of fruit you wish. The fruit can be any size or shape. But no new fruits are formed. Each piece of fruit can be removed from the mixture. Each piece of watermelon is still watermelon. Each strawberry is still a strawberry.

You can make different kinds of mixtures. A fruit salad is a mixture of solids. You can separate the solid pieces by hand, as the picture shows.

Mixing salt and sand in water makes a mixture of two solids and a liquid. You can separate the sand from the water and salt by filtering. The salt and water separate during evaporation. Water evaporates into the air. The salt is left behind.

Antifreeze is a mixture of two liquids

You can also make a mixture of two liquids. The man in the picture is adding antifreeze to water in the car radiator to keep it from freezing. Antifreeze is a kind of alcohol that is mixed with the water. The two liquids can be separated by boiling the mixture. Each liquid will boil off at its own boiling point. Water will boil at 100° Celsius. The alcohol will boil at 199° Celsius.

The air around you is a mixture of gases. The air you breathe is made of about one-fifth oxygen. Another gas, nitrogen, makes up about four-fifths of the air. Air has small amounts of other gases, including water vapor, as shown in the graph. When the molecules of oxygen, nitrogen, and other gases mix together in the air, no new gases are formed. Each gas can be separated from the others. When it rains or snows, some of the water vapor in the air has separated from the other gases.

Air is a mixture of gases

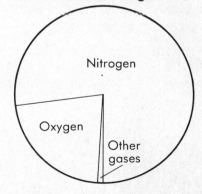

Nitrogen

Oxygen

Other gases

209

What Are Other Kinds of Mixtures?

Mixtures of gases and liquids can also be formed. The bubbles in the glass of soft drink show that a gas is mixed with the liquid. If you let a glass of soft drink sit for a while, most of the gas escapes. You can see the gas escape in the bubbles that rise to the surface of the liquid. The mixture separates by itself.

Solids and gases can be mixed too. Dust particles and pollen grains that float in the air are an example of a mixture of solids and gases. Filters on air conditioners separate the solids from the gases in the air.

Think About It

1. What is a mixture?
2. Give three examples of mixtures.
3. Name three ways to separate mixtures.
4. **Challenge** How could you separate a mixture of sawdust, sand, and water?

Mixture of gas and liquid

Do You Know?

Air Can Be Taken Apart

Removing liquid oxygen from the tank

Can you name the most common mixture in the world? If you answered "air," you are correct. Maybe you do not often think about air. You cannot see or smell this mixture of gases. You can feel air only when the wind blows.

You know that people need air for breathing. But did you know that air has many uses in industries? Oxygen and nitrogen, the two gases that make up more than 99% of air, are both widely used in industry.

The most common use of oxygen is in steelmaking, as shown. Hospitals also use oxygen to help people with breathing problems.

Nitrogen is used to make fertilizers and explosives. It is also used in refining metals. In 1981 nitrogen was the third most widely used chemical in the United States.

Oxygen and nitrogen can be separated from an air mixture. First, a tank of air is cooled to a very low temperature. At about −183° Celsius the oxygen changes from a gas to a liquid. Then, at the colder temperature of −196° Celsius, the nitrogen also changes to a liquid. At temperatures below −200° Celsius, the tank of air has become liquid. The mixture is known as *liquid air.*

Next, the liquid air is allowed to warm up very slowly. As the temperature reaches −196° Celsius, the nitrogen changes back to a gas. If you could see the tank of liquid air, you might say that the nitrogen is boiling away.

The temperature is kept at −196° Celsius. At this temperature all the nitrogen will change to a gas. But the oxygen will stay as a liquid. The nitrogen gas can be piped off, while the oxygen is still a liquid in the tank. The two major parts of air have been separated from each other.

Oxygen furnace

3 Which Mixtures Are Solutions?

dissolve (di zolv'), cause a substance to become part of a solution.

You can make a mixture by stirring sand and water together. When you stop stirring, the sand settles to the bottom. The parts of the mixture are still unchanged. In the picture of the sand and water mixture, you can still see the separate parts.

If you mix sugar and water together, something different happens. The sugar and water still stay unchanged. But the sugar seems to disappear. The sugar **dissolves** in the water. In the picture of the sugar and water mixture, you cannot see the sugar. The sugar has broken into such small pieces that they cannot be seen. In fact the pieces are really molecules of sugar. Since you cannot see the molecules, it looks as if the sugar has disappeared. But you know the sugar is still there because the water tastes sweet. If you evaporate the water, the sugar is left behind.

Not all substances dissolve in water

Sugar dissolves in water

Sometimes you cannot see the individual parts of a mixture. When the substances are spread evenly through the mixture, you say the mixture is **homogeneous.** A homogeneous mixture looks as though it is made of only one substance, even though it has two or more substances in it.

A mixture that is homogeneous is called a **solution.** In a solution one substance is spread evenly throughout the other substance. In the solution of sugar and water, the sugar molecules are spread evenly through the water.

The picture shows that, in a solution, one substance dissolves in another. Sugar dissolves in water. The substance that dissolves is the **solute.** The substance that does the dissolving is the **solvent.** When sugar dissolves in water, sugar is the solute. Water is the solvent.

homogeneous (hō/mə jē/nē əs), distributed evenly or uniformly throughout.

solution (sə lü/shən), a homogeneous mixture formed by dissolving.

solute (sol/yüt), a substance that dissolves in another substance.

solvent (sol/vənt), a substance that dissolves another substance.

213

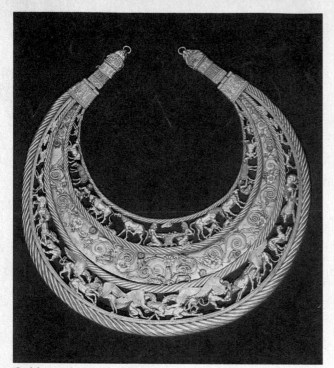

Gold jewelry is an alloy

What Kinds of Solutions Are There?

The most common kind of solution is a solid dissolved in a liquid. Salt or sugar dissolved in water forms this kind of solution.

Water is a liquid that will dissolve many different substances. Other liquids, such as alcohol, will dissolve in water. This kind of solution is a liquid dissolved in a liquid.

Gases, such as ammonia, oxygen, and nitrogen, also dissolve in water. Ammonia dissolved in water is used for cleaning. Oxygen and nitrogen from the air dissolve in the water of lakes, oceans, and rivers. Without the dissolved oxygen in the water, fish would not be able to live.

Solutions can also be formed by dissolving a solid in another solid. These solid solutions are usually made of two or more metals and are called alloys. The jewelry in the pictures is made of copper or silver dissolved in gold.

Have You Heard?

The United States 5-cent coin is an alloy of the metals nickel and copper.

214

What Things Affect Solutions?

How fast a solute dissolves in a solvent depends on the amount of surface of the solute. The greater the surface of the solute, the faster it mixes with the solvent. If sugar and water are mixed, small grains of sugar will dissolve faster than the same amount of sugar in a cube. The grains have much more surface that comes into contact with the water.

The temperature of the solvent affects how much solute will dissolve in the solvent. More solid will usually dissolve in a liquid if the temperature is raised. For example, more sugar will dissolve in hot water than in cold water. The picture shows two glasses of water. The same amount of sugar was added to both glasses. You cannot see any sugar in the glass of hot water because all the sugar dissolved. Only some of the sugar dissolved in the cold water. Notice the grains of sugar on the bottom of the glass.

Think About It

1. What is a solution?
2. What is the difference between a solute and a solvent?
3. List three different kinds of solutions.
4. Name two things that affect solutions.
5. **Challenge** If you mix chalk dust in water, does a solution form? Explain.

Sugar in hot water

Sugar in cold water

215

4 What Are Acids and Bases?

acid (as′id), substance with a sour taste that turns litmus red.

base, substance with a bitter taste that turns litmus blue.

Have You Heard?

Lemons, limes, oranges, and grapefruit all contain citric acid. The acid was named because it is found in citrus fruits.

The foods you eat contain many kinds of substances. Some of these substances have a particular taste. The sour taste of this lemon comes from an **acid** in the fruit. An acid is a chemical that tastes sour. Grapefruit, tomatoes, and vinegar are other foods that contain acids.

Other substances have a bitter taste. If you have ever tasted milk of magnesia, you know it has a bitter taste. Some other medicines also have a bitter taste. Substances that taste bitter are called **bases.**

Other acids and bases should only be used by adults. Acid in car batteries conducts electricity. Acid is also used to etch designs in metal. Ammonia, drain cleaner, and oven cleaner are strong bases that are good for cleaning. These acids and bases are dangerous chemicals. Scientists use other chemicals to find out if a substance is an acid or base. *CAUTION: Never taste a substance to find out if it is an acid or a base.*

Lemons contain an acid

Acids and bases change the color of litmus

Litmus is a chemical dye used to test acids and bases. The picture shows that litmus dye on paper will turn red if an acid touches it. It will turn blue if a base touches it. Litmus is called an **indicator.** It indicates, or shows, whether a substance is an acid or a base. Litmus is one of many indicators that scientists use.

Some substances do not change the color of litmus. Such substances are **neutral.** These substances are neither acids nor bases. Pure water is a neutral substance.

If an acid and a base are combined, a chemical change takes place. New substances that are neither acids nor bases are formed. This chemical change is called **neutralization.** Knowing about neutralization can be useful. If you spilled a strong acid, it would be dangerous to clean up. Adding a base to the spilled acid would cause neutralization to occur. The neutral substances would be safe to clean up.

Think About It

1. How do foods that contain acids and bases taste?
2. What happens to litmus paper when an acid touches it? When a base touches it?
3. What happens during neutralization?
4. **Challenge** Sometimes rainwater near large cities will turn litmus dye red. What does this tell you about the rainwater?

litmus (lit′məs), chemical that turns red when touched by an acid and blue when touched by a base.

indicator (in′də kā′tər), substance that changes color when touched by an acid or base.

neutral (nü′trəl), neither acid nor base.

neutralization (nü′trə lə zā′shən), chemical change in which an acid and a base combine to form substances that are neither acids nor bases.

Find Out
What are some other indicators that scientists use to test acids and bases? Find out what colors they turn.

Activity

Testing with an Indicator

Purpose
To infer whether substances are acids, bases, or neutral substances, based on their reaction with red-cabbage indicator.

You Will Need
- 6 clear-plastic glasses
- red-cabbage indicator
- 5 samples of household products, such as lemon juice, vinegar, ammonia, liquid detergent, and bleach
- water
- masking tape

Directions
1. Label the first 5 glasses with the names of your household products, as shown in the picture. Label the sixth glass *water.*
2. Pour about 1 cm of red-cabbage juice into each glass. Notice the color of the juice. Red-cabbage juice turns red or purple in acids, blue in neutral substances, and green or yellow in bases.
3. Add a small amount of vinegar to the correct glass. Observe any color change.
4. Add a small amount of each of your other household products to the correct glass. Observe any color change.
5. Add a small amount of water to the sixth glass. Observe any color change.

Think About It
1. List the color the red-cabbage indicator turned in each substance.
2. Which of the tested substances were acids?
3. Which substances were bases?
4. Which substances were neutral?
5. **Challenge** If you had an unknown substance that turned red-cabbage juice yellow, what could you add to neutralize the substance?

Tie It Together

Sum It Up

1. Identify five mixtures that you can find at home.

2. Name a mixture that you can separate by using filter paper.

3. Name a mixture that you can separate by evaporation.

4. List three examples of solutions. Name the solute and solvent in each solution.

5. Copy the chart below, and fill in the blank spaces on your copy.

Science Words

acid   mixture

base   neutral

dissolve   neutralization

homogeneous   solute

indicator   solution

litmus   solvent

Substance	Color of Litmus	Color of Red Cabbage Juice	Acid, Base or Neutral
Lemon Juice	red		acid
Water		blue	
Detergent			base

Challenge!

1. Explain how you could separate a mixture of sugar and sand.

2. Is oil-and-vinegar salad dressing a solution? Explain.

3. How can you tell if salt is dissolved in a glass of water without tasting it?

4. Can a solution be separated by filtering? Give an example to prove your answer.

5. If oven cleaner were accidentally spilled on the kitchen floor, what would make it safe to clean up?

Laboratory

Dissolving a Bouillon Cube

Purpose
To demonstrate how dissolving time and surface area are related.

You Will Need
- plastic-foam cup
- very hot or boiling water
- 3 bouillon cubes
- clock with second hand
- paper
- table knife

a

b

Stating the Problem
It is cold outside, and you have not had time to eat a hot lunch. But, before you return to school, you want to drink a warm cup of bouillon (bül´yon). What is the fastest way to dissolve the cube? Do you think that a whole cube or a cube cut into pieces would dissolve faster? Record your prediction.

Investigating the Problem
1. Half fill a plastic-foam cup with hot water. Record the time. Then, drop 1 whole bouillon cube into the water. When the cube is completely dissolved, the liquid will look like

the liquid in picture *a*. Record how long it takes for the cube to dissolve completely. Pour the bouillon into a container provided by your teacher. Rinse out the cup.

2. Place another bouillon cube on a piece of paper. Cut the cube into 4 pieces as shown in picture *b*.

3. Half fill the cup with hot water. Record the time. Then, drop the 4 pieces of bouillon cube into the cup. Record how long it takes for the pieces to dissolve completely. Pour the bouillon into another container, and rinse out the cup.

4. Place a bouillon cube on a sheet of paper. Cut or crush the cube until it crumbles into tiny pieces. See picture *c*.

5. Half fill the cup with hot water. Record the time. Pour the crushed bouillon cube into the cup. Record the time that it takes the pieces to dissolve completely.

Making Conclusions

1. Compare the time that it took to dissolve the whole cube, the quartered cube, and the crushed cube. Was your prediction correct?

2. In step 1 the hot water touched the 6 sides of the cube. Cutting and crushing the cube changed the amount of surface or surface area that touched the water. Compare the surface areas of the whole cube, the quartered cube, and the crushed cube.

3. How are the dissolving time and the surface area of the bouillon cube related?

4. Imagine that you are trying to melt a stick of butter in a pan. How could you make the butter melt faster, without changing the setting on the stove?

c

Careers

Physicist

"I was always interested in building things and knowing how they worked," says Lee. "I liked observing the properties of objects. Today, I am a physicist (fiz'ə sist) and I help to build something many people often use."

Lee works for a television company. He designs picture tubes for color televisions. "Most people seem surprised when they find out a physicist works for a television company. But almost every kind of industry needs one or more physicists. They help design things from rockets to bridges. They even design certain toys. Physicists also study the properties of matter. So, they can help decide what materials will be used to build certain things."

Physicists often work with other scientists, such as geologists, to help find and pump out oil. Physicists working with chemists and biologists have helped to make many gains in the field of medicine.

"What I like best about my job," says Lee, "is the challenge. Many scientists who work in industry are always trying to make a product better. You often see *New and Improved* written on the package. For the product to become new and improved, scientists may have to research and experiment for many years. In the television industry, we are always trying to make picture tubes that give sharper and brighter pictures."

A college education is necessary for anyone interested in working in physics. Most physicists go to college for five to seven years. They must do a lot of reading to keep up with the new discoveries in this exciting field. "I think that anyone who has a strong curiosity and who likes exploring new areas might enjoy a career in physics."

Uranium miner

When people think of matter and the atom, they often think of nuclear energy. Many jobs can be found in the field of nuclear energy.

Uranium is the raw material used for fuel in nuclear power plants. **Ore controllers** help locate the uranium underground. They learn about earth science during two years of college.

Heavy-equipment operators and **miners** remove the uranium ore from the ground. These workers get a lot of on-the-job training.

At a nuclear power plant, a **safety technician** makes sure the plant is safe for the workers. This person checks the amount of radiation inside and outside the plant. The safety technician tests samples of air and water to be sure they do not contain enough radiation to harm the environment.

Safety technicians learn their skills during a four-year training program.

A **public affairs officer** is a very important person in the field of nuclear energy. This person is responsible for answering questions that the public has about nuclear energy. A public affairs officer must translate technical language into a language most people will understand. This person should have good knowledge about nuclear energy and be able to talk with people.

A lot of radiation is harmful to living things. But certain kinds and amounts of radiation are used to fight cancer. A **radiation therapist** concentrates X rays or other radiation on the diseased parts of a cancer patient's body. The radiation might destroy or stop the growth of cancer cells.

A student who wants to be a therapist must train at a college or hospital for two years.

Safety technician

On Your Own

Picture Clue

To discover what the picture on page 162 shows, look at the picture on page 195, and imagine waiting for several hours.

Projects

1. Get soil samples from several different places. Mix each soil sample with water. Pour a small amount of the soil-and-water mixture into red-cabbage indicator to find out if the soil is acidic, basic, or neutral.

2. Examine different kinds of crystals with a hand lens. Make labeled drawings of the different crystal shapes you find.

3. Use library books to prepare a report on the way different colored fireworks are made.

Books About Science

Fascinating Experiments in Chemistry by Francois Cherrier. Sterling, 1978. Explore crystal structure, or make invisible ink!

Heat by Harlan Wade. Raintree, 1977. Learn about the sources and effects of heat.

Water: Experiments to Understand It by Boris Arnov. Lothrop, Lee & Shepard, 1980. Find out about the properties of water through experiments.

What Makes a Lemon Sour? by Gail Kay Haines. Morrow, 1977. Learn how acids and bases can be neutralized and how they are used commercially.

Unit Test

Multiple Choice

Number your paper from 1–5. Next to each number, write the letter of the word or words that best complete the statement or answer the question.

1. Which is a mixture?
   a. sugar dissolved in water
   b. air
   c. fruit salad
   d. all the above

2. Which is a solution?
   a. salt and pepper
   b. sand in water
   c. sugar in water
   d. all the above

3. Acids
   a. turn litmus red.
   b. neutralize bases.
   c. are found in lemons and limes.
   d. all the above

4. Neutrons
   a. are outside the nucleus and have no charge.
   b. are inside the nucleus and have no charge.
   c. are inside the nucleus and have a positive charge.
   d. are outside the nucleus and have a negative charge.

5. Which of the following is a chemical property?
   a. color
   b. state of matter
   c. ability to burn
   d. hardness

True or False

Number your paper from 6–10. Next to each number, write *true* if the sentence is correct and *false* if the sentence is incorrect. Make each false statement true by changing the underlined word or words and writing the correct word or words on your paper.

6. The alcohol in a thermometer <u>expands</u> when the temperature increases.

7. When one end of a metal spoon is heated, heat flows toward the other end by <u>convection</u>.

8. The formation of dew on the grass is a <u>physical change</u>.

9. A <u>solid</u> has a definite volume but not a definite shape.

10. A <u>compound</u> contains at least two different kinds of atoms.

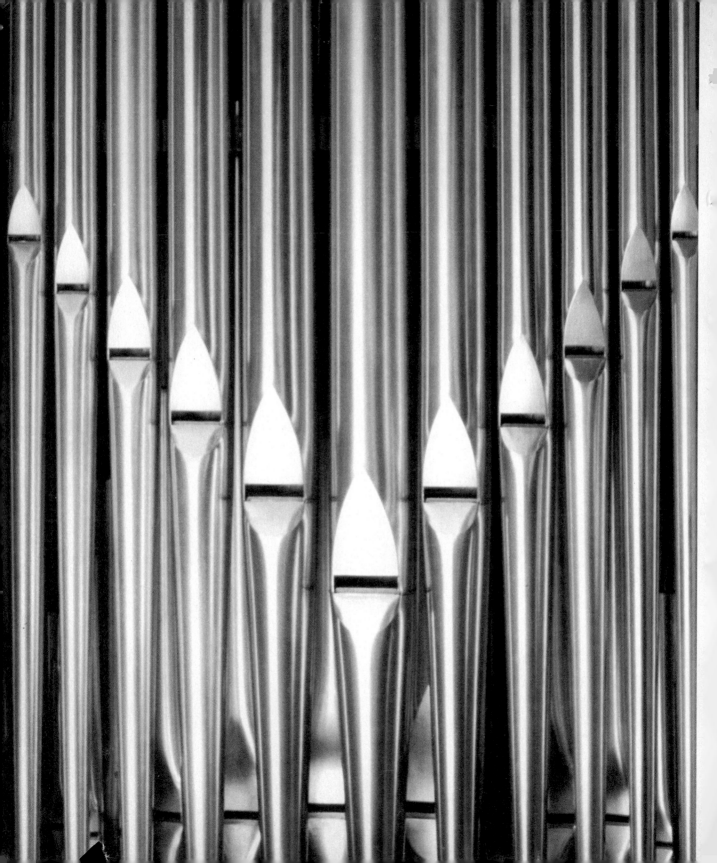

UNIT FIVE
SOUND

It is silver.
   Though it shines,
It plays music.
It plays loud
   For the crowd.

Ezechiel Valenzuela *age 10*

Chapter 14
Sound

A loud, crashing sound awakens you in the night. Startled, you sit up in bed and listen closely. Suddenly you hear the sound of raindrops splattering on the roof. In the distance you hear a low, rumbling sound. You lie back down—it is only a summer storm.

The lessons in this chapter describe other familiar sounds, such as a ringing bell or the strum of a guitar. You can hear many different sounds, but you will find that all sounds are alike in some ways.

1 Inferring What Causes Sound

You hear many different sounds every day. The voices of your friends, a dog's bark, and music are just a few of the sounds you hear. But before any sound can be made, something must happen. To find out how sounds are made, try the activities shown in the picture.

First, gently stretch a rubber band. Pluck it with one finger. Notice what happens to the rubber band when it makes a sound.

Next, place a plastic ruler on your desk so that part of it hangs over the edge. Hold the ruler tightly on the desk with one hand. Gently push down on the free end of the ruler with the other hand. Release the free end, and observe the ruler as it makes a sound.

Blow up a balloon. Let the air escape while you stretch the neck of the balloon. Carefully observe the neck of the balloon when you hear a sound.

Think About It

1. How are the actions of the rubber band, ruler, and balloon alike?
2. What happens when a sound is produced?
3. **Challenge** What causes the sounds made by a guitar?

2 How Do Vibrations Cause Sound Waves?

Many objects around you produce sound. You have heard the sound of a ringing telephone, a doorbell, and an alarm clock. All three objects contain bells. When the bells ring, they **vibrate**—or move rapidly back and forth. If you pick up a ringing alarm clock, you can feel these vibrations.

The drawings show how a ruler moves when it vibrates. As the ruler moves up, particles of air above the ruler are squeezed together to form a **compression.** When the ruler moves down, it makes a second compression below it. The space left above the ruler has few air particles in it. This space is called a **rarefaction.** The ruler moves up again, forming another compression above it and a rarefaction below it. As the picture shows, the back and forth movement of the vibrating ruler causes a series of compressions and rarefactions. These series of compressions and rarefactions are sound waves.

vibrate (vī′brāt), to move rapidly back and forth.

compression (kəm presh′ən), the place in a sound wave where particles are squeezed together.

rarefaction (rer′ə fak′shən), the place in a sound wave where particles are spread farthest apart.

Vibrations cause sound waves

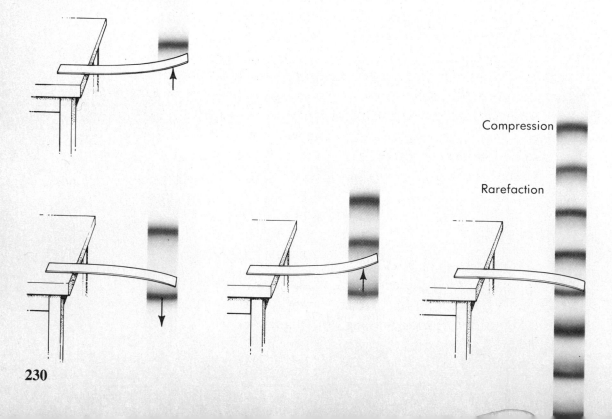

Compression

Rarefaction

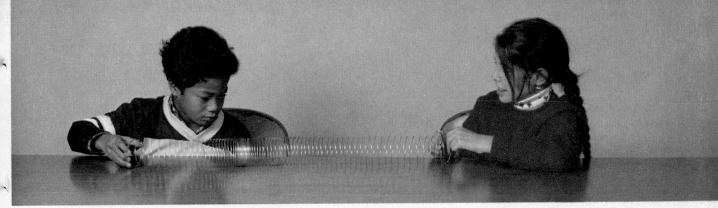

A compression moves through the coil

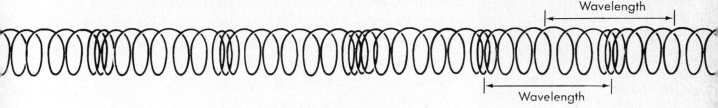

Wavelength

Wavelength

Sometimes a coil spring is used to show compressions and rarefactions. The boy in the picture is holding one end of the spring. The girl on the other end pinches several coils together to form a compression. When she lets go of the pinched coils, the compression moves through the coil. The compression is followed by a rarefaction. In a similar way, sound waves travel away from a vibrating object.

The drawing above shows what the coil spring would look like if a series of compressions were moving through it. Notice that, between neighboring compressions, you see rarefactions. The compressions and rarefactions are evenly spaced. The distance between two neighboring compressions or rarefactions is the **wavelength.**

wavelength (wāv′lengkth′), the distance between two neighboring compressions or rarefactions.

Find Out

How does a cricket make its chirping sound?

Think About It

1. How does a vibrating ruler cause waves?
2. How do you find the wavelength of a sound wave?
3. **Challenge** What do you think would happen if you put the prongs of a vibrating tuning fork in a cup of water? Explain.

231

3 How Does Sound Travel?

Big Ben, the bell of the large clock in the picture, rises more than 100 meters over the city of London. The clock's bell rings every hour, announcing the time.

Big Ben weighs 12 metric tons—more than 2 elephants. When this bell rings, people several blocks around it can hear the sound, no matter where they stand. The bell vibrates when it is struck, sending sound waves through the air around it. The sound of the bell goes out in all directions, just as a balloon expands in all directions. The picture shows what the sound waves might look like if you could see them. The balloons would be like the compressions of the sound waves. The spaces between the balloons would be like the rarefactions.

Big Ben

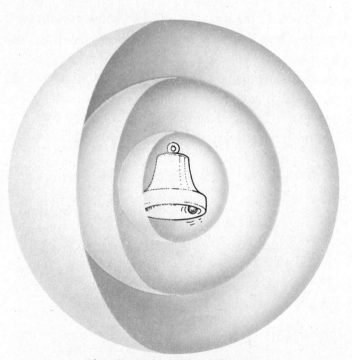

Sound travels out in all directions

Perhaps you have heard the sound of a distant object, such as an airplane flying high above you. The sound waves of the airplane travel to your ears through the air. No sound can reach you unless air, or some other matter, is between you and the object making the sound.

Long ago, a scientist named Robert Boyle hung a watch inside a large glass jar like the one in the picture. He could hear the ticking clearly because the sound traveled through the air and the glass jar. When the air was removed from the jar, however, Boyle found that he could not hear the watch ticking.

Boyle discovered that sound can be heard only when it travels through some matter. When he removed the air from the jar, the sound waves could not travel through the space where there was no air. Usually, we hear sound traveling through air. But sound can travel through any matter—gases, liquids, and solids.

Have You Heard?

Astronauts on the moon cannot speak directly to one another because there is no air through which the sound waves can travel. They must communicate by radio.

How Fast Does Sound Travel?

Sound can travel through any matter, but it travels through different matter at different speeds. The speed of sound in air is about 340 meters per second. Sound travels about 4 times as fast in water as in air. And sound travels fastest through solids, such as steel. The speed of sound in steel is about 15 times as fast as in air.

In air, you can tell the direction from which a sound is coming. Sound waves reach your ear that is closest to the source of the sound just slightly before they reach your other ear.

This swimmer underwater could hear the sound of a boat motor. But she would not be able to tell where the boat was. Since sound travels so much faster in water, the sound waves would reach both her ears at almost the same time.

Think About It

1. How does sound move from Big Ben to people on the street?
2. Through what kind of matter does sound travel fastest?
3. **Challenge** In western movies you might have seen the outlaw put his ear to the ground to listen for the approaching posse. Explain.

Activity

Observing How Sound Waves Travel

Purpose

To infer, based on observations, that sound waves are a series of vibrations which travel through matter.

You Will Need

- large plastic-foam cup
- pencil
- 2 rubber bands
- plastic food wrap
- salt

Directions

1. Use a pencil to punch a tiny hole in the bottom of the cup.
2. Cut the rubber band, and push one end through the hole. Tie a knot so the rubber band cannot be pulled out of the hole.
3. Stretch a piece of plastic wrap over the top of the cup. Stretch a small rubber band around the sides of the cup to hold the plastic wrap tight.
4. Sprinkle a few grains of salt on the wrap. Hold the cup while your partner gently stretches the cut rubber band. Pluck the stretched rubber band and observe what happens to the grains of salt.
5. Remove the plastic wrap from the cup.
6. Hold the cup near your ear while your partner stretches the rubber band. *CAUTION: Loud sound can injure your hearing. Do not hold the cup too close to your ear or stretch the rubber band so far that it breaks.*
7. Ask your partner to pluck the rubber band with one finger.
8. Ask your partner to rub one finger along the rubber band.
9. Switch places with your partner, and repeat steps 6 through 8.

Think About It

1. What happened to the grains of salt when you plucked the rubber band?
2. Describe the sound you heard when your partner plucked the rubber band.
3. Describe the sound you heard when your partner rubbed the rubber band.
4. **Challenge** How would the sounds you heard be different if the rubber band were not attached to the cup?

4 How Do Sounds Differ?

amplitude (am′plə tüd), the distance a vibrating object moves from its resting position.

The vibrating strings of a guitar produce sounds. When you pluck the string, it moves. The distance the string moves from its resting position is its **amplitude.** The string has more energy when it has a large amplitude.

Notice the picture of the vibrating guitar string. If you pluck the guitar string hard, the string moves far and makes a loud sound. As the string moves back and forth through a smaller distance, the sound becomes softer. Finally, the string stops vibrating, and you do not hear a sound.

If you sing softly, the sound's amplitude is small, and the sound is soft. But if you use more energy to sing, the amplitude is greater, and the sound is louder.

The vibrating string makes a sound

Scientists usually measure the strength of a sound by using a sound-level meter. The unit used in measuring strength is called the **decibel.** A sound of 0 decibels is a sound that most people can barely hear. A sound of 10 decibels has 10 times the energy of a 0-decibel sound. A sound of 20 decibels has 100 times as much energy as a 0-decibel sound. The table below shows the strength (in decibels) of some common sounds.

decibel (des′ə bəl), unit used in measuring the strength of a sound.

Strength of some sounds in decibels

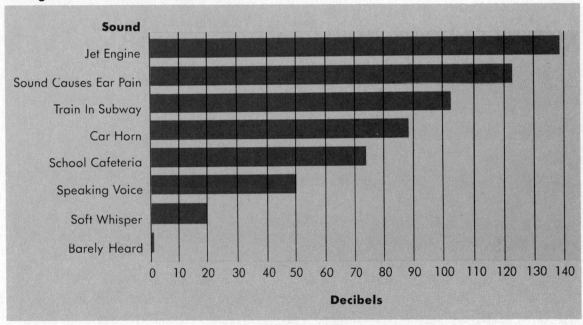

Many scientists think that loud noises are harmful to your health. Studies show that loud noises can make people ill. Too much noise can make you tired, cranky, or even sick to your stomach. Noise can make you lose your appetite or get a headache. Noise also disturbs your sleep, even if the noise is not loud enough to awaken you. Noise keeps you from sleeping soundly, and the next morning you still feel tired. Many people say that they cannot think clearly with loud noises around them.

What Determines a Sound's Pitch?

pitch (pich), the highness or lowness of a sound.

Sounds also differ in how high or low they are. When you sing a song, you sing different notes. Some notes are high, and others are low. The lowness or highness of a sound is its **pitch.** As you sing different notes, you sing different pitches.

The pitch of a sound is determined by how rapidly the source of the sound is vibrating. A string that vibrates slowly produces a lower note. A string that vibrates quickly produces a higher note. The speed at which something vibrates is its **frequency.** The lowest tone on a piano has a frequency of 27 vibrations per second. The frequency of the piano's highest tone is about 4,000 vibrations per second.

frequency (frē′kwən sē), the speed at which something vibrates.

The drawing shows how air particles are compressed and spread apart in a high-pitched sound and a low-pitched sound. Notice that the compressions in the high-pitched sound are closer together than the compressions in the low-pitched sound.

Low-pitched sound

High-pitched sound

Think About It

Have You Heard?
Dogs can hear high-pitched sounds that most people cannot hear. "Silent" dog whistles are silent only to people.

1. Explain two ways in which sounds can differ.
2. List three ways that loud sounds can affect you.
3. **Challenge** Compare the frequencies of the sounds made by a bass fiddle with those made by a violin.

Discover!

Scientists Use Sounds You Cannot Hear

Some medical research uses sounds that you cannot hear. The word *ultrasonic* is used to describe sounds with very high frequencies.

Ultrasonic sounds range from twenty thousand to more than a billion vibrations per second. These sounds are too high for humans to hear. But dogs and other animals can hear some ultrasonic sounds.

Scientists have found many uses for ultrasonic sounds. For example, doctors use ultrasound to study the health of babies before they are born. Ultrasonic sounds are sent through the mother's abdomen. The waves reflect off the baby's body into a microphone that picks up these waves. The reflected sounds can also be made into a picture and shown on a television screen.

The ultrasonic wave patterns show some of the health problems a baby might have. Heart

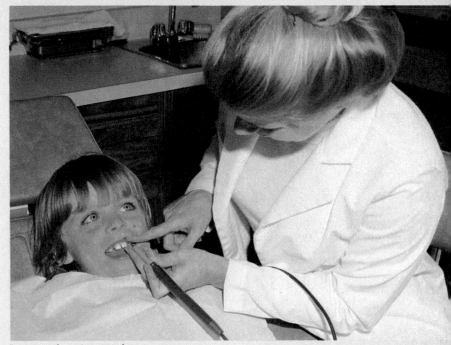

Dentist cleaning teeth

problems and slow growth are some problems that can be detected with ultrasonics. This information can help doctors plan ahead for what a baby might need as soon as it is born. Doctors can also use this method to let the mother know if she is expecting twins or triplets. Doctors think that they will soon be able to learn a great deal more about problems in unborn children by using ultrasonics.

Many industrial uses of ultrasonics have also

been found. Some factories use ultrasonic waves to look for hidden cracks in metals. Ultrasonic waves can be used to find gas and oil deposits underground. Paint and homogenized milk can be mixed by ultrasonic waves. Dentists can even clean your teeth with these waves, as shown in the picture.

This "unheard sound" has become a useful tool in many areas of medicine, industry, and science research.

5 How Is Sound Absorbed and Reflected?

Carpets, curtains, and furniture absorb sounds

absorb (ab sôrb′), to take in without reflecting.

reflect (ri flekt′), to turn back or to throw back.

Ceiling tiles absorb sounds

Have you ever walked through an empty house such as the one in the picture? Footsteps and soft voices can be heard easily. When carpets, curtains, and furniture are added, the noise is reduced. These materials take in—or **absorb**—sounds.

The ceiling in this office building is covered with a material that absorbs sounds. If these materials were not used, the sounds would bounce around, causing a great deal of noise.

Sounds that are not absorbed are bounced back—or **reflected.** If you have ever shouted and then heard your voice come back to you, you have observed the reflection of sound. When the sound waves of your voice hit a hard surface and reflect back, you hear an echo.

A long hallway that does not have a carpet on the floor would produce echoes of your footsteps. As you walked toward a smooth wall at the end of the hall, you would notice several things. First, the echoes would sound louder as you got closer to the wall. You would also hear the echoes closer and closer to the sounds of your footsteps. Finally, the echoes would seem to stop. The echoes would still be there. But they would be returning to you too fast to hear as an echo. You would not be able to tell the difference between the echoes and the sounds of your footsteps.

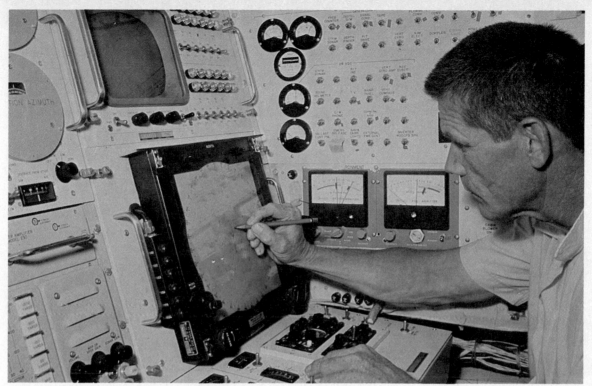
Sonar is used to find the depth of the water

People use echoes to find distances to objects. This person is looking at a **sonar** screen. Sailors use sonar to find the depth of water or to locate underwater objects.

Sound waves travel through seawater at about 1,530 meters per second. Sonar sends sound waves from the ship to the ocean bottom. The time that it takes for the echo of the sound wave to return to the ship is recorded. Using this information, the depth of the water can be found. For example, if it takes 4 seconds for a sound wave to be sent out and reflected back to the ship, the depth of the water is about 3,060 meters.

Finding fish in the oceans has never been an easy task. But with sonar, large schools of fish are not as hard to find. Using sonar, a fishing ship sends out sound waves. The sound waves hit the bottom and return in a certain time. If the sound waves hit a school of fish, the waves return to the ship sooner. Then, the fishing nets are lowered, and the fish are brought aboard.

sonar (sō′när), a system for finding the depth of water and for locating underwater objects by using the reflection of sound waves.

241

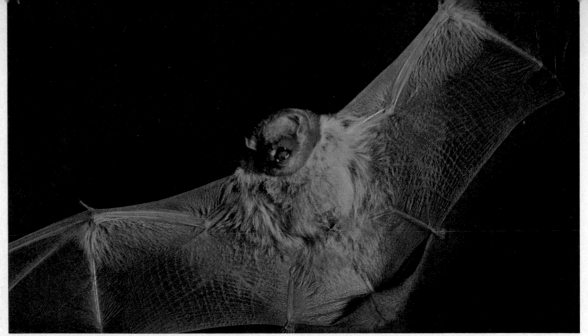

The little brown bat uses echoes to find food

How Do Animals Use Reflected Sound?

Most of the 2,000 different kinds of bats eat insects. Insect-eating bats, such as the little brown bat in the picture, use echoes to find their food at night. The bat sends out sounds that are too high-pitched for people to hear. These high-pitched sounds are called **ultrasonic** sounds. Echoes of the bat's sounds reflect from the bodies of insects. Using this method, called **echolocation,** the bat can find and eat up to 5,000 small insects each hour. Bats also use echolocation to fly around in dark caves without bumping into the walls.

Some moths, which bats feed on, can also send out ultrasonic sounds. Scientists think these sounds disturb the bat's echolocation. Bats hunting for food often miss catching this kind of moth.

ultrasonic (ul′trə son′ik), too high-pitched for the human ear to hear.

echolocation (ek′ō lō kā′shən), method of finding objects by using sound waves that are reflected off the objects.

Think About It

1. Give an example of how sound waves can be absorbed.
2. How does an echo occur?
3. **Challenge** How might sonar help protect a ship?

242

Tie It Together

Sum It Up

Number your paper from 1–8. Complete the statements below on your paper. The boxed letters will spell the name of another group of animals that uses echolocation.

1. The ☐ _ _ _ _ _ _ is the unit used to measure the strength of sounds.

2. The part of a sound wave where the particles are squeezed together is a _ ☐ _ _ _ _ _ _ _ _ .

3. A high-pitched sound has a shorter _ _ _ _ ☐ _ _ _ _ _ than a low-pitched sound.

4. The frequency of a sound determines its ☐ _ _ _ _ .

5. An _ _ ☐ _ occurs when a sound wave is reflected back to you.

6. Sound is produced only when an object _ ☐ _ _ _ _ _ _ .

7. Fishing ships can use _ _ ☐ _ _ to find schools of fish.

8. ☐ _ _ _ _ travels faster through water than through air.

Challenge!

1. Why can you hear some sounds but not see the vibrations?

2. How could you show that sound travels faster through solids than through air?

3. How could you change the pitch of the sound made by a vibrating ruler?

4. Why are the sounds in a school gym so loud?

5. How can a submarine travel safely beneath a polar icecap?

Science Words

absorb

amplitude

compression

decibel

echolocation

frequency

pitch

rarefaction

reflect

sonar

ultrasonic

vibrate

wavelength

Chapter 15
Sounds in
Our World

Many people, such as the students in this chorus, enjoy singing. Other people just like to listen to the songs. Hearing allows you to enjoy many of the sounds around you.

The lessons in this chapter describe how sounds are sent and received.

1 Listening and Comparing

2 How Do You Speak and Hear?

3 How Do Different Animals Send and Receive Sounds?

4 How Can Sounds Be Made with Musical Instruments?

5 How Can Sound Waves Be Reproduced?

1 Listening and Comparing

The voices of these cheerleaders can be heard over the roar of the crowd. The cheerleaders are using something that makes their voices seem louder. You can find out how sounds can be more easily heard by using a paper cone.

First, twist a large piece of heavy paper to form a cone. Make sure the cone is open at both ends. Use tape to make your paper keep its cone shape.

Ask a classmate to work as your partner. Your partner should stand or sit about 1 meter away from you. Your partner should whisper *hello*. Notice how loud your partner's voice sounds. Now, ask your partner to whisper *hello* into the small end of the paper cone. Notice any difference in loudness of your partner's voice.

Ask your partner to whisper *hello* again without using the paper cone. Now, place the small end of your cone to your ear. Listen as your partner whispers *hello*. Compare the loudness of the two sounds. Finally, repeat the activity so that you can whisper and your partner can listen.

Think About It

1. Describe and explain how your partner's voice changed when it came through the cone.
2. Describe and explain how your partner's voice sounded when you listened through the cone.
3. **Challenge** Why do you think trumpets and trombones have cone-shaped ends?

Cheerleaders with megaphones

2 How Do You Speak and Hear?

vocal cords (vō′kəl kôrdz), two pairs of thin tissue at the top of the windpipe.

Review: Why might you cup your hands around your mouth when shouting to a friend across the street?

All sounds, even our voices, are produced only when something vibrates. You are able to speak because your **vocal cords**—two pairs of thin tissue in your windpipe—can vibrate. Your vocal cords are like thin sheets of stretched rubber. You can feel the vibrations that your vocal cords make. Place your fingers lightly across your throat when you speak.

When you are not speaking, your vocal cords are relaxed. The first drawing shows relaxed vocal cords. When you speak, your vocal cords tighten and vibrate as air passes through a narrow opening between them. The tighter your vocal cords get, the higher the pitch of your voice becomes. A lower pitch is produced as your vocal cords relax. The second drawing shows the stretched vocal cords of a person who is speaking.

Top view of relaxed vocal cords

Top view of stretched vocal cords

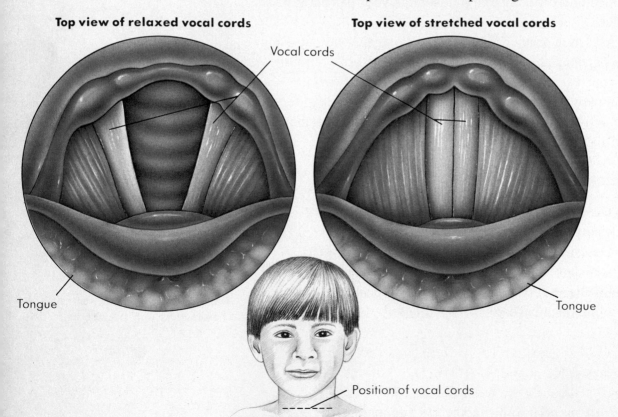

Vocal cords

Tongue

Tongue

Position of vocal cords

246

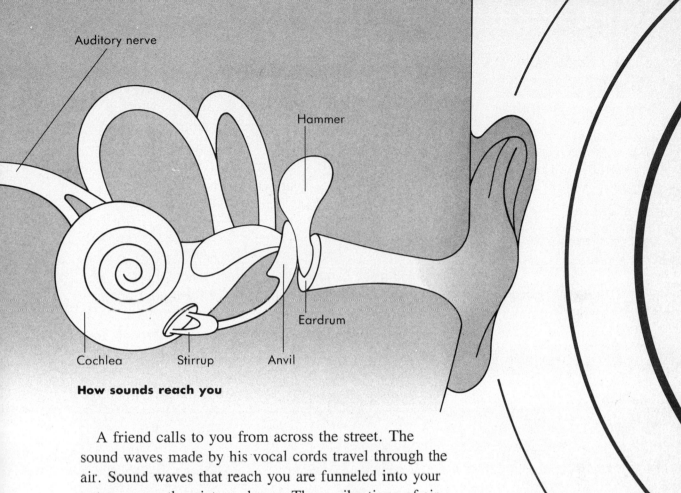

Auditory nerve

Hammer

Cochlea Stirrup Anvil Eardrum

How sounds reach you

A friend calls to you from across the street. The sound waves made by his vocal cords travel through the air. Sound waves that reach you are funneled into your outer ear, as the picture shows. These vibrations of air travel into your outer ear until they reach a thin tissue called the **eardrum.** When sound waves hit your eardrum, it begins to vibrate in rhythm with the waves.

The eardrum separates your outer ear from your **middle ear.** When your eardrum vibrates, it causes three small bones in your middle ear to vibrate. These three bones are called the hammer, anvil, and stirrup because they are shaped like those objects.

The hammer, which is attached to your eardrum, picks up sound vibrations. These vibrations are then passed along by the anvil and stirrup to your inner ear. All the parts of your middle ear take up a space the size of a marble.

eardrum (ir′drum′), a thin tissue in the outer ear that vibrates when sound waves strike it.

Have You Heard?
Your eardrum is only about 0.1 mm thick—about as thick as a sheet of notebook paper.

middle ear, space containing 3 small bones that pass sound waves from the eardrum to the inner ear.

How Does Sound Reach the Brain?

cochlea (kok′lē ə), the fluid-filled, snail-shaped part of the inner ear that sends sound signals to the auditory nerve.

auditory nerve (ô′də tôr′ē nėrv), nerve that carries sound signals from the inner ear to the brain.

Find Out

Find out the role of the canals that rest atop the cochlea.

Part of your inner ear—the **cochlea**—is shaped somewhat like the shell of a snail. The fluid-filled cochlea picks up vibrations from the stirrup, which is attached to it. The energy of the vibrations is changed into electrical signals. Notice that the cochlea attaches to the **auditory nerve.** This nerve carries electrical signals to your brain. Your brain sorts them out and interprets them as sounds that you hear.

Think About It

1. How are the sounds of your voice made?
2. Describe the path of a sound wave from your outer ear to your brain.
3. **Challenge** Would sound waves traveling through the outer ear travel faster or slower than those traveling through the inner ear? Explain.

Inner ear

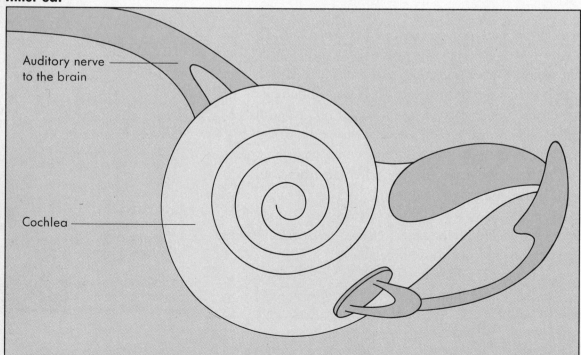

Auditory nerve to the brain

Cochlea

248

Discover!

There Are Many Ways to Communicate

Feeling vibrations from sounds

Many people take talking for granted. But talking is a challenge for a person who cannot hear words. Deaf people learn to communicate in ways very different from hearing people.

Perhaps you have noticed that some sounds can make a table vibrate. Sometimes deaf people can learn to talk by feeling the vibrations from sounds instead of hearing the vibrations. The picture shows someone feeling vibrations from words by putting his hands on the chin of the person who is speaking. He then makes sounds that produce vibrations which feel like the vibrations of the sound he felt spoken.

A deaf person can also learn to talk by watching the way that a speaking person's mouth moves. A person learning to speak this way tries to make the same movements with his or her mouth.

A computer can also teach people to understand spoken language. The pictures show the position of the lips, teeth, and tongue when certain speech sounds are made. A deaf person can study these pictures. Then, the person might watch his or her mouth in a mirror and learn to make the sounds.

People communicate in ways other than by speaking. Signing is a way of communicating with hand and finger movements. Each movement is called a

Computer pictures of mouth

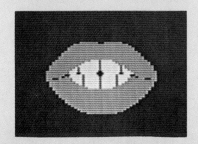

sign. One kind of signing is called finger spelling. In finger spelling each letter has a sign. A person makes the signs of the letters to spell words.

The second kind of signing uses a sign to represent a word or set of words. Spread the fingers of one hand. Then, fold down the third and fourth fingers. This sign means "I love you."

People who are not deaf often learn to sign. Then, deaf and hearing people can communicate by signing.

3 How Do Different Animals Send and Receive Sounds?

Describe the sound the wolf in the picture is making. Most people know the sounds made when animals vibrate their vocal cords. You have probably heard a dog's bark or a cow's moo. But not all animals make sounds by using only vocal cords. Woodpeckers use their beaks to tap out sounds on tree trunks. Another bird, the male ruffed grouse, beats his wings rapidly to make a whirring sound.

Wolf howling

Cicada

Grunts

Insects, such as the cicada (sə kā′də) in the picture, use different body parts to make sounds. A cicada makes loud sounds by vibrating thin membranes on its abdomen. Flies make sounds by rapidly vibrating their wings.

The fish in the picture are called grunts. The name comes from the sounds the fish make. Many fish make sounds by vibrating a gas-filled pouch inside their bodies.

Large ears gather in faint sounds

Many animals have very large ears. Notice the size of the ears on the rabbit and the deer. The rabbit holds its ears up and moves them when it senses danger. Its ears can gather faint sounds. If a fox tries to sneak up on it, the rabbit might hear the sounds with its large ears. Then, the rabbit might dash away before the fox can catch it.

Insects' hearing organs are different from those of other types of animals. Some insects, such as the grasshopper, have ears on the sides of their bodies. Some butterflies have ears at the bases of their wings. The bee's ears are on its legs! Bees cannot hear sound vibrations that travel through the air. They can only hear sound vibrations that move through things on which they are standing.

Jack rabbit

Find Out
Use library books to find out how fish hear.

Think About It

1. List three ways animals make sounds.
2. Describe three different kinds of animal ears.
3. **Challenge** Do you think a bird's ear would be more like a deer's ear or an insect's ear? Explain.

251

4 How Can Sounds Be Made with Musical Instruments?

Musical instruments make sounds in several different ways. Some instruments, such as the harp or banjo, produce sounds from vibrating strings.

The violin in the picture is another stringed instrument. If you look closely, you will notice that each string has a different thickness and length. These strings will vibrate when plucked or rubbed by a bow. Length, thickness, and tightness affect the pitch of a vibrating string. Short, thin, or tight strings vibrate rapidly, producing high-pitched sounds. Long, thick, or loose strings vibrate slowly, producing low-pitched sounds. Each string can be made tighter or looser to change the pitch. You can also change the pitch by pressing down on the string with the tip of your finger. When you press down on a string, you shorten its vibrating length, so the sound will have a higher pitch.

Wind instruments, such as this clarinet and trumpet, produce sounds when a column of air vibrates in a tube. A long air column produces a low-pitched sound, and a short air column produces a high-pitched sound.

When air is blown into a clarinet, a thin strip of wood or plastic—a **reed**—begins to vibrate. This vibrating reed causes the air in the tube to vibrate, and a sound is produced. When all the holes are covered, the air column is as long as it can be, and the clarinet produces its lowest note. Uncovering the last hole allows air to escape and makes the air column shorter. The pitch of the sound is higher. When the next hole is uncovered, the pitch is raised again.

The trumpet produces sounds in a different way from the clarinet. The trumpet has a mouthpiece at one end and a cone-shaped opening at the other end. You make music on a trumpet by forming your lips in different ways while blowing and by changing the length of the air column in the tube.

Notice that the trumpet has three valves. When a valve is pressed down, the air is sent through an extra length of tubing. The longer length of vibrating air produces a lower-pitched sound. The vibrating lips of a trumpet player can also produce sounds of different pitches. If the trumpet player's lips vibrate rapidly, high-pitched sounds are produced. Low-pitched sounds are produced when the player's lips vibrate slowly.

reed, a thin piece of wood or plastic in a musical instrument that vibrates when air moves over it.

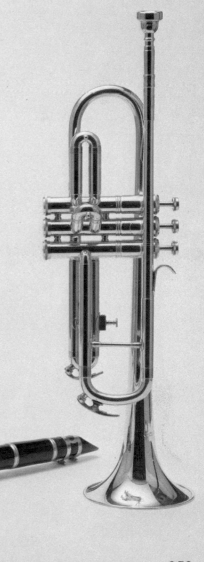

What Are Percussion Instruments?

Drums are probably the oldest musical instruments known. Cave art shows that early humans thumped on hollow logs to produce sounds.

Percussion instruments, such as this kettledrum, produce sounds when they are struck and the cover vibrates. Most drums produce only one pitch. But kettledrums are different. They can be tuned to produce different pitches. Stretching the drum's cover makes the cover tight and raises the pitch. As the cover is loosened, the pitch is lowered.

Think About It

1. How is the pitch of a sound changed in a stringed instrument?
2. How can the pitch of wind instruments be changed?
3. How is sound produced in percussion instruments?
4. **Challenge** What happens in all musical instruments to produce sound?

Kettledrums produce different pitches

Activity

Listening for Changes in Pitch

Purpose
To identify causes for changes in pitch.

You Will Need
- several rubber bands of different sizes and thicknesses
- plastic margarine tub with lid
- toothpick
- scissors
- centimeter ruler

Directions
1. Cut 2 slits each 1 cm long and 1 cm apart on opposite sides of the margarine tub, as shown in the picture.
2. Fasten a rubber band through the slits as the picture shows.
3. Cut a circular hole about 5 cm in diameter in the center of the lid. Place the lid on the tub.
4. Pluck the rubber band with the toothpick, and note the pitch.
5. Repeat steps 2 through 4 with the other rubber bands.

Think About It
1. Describe the thickness and length of the rubber band that made the sound with the highest pitch.
2. Describe the thickness and length of the rubber band that made the sound with the lowest pitch.
3. What differences in the rubber bands caused the pitch to change?
4. **Challenge** How could you find the cause of changes in pitch in a column of air?

5 How Can Sound Waves Be Reproduced?

You hear many sounds every day. Sounds wake you in the morning. Perhaps bells ring at school when classes start. You hear the voices of your teachers and friends. You may even hear the voices of people who live far away from you—if you use the telephone.

A telephone like the one in the picture has two main parts. You speak into the **transmitter** and listen to the **receiver.**

The sound waves of your voice vibrate a thin, metal disk in the transmitter. A small cup of carbon grains is attached to the back of the disk. When the vibrating disk pushes these grains together, an electric current flows. Telephone wires carry the electric current from your phone to the receiver in the listener's telephone.

Current flowing through a piece of metal in the receiver vibrates a metal disk. These vibrations reproduce the sound waves of the speaker's voice.

A telephone has two main parts

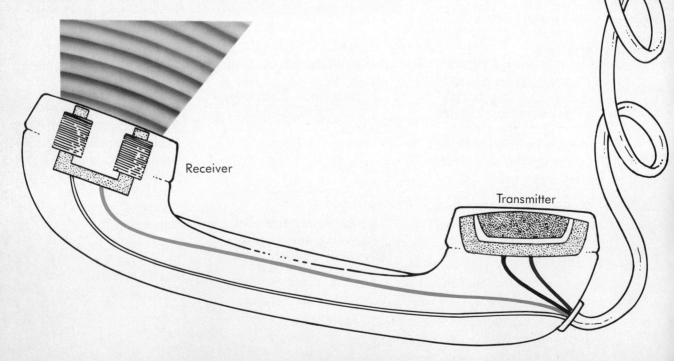

Receiver

Transmitter

Grooves in a phonograph record

Other sounds that you hear might come from a phonograph record. If you use a hand lens to look closely at a record, you can see grooves like those in the picture. These grooves look like thin, wavy lines. The sounds that you hear are the vibrations which were stored on the record when it was made.

If you place a needle in the grooves of a spinning record, the grooves will vibrate the needle. These vibrations are then changed into weak electrical signals. These signals travel from the needle to a device called an **amplifier,** which magnifies changes in the electrical signals. When these amplified signals reach the speaker of a phonograph player, the speaker vibrates. Sound waves that have been stored on the record are then reproduced so you can hear them.

amplifier (am′plə fī′ər), a device that magnifies changes in electrical signals.

Magnetic patterns on tape produce sound waves

How Is Sound Produced from a Tape?

Sounds can also be recorded on a ribbon of plastic tape. This tape is coated with a powdery substance, iron oxide, that is easily magnetized. An electric current carries sound waves from a microphone to a tape recorder. The electric current magnetizes the powder into different sound wave patterns. The picture shows how the tape moves through the player.

When the tape is played back, the magnetic patterns on the tape create a current that is sent to the speaker. The speaker vibrates, producing sound waves that match the waves which went into the microphone.

Think About It

1. How does a telephone transmit and receive sound?
2. What is the role of an amplifier in a record player?
3. **Challenge** How are record players and tape players alike?

Tie It Together

Sum It Up

On the telephone buttons below, three letters are placed with a number. Fill in the missing words below, using the numbers as clues.

1. Your 3273786 vibrates when sound waves strike it.

2. You make sounds by vibrating your 86225 26737.

3. The 722248 uses its large ears to listen for sounds of predators.

4. The length, thickness, or tightness of a string determines the 74824 of the sound.

5. You can speak to someone far away by using your 835374663.

6. The 28348679 nerve carries impulses to your brain that you interpret as sounds.

7. A paper cone can be used to make sounds seem 568337.

8. Not all animals have their ears on their 43237.

9. The trumpet and clarinet are examples of 9463 instruments.

10. The 4766837 on a phonograph record cause the needle to vibrate.

Challenge!

1. Men usually have lower-pitched voices than women. Would a man's vocal cords be thicker or thinner than a woman's? Explain.

2. If you blow across the top of a soft-drink bottle, you will hear a musical note. How will the pitch change if you pour some water into the bottle? Explain.

3. If you lightly hold a pin in a groove of an old record while the turntable is turning, you will hear a faint sound. What do you think will happen to the sound if you push the pin through the small end of a paper cone and then put it in the record groove? Explain.

4. What part of the telephone is like your eardrum? Explain.

5. Why would it be helpful for a predator, such as a fox, to have large ears?

Science Words

amplifier	receiver
auditory nerve	reed
cochlea	transmitter
eardrum	vocal cords
middle ear	

Laboratory

Vibration Rate and Pitch

Purpose
To make a device that shows how the vibration rate of a sound changes when the pitch of the sound changes.

You Will Need
- round container, such as an oatmeal box or salt box
- scissors
- large balloon
- rubber band or string
- glue
- small mirror
- flashlight

Stating the Problem
Sounds are produced when matter vibrates. Your vocal cords vibrate to help you produce sound. You can produce sounds that differ in pitch. Predict how the pitches of sounds that you make and the rates of vibration of the air that the sound waves travel through are related. Write down your prediction.

Investigating the Problem
1. Remove one end from the container. Cut a hole about the size of a quarter in the center of the closed end of the container. See picture *a*.
2. Cut off the neck of a balloon so that the remaining balloon will stretch over the open end of the container. Cover the open end of the container with the balloon. Secure the balloon with a rubber band or string.
3. Glue a small piece of mirror to the outside of the balloon as shown in picture *b*.

a

b

c

4. Darken the room. Stand 2 or 3 meters from the chalkboard. Facing the chalkboard, hold the container so that the small hole is near your mouth. The mirror will be facing away from you with its shiny side toward the chalkboard.

5. Ask someone to stand to the side and to shine the flashlight on the mirror so that the reflected light strikes the chalkboard. See picture c. Hold the container steady, so the spot of light on the chalkboard is still.

6. Hum a low-pitched note into the small hole in the container. Observe the reflected light on the chalkboard. Hum a high-pitched note. Observe the reflected light.

Making Conclusions
1. Explain what you see on the chalkboard when you hum into the container. Why does this happen?
2. What caused the mirror on the balloon to vibrate?
3. Compare the rate of vibration of the light when you hummed a low-pitched note with the vibration rate when you hummed a high-pitched note. Was your prediction correct?
4. Compare the rates of vibration of your vocal cords when you produce a high-pitched sound and when you produce a low-pitched sound. How are pitch and vibration rate related?
5. How is the balloon like your eardrum? What happens to your eardrum when you hear a high-pitched sound followed by a low-pitched sound?

Careers

Disc Jockey

How long can you talk? Many people have no trouble talking for an hour on the telephone. But Louise remembers a day when she talked for 24 hours!

Louise is a disc jockey at a radio station. "It was on one of those heavy snow days in 1979," says Louise. "I arrived at the station at 2:00 in the afternoon to do my show. By early evening, I was ready to go home. But no one else ever showed up! The snow stopped the other disc jockeys and engineers from getting to work. I did not want to shut down all of the broadcasting, so I just got some coffee and stayed on the air."

Of course, disc jockeys do not talk every minute they are on the air. They often relax while the songs are playing.

"At some radio stations, the engineer prepares the records and tapes to be played. But at other stations, that is the job of the disc jockey. Some disc jockeys write many of the commercials you hear on the radio. I have written a few myself.

"A disc jockey often has to do different jobs at

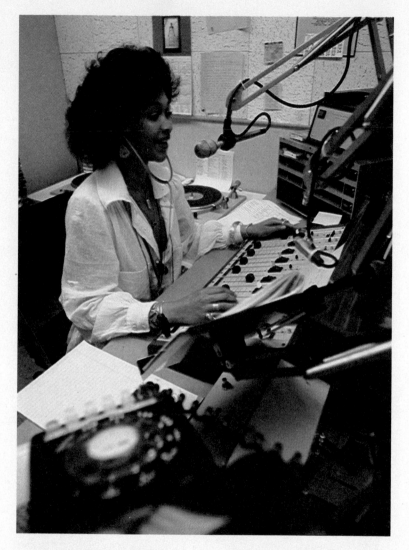

a radio station. So, a person who wants to do this kind of work should try to do well in all school subjects. A disc jockey should also have a friendly personality and not be afraid to talk to people.

"I like this job because it allows me to be creative. I usually have a lot of freedom to talk about different things on the air. I also get to meet and interview a lot of famous musicians."

If you enjoy listening to a disc jockey or music on the radio, you should thank a **broadcasting engineer.** This person sits in the control room next to the studio. The engineer uses a variety of buttons, dials, and switches to be sure the sound is correct. The engineer often operates the record turntables and tape recorders that play the music and commercials.

To be a broadcasting engineer, students go to a special school for two years after high school.

Sound is a very important part of an engineer's job. But many people have jobs that involve sound in a different way.

Audiologists work with people who have hearing problems. Patients are given tests to see how much hearing ability they have. The audiologist can then plan a program to help the patient.

Speech and hearing therapists often work with hearing-impaired people in schools. The therapist often teaches a person how to communicate in different ways. The patients may use electronic equipment to help make the sounds they hear louder and clearer.

People who want to be an audiologist or therapist go to college for four to six years.

If a person is deaf or almost deaf, he or she might learn sign language. In sign language, a person uses the fingers to form letters or arm movements to express an idea. A **sign language interpreter** teaches sign language and communicates with the deaf. Interpreters work in schools, churches, and businesses.

Broadcasting engineer

Therapist

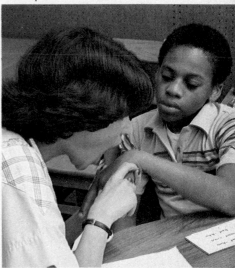

On Your Own

Picture Clue

The picture on page 226 shows part of a musical instrument. This instrument has a keyboard like a piano's but makes its musical sounds with vibrating air columns of different sizes.

Projects

1. Make a stethoscope from a large funnel and a piece of plastic or rubber hose. Use the stethoscope to listen to your heartbeats.

2. Use a set of eight glasses or jars to make the tones of a music scale. Make different pitches by varying the amounts of water in the glasses. Tap each glass lightly with a spoon to make it vibrate.

3. Find out how far you must stand from a building in order to hear an echo. Stand near the flat wall of a building, and shout *hello* at the wall. Repeat this as you move farther and farther away from the wall. Mark the spot where you first hear an echo. Measure the distance from the spot to the wall.

Books About Science

Deafness by Jane Hyman. Watts, 1980. Discover types of hearing loss and ways the hearing-impaired learn speech.

Silent Sound by David C. Knight. William Morrow & Co., Inc., 1980. Find out about the uses of ultrasound—from dog whistles to eye surgery.

The Dangers of Noise by Lucy Kavaler. Crowell, 1978. Learn how the noise around you affects you.

The Story of Your Ear by Alvin and Virginia Silverstein. Coward, 1981. Read about how your ears work and how they can be damaged.

Unit Test

True or False

Number your paper from 1–5. Next to each number, write *true* if the sentence is correct and *false* if the sentence is incorrect. Make each false statement true by changing the <u>underlined</u> word and writing the correct word on your paper.

1. <u>Vibrations</u> are needed to produce sounds.

2. Sound travels fastest through <u>gases</u>.

3. Sounds made by <u>wind</u> instruments do not change in pitch.

4. The part of the telephone into which you spcak is the <u>receiver</u>.

5. A sound with a large amplitude is a <u>loud</u> sound.

Matching

Number your paper from 6–10. Read the description in Column I. Next to each number, write the letter of the word or words from Column II that best match the description in Column I.

Column I

6. can help you hear very soft sounds

7. picks up sound vibrations from the stirrup

8. produces a sound by means of a vibrating reed

9. increases the loudness of a sound by increasing the strength of an electrical signal

10. sounds that are too high-pitched for people to hear

Column II

a. cochlea

b. eardrum

c. paper cone

d. clarinet

e. amplifier

f. ultrasonic

UNIT SIX
LIGHT

Here are some silver dots,
Maybe filled with
        colored spots . . .
But what I see,
because I'm me,
May not be
what you would see.

Tiffany Washington *age 10*

Chapter 16
Light and Optics

Your eyes help you learn about the world around you. You get more information through your eyes than any other way. But can you always believe what you see? Your eyes receive light, and sometimes light can make you see unexpected things.

The lessons in this chapter will help you understand how light causes you to see things the way you do.

1 Observing Spoon Images

Fun-house mirrors can make you look much different than you really are. You can get some idea of how mirrors form these odd-looking images by observing images on spoons.

Hold a spoon by its handle with the front part facing you. Look at your face in the spoon. Describe the image you see, and record your observation.

Now, hold the spoon with the back part facing you. Record what your image looks like now. Hold the spoon so the handle is to one side, as shown in the picture. Describe how your image changes.

Think About It

1. Examine the front and back of the spoon. How are they different?
2. **Challenge** What do you think caused the different images on the spoon?

2 How Is Light Reflected?

Notice the images in the picture below. The images are formed when light bounces off a smooth surface. When light is bounced back, it is **reflected.**

Some surfaces reflect light to form images better than others. Smooth, shiny surfaces reflect light to form the best images. When light rays hit a smooth piece of aluminum foil, all the rays reflect in the same direction. Rough surfaces also reflect light, but images do not form. Wrinkled foil causes the rays to scatter—or reflect in many different directions. The drawings show how light rays are reflected from the foil.

People use reflected light in many ways every day. Cars, trucks, department stores, and cameras use mirrors to let people see images reflected from other places.

reflect (ri flekt′), give back a likeness or image; turn back or throw back.

Find Out

Your bicycle has reflectors on it so drivers can see you easily. Examine a reflector to see how it is made.

Smooth foil

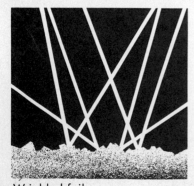

Wrinkled foil

Reflections in building and water

Ball bouncing off floor

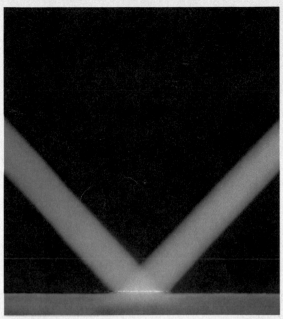

Light reflecting off mirror

Mirrors are very smooth surfaces made of polished metal or silver-coated glass. Notice in the pictures above that a beam of light bounces off a flat mirror the same way a ball bounces off the floor. The drawing shows that light reflects off a mirror in straight lines at the same angle that the light hits the mirror.

Curved mirrors also reflect light rays at the same angles at which they hit the surface. Because the surface is curved, the rays that hit in different places bounce off in different directions. The directions the rays reflect depend on how the surface is curved. As you saw when observing spoons, curved mirrors can make images look larger or smaller than the real things.

Think About It

1. Explain why a wrinkled piece of aluminum foil does not produce an image.
2. How do mirrors change the direction of light?
3. How does the angle at which light hits a mirror compare to the angle at which it leaves the mirror?
4. **Challenge** What are some uses for curved mirrors?

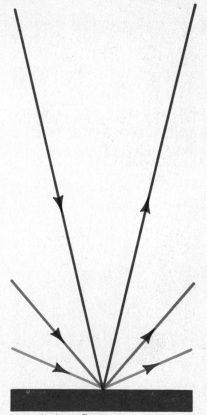

How light reflects

271

3 What Happens When Light Bends?

Pencil appears to be bent

It seems as if the turtle in the picture has lost part of its head. The odd image was made because light sometimes bends.

Light bends as it moves from one material into another at an angle other than 90° from the surface. The pencil in the picture looks bent at the water line. Light travels through some materials faster than it does through others. Light travels faster through air than it travels through water. The light bends, or changes direction, as its speed changes when it moves from air to water. This change in direction is **refraction.**

Refraction of light

Some lenses magnify

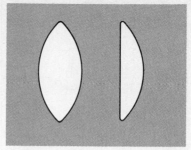

Convex lenses

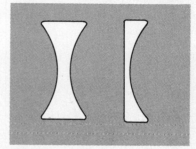

Concave lenses

Light is also refracted when it passes from air into clear glass or plastic. A **lens** is a smoothly curved piece of glass or plastic. Lenses refract light in special ways. Some lenses, such as the one in the picture, refract light and make things look bigger. People call this kind of lens a magnifying glass.

Lenses are grouped by shape into two kinds. **Convex** lenses are thicker in the middle than at the edges. **Concave** lenses are thinner in the middle than at the edges. The pictures on the right show some convex and concave lenses.

lens (lenz), piece of glass or other clear material that brings together or spreads apart rays of light passing through it.

convex (kon veks′), curving outward.

concave (kon kāv′), curving inward.

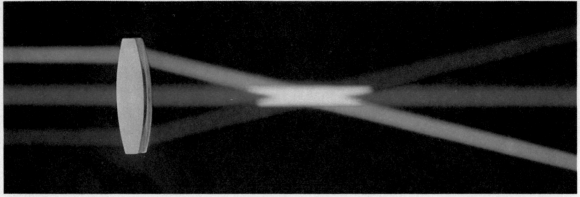

Light passing through a convex lens

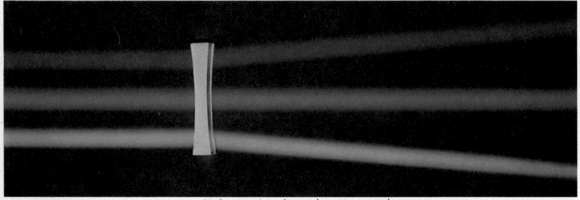

Light passing through a concave lens

How Do Lenses and Prisms Bend Light?

focus (fō′kəs), point at which rays of light meet.

The top picture shows how a convex lens refracts light rays. The rays are bent so they come together at a point behind the lens—the **focus**. Cameras, microscopes, and telescopes have convex lenses in them. People who do not see nearby things well wear glasses with convex lenses.

The lower picture shows how a concave lens refracts light rays. Notice that the light rays do not come to a focus. Instead, the rays are bent and spread apart as they pass through the lens. People wear glasses with concave lenses to see distant things clearly.

Here is an easy rule to remember about how light rays travel through lenses: Light rays passing through a lens always bend toward the thickest part of the lens.

A triangular glass **prism,** shown in the drawing, also refracts light. The light rays bend toward the base of the prism. Isaac Newton studied prisms over three hundred years ago. He discovered that prisms could separate sunlight into different colors.

prism (priz′əm), a clear piece of glass or plastic with triangular ends, used for separating white light.

Think About It

1. What is refraction?
2. Compare how concave and convex lenses refract light.
3. Name three uses of lenses in daily life.
4. **Challenge** Explain why you might reach for a rock in a pond and find that it was not where you expected it to be.

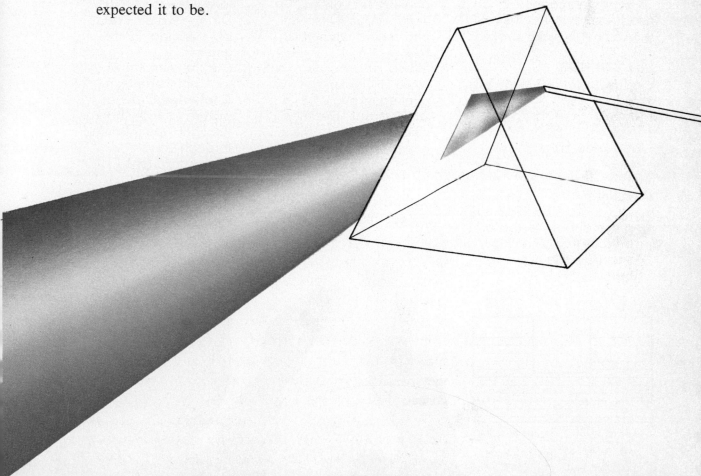

Activity

Observing Refraction Through Water Drops

Purpose
To observe images produced by refraction of light through water drops.

You Will Need
• index card
• clear plastic
• tape
• scissors
• magazine page
• water

Directions
1. Cut a 4-cm by 4-cm piece out of the top of an index card, as shown in the drawing below.

2. Cut a piece of clear plastic large enough to cover the cutout. Tape the plastic to the card.
3. Place the index card on a magazine page so that you can see words through the plastic.
4. Drop several small drops of water onto the plastic. Look at the printing through the water drops. Describe and record what you see.
5. Slowly lift the card while still looking at the printing through the water drops. Describe what happens to the letters.

6. Hold the card at eye level, as shown in the picture. Look at the shape of the water drops from the side. Draw the shape of the water drops.

Think About It
1. The water drops acted as lenses. What kind of lens were they?
2. Did the water drop always magnify the letters?
3. Did the letters always look right side up?
4. **Challenge** Draw a picture to show how the light was refracted through your water-drop lens.

Do You Know?

How Do You See Things That Are Not Really There?

Mirage on a highway

When is a puddle not a puddle? While riding in a car, you might have seen a puddle of water on the road ahead of you. But when you rode farther, the puddle disappeared. What you saw was a mirage.

A mirage is produced when light passes through air of different temperatures. How is a mirage formed? The drawing will help explain. The air close to the ground is hot. The air higher up is cool. When light passes from one layer of air to another, the light is bent. You can follow the path of the light in the drawing.

Your mind expects light to travel in straight lines. The dotted line shows the path that you expect the light to take. So when these light rays reach your eyes, your brain "sees" them differently. The object that your brain sees is the mirage rather than the real object.

Mirages are common on the desert where the air is hot. Someone sees a tree and its reflection. Their brain tells them the tree is being reflected in a lake. But the double image is a mirage. The thirsty traveler in the desert has been fooled by a trick of light!

How a mirage forms

Cool air

Warm air

Actual object

Expected image

4 How Do You See?

You see the sun, other stars, and candle flames because they give off their own light. Most things do not give off light. For you to see most things, light must be reflected from them to your eyes. Your eyes receive the light and send a message about it to your brain.

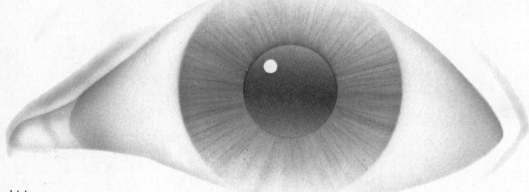

Pupil and iris

cornea (kôr′nē ə), the clear part of the outer coat of the eyeball.

iris (ī′ris), the colored part of the eye around the pupil.

pupil (pyü′pəl), the opening in the center of the iris.

The drawing shows the front of your eye. Light enters your eye through a clear layer called the **cornea.** The colored part of your eye—or **iris**—is behind the cornea. In the center of the iris is a black circle—the **pupil.** This black circle is really an opening that lets light enter your eye.

The iris is made of tiny ring-shaped muscles. The iris makes the pupil larger or smaller. Notice the difference in the sizes of the pupils in the pictures below. In dim light the pupils become larger to let more light into your eyes. In bright light the pupils become smaller. When your pupils are smaller, the insides of your eyes are protected from too much light.

Pupil in bright light

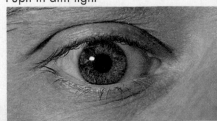

Pupil in dim light

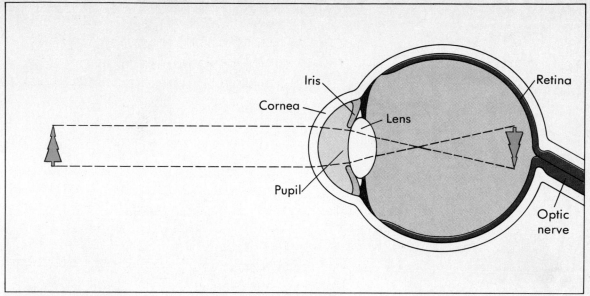

Structure of the eye

A convex **lens** lies behind the iris and pupil. This lens focuses light just as a glass lens does. Light comes into your eye through the pupil and passes through the lens. The lens can change its shape to become thicker or thinner. The lens becomes thicker when you look at a close object. When you look at something far away, the lens becomes thinner.

The lens turns the image of what you see upside down. The drawing shows how the image is formed. The upside-down image forms on a layer at the back of your eye—the **retina.** Special cells in the retina send a message of the image along the **optic nerve** to your brain. Your brain turns the image right side up so you see everything the right way.

lens (lenz), the part of the eye that focuses light rays on the retina.

retina (ret′n ə), layer at the back of the eyeball that is sensitive to light and receives the images of things you look at.

optic nerve (op′tik nėrv), the nerve that goes from the eye to the brain.

Find Out

Find out how the eyes of spiders and cats are different from yours.

Think About It

1. Name three parts of your eye. Explain what each part does.
2. How would your pupils change if you walked into a dark room from outside on a sunny day?
3. **Challenge** What would happen if the lens in your eye was not able to change its shape?

5 How Does a Camera Work?

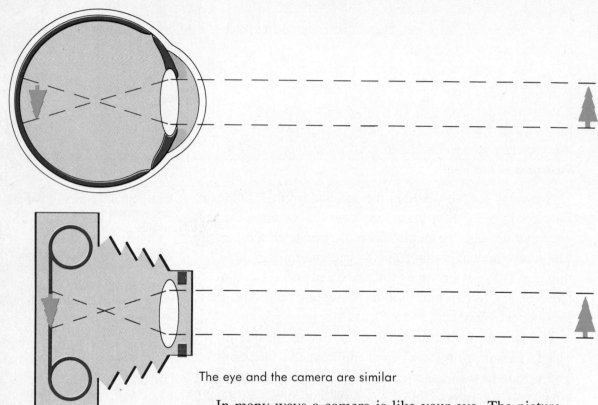

The eye and the camera are similar

In many ways a camera is like your eye. The picture shows how much alike they are. A camera and your eye both use light rays to record an image. Rays of light reflect off an object to the camera. Light enters the camera through a convex lens. The lens in a camera cannot change its shape as the lens in your eye can. In order to get a clear picture, you must focus the camera—or move the lens backward or forward.

The lens focuses the light rays on film inside the back of the camera. The image formed on the film is upside down, just as the image formed on the retina of your eye is upside down.

To get the best picture, you must make sure that the right amount of light enters the camera. An opening that can be made larger or smaller controls the amount of light that goes into the camera. This opening is like the pupil in your eye. The iris of your eye controls the size of your pupil. In the camera, movable plates control the size of the opening. Notice the difference in the sizes of the openings on the right.

In dim light you must make the opening larger to let in more light. If you do not, the picture will be too dark. In bright light you must make the opening smaller, or the picture will be too light. Decide which of the pictures below was taken with a large opening.

The opening in a camera can be changed

Picture taken in dim light

Picture taken in bright light

How Do You See Moving Pictures?

Suppose you want to take a picture of something that is moving. The person in the picture is juggling three balls. But the picture does not show that the balls are moving. If you want pictures that show things moving, you need to use a movie camera.

A movie camera takes pictures the same way a still camera does. But it takes many pictures of a moving object, one right after another. The pictures on the left show a running animal on a piece of movie film. When these pictures are shown on a movie screen, your eyes see each picture for a moment after the picture has been taken away. The screen actually goes black between pictures. But these pictures flash on the screen so quickly, your eyes see the animal moving.

Think About It

1. How is a camera like your eye?
2. How is a camera different from your eye?
3. **Challenge** If you could not move the lens inside a camera, what could you do to focus the image on the film?

Tie It Together

Sum It Up

1. Which of the drawings below correctly shows how light reflects from a mirror?

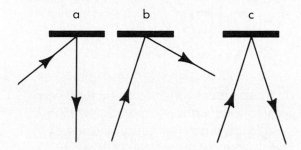

2. Make a drawing to show how light rays travel through a convex lens.

3. Make a drawing to show how light rays travel through a concave lens.

4. Make a drawing of the eye, and label these parts: cornea, iris, pupil, lens, retina, and optic nerve.

5. Describe the images formed on the front and back of a spoon.

6. Explain how you see moving pictures.

Challenge!

1. Is the back of a spoon a concave or convex mirror? Explain.

2. Explain what happens to the beam of light from the flashlight in the picture below.

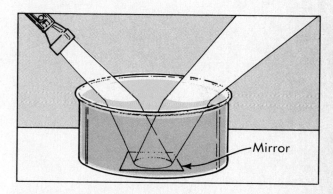

3. How could you print your name so that it looks correct when you view it in a mirror?

4. Explain why you would not see reflections in a pond on a windy day.

5. How does the amount a lens is curved affect the way the lens bends light rays?

Science Words

concave	optic nerve
convex	prism
cornea	pupil
focus	reflect
iris	refraction
lens	retina

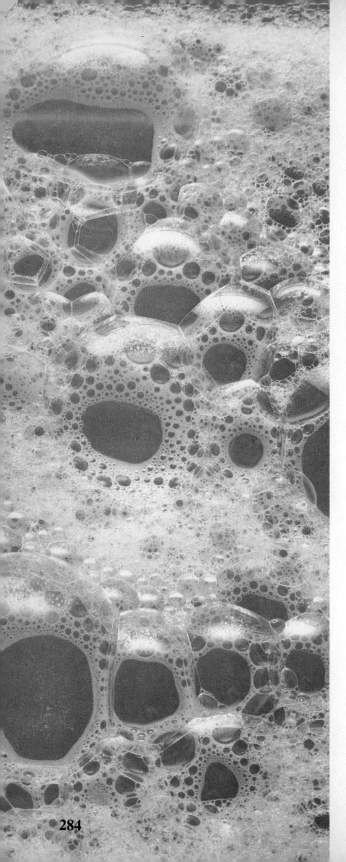

Chapter 17
Light and Color

Imagine how the world around you would look without color. Everything would be black, white, or shades of gray. Your world would look like a black-and-white photograph.

Perhaps you have never thought about what color is. The bubbles in the picture have no color. But the light you see reflected from them looks colored. Without light, there would be no color.

The lessons in this chapter describe how color is produced and seen.

1 Observing Soap Bubbles

The light in your classroom is made of colors. But you cannot see the colors until something happens to the light. You can see the colors when light passes through water drops in the air. This band of colors, like the one in the picture, is a rainbow.

You can make some colors yourself. Take a small jar half full of soapy water. Make sure the lid is tightly on the jar. Next, shake the jar, as shown, until bubbles form. Remove the lid, and look down into the jar at the bubbles. You should be able to see colors in the bubbles. Keep observing to see if the colors change.

Think About It

1. What colors did you see in the bubbles?
2. How were the colors you saw in the soap bubbles different from those in the rainbow?
3. **Challenge** What other ways can you make the colors in light visible?

Shaking the soapy water

2 What Is the Spectrum?

Have You Heard?

An easy way to remember the order of the colors in the spectrum is to think of a boy named Roy G. Biv!

Light from the sun, a flashlight, or a movie projector is called white light. But white light is really made of many colors. You can see these colors in a rainbow or when white light passes through a prism. The band of colors is the **visible spectrum.** You may have seen a spectrum made when light passes through glass beads or cut-glass dishes like the ones in the picture.

Although they cannot see how light moves, scientists think that it moves through space in a wavelike motion. Some parts of light have shorter wavelengths than others. The differences in the lengths of the waves produce the different colors in light.

The visible spectrum is made of seven colors—red, orange, yellow, green, blue, indigo, and violet. Light is refracted—or bent—as it leaves a prism. Each color of the spectrum is refracted a different amount. This refraction separates the colors that make up white light.

Violet light has the shortest wavelength and is refracted the most. Red light has the longest wavelength and is refracted the least. Look at the spectrum in the picture on the right. Notice that there are no dividing lines between the colors. It is sometimes hard to pick out all the colors. The spectrum is a gradual change from one color to another.

A spectrum can be produced by different objects

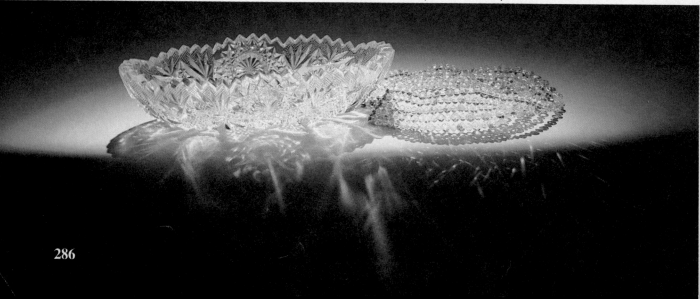

Find Out

Look in an encyclopedia to find out how Wilhelm Roentgen discovered X rays.

Have You Heard?

When ultraviolet rays hit certain minerals, the minerals "glow in the dark." These minerals take in the ultraviolet rays and give off visible light.

X ray of teeth

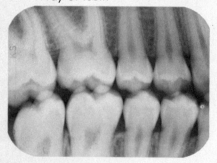

Can You See All the Spectrum?

The pictures show the visible spectrum and other wavelengths in the spectrum that you cannot see. Beyond the red end of the visible spectrum are infrared and radio waves. They have longer wavelengths than red light. Infrared waves are used in hospitals for heat treatments. Radio waves are used in communication.

Notice that beyond the violet end of the visible spectrum are ultraviolet rays and X rays. They have shorter wavelengths than violet light. Ultraviolet rays can tan or burn your skin. Doctors use X rays to take pictures of the inside of your body. Notice the X-ray picture of teeth on the left.

Think About It

1. What are the colors in the visible spectrum?
2. Name two parts of the spectrum that you cannot see.
3. **Challenge** Why do you think the discovery of X rays was important?

Spectrum

X rays   Ultraviolet rays   Visible rays   Infrared waves   Radio waves

Discover!

A New Kind of Light in Your Life

Scientists have found a new kind of light. This light is called laser light. You might have seen laser shows at school. Lasers are also being used in medicine, industry, and science research.

How is laser light different from other kinds of light? White light contains all the colors of the rainbow. And the "red" light in a traffic signal contains red light of many different wavelengths. But the waves of laser light are all the same wavelength.

Laser beam drilling a hole in metal

So the light from a laser is one pure color. Another difference between laser light and other light is that a laser makes a thin beam of light that travels only in one direction. Finally, the waves of laser light are lined up as shown in the picture.

Because the waves of laser light are the same length, travel in one direction, and all line up, a beam of laser light can be very powerful. A laser beam can even drill holes in metals, as the picture shows. The lens focuses the beam to hit the point where the hole is to be drilled.

Laser light is useful in many other ways. Laser beams can be used to carry radio and telephone messages. Lasers can even prevent some people from going blind. Doctors can use laser beams to reattach a person's retina if the person's eye has been damaged in an accident. A laser might even have been used to cut the cloth for your clothes!

Laser light waves line up

3 How Does Artificial Light Differ from Sunlight?

filament (fil′ə mənt), very slender, threadlike part.

In the past, people used candles and oil lamps to light their homes. Today, we have many sources of artificial light. But each kind of artificial light is a little different from sunlight. You might have noticed that colored objects look slightly different in artificial light than they do in sunlight. Each kind of light is a different mixture of colored light.

A light bulb gives off light from a glowing metal wire. In the picture, notice the thin, coiled wire—the **filament**—inside the glass bulb. The filament is made of a metal that can be heated to high temperatures. All the air is taken out of the bulb. A special gas is then put in, and the bulb is sealed tightly. If air were left in the bulb, the filament would burn up very quickly.

A light bulb contains a filament

When the light switch is turned on, electricity flows through the filament. The filament gets so hot that it glows and gives off light. The glowing filament gives off light that contains more red rays than blue ones.

Perhaps your classroom has lights like those in the picture. These lights do not contain a filament. Each light is a glass tube with a coating of special powder on the inside. The powder coating glows when ultraviolet rays hit it. The glowing powder gives off light that contains more blue and green rays than red ones. These lights, called **fluorescent** lights, are used in many schools and offices. They use less electricity and stay cooler than light bulbs.

The pictures on the right show the amount of each color given off by different light sources. Notice how the pictures are different.

Think About It

1. Describe the differences between a light bulb and a fluorescent light.
2. List two reasons why schools would use fluorescent lights instead of light bulbs.
3. **Challenge** How is the light given off by the sun different from the light given off by artificial lights?

Fluorescent lights in a classroom

fluorescent (flů res′nt), able to give off light when exposed to ultraviolet rays or X rays.

Sunlight

Light bulb

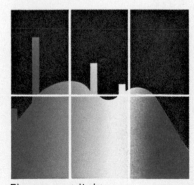

Fluorescent light

291

4 How Do You See Color?

White light contains all the colors of the visible spectrum. When white light shines on objects, you see colors.

You see the flowers in the picture as red and the leaves as green. You see the plant because light is reflected from it to your eyes. But not all the light that reaches the plant is reflected. Most of the light is absorbed—or taken in without being reflected. The flowers absorb all the colors of light except red. They reflect mainly red light to your eyes. The leaves absorb all colors except green. They reflect mainly green light to your eyes.

Colors absorbed and reflected by white, black, and gray objects

White objects reflect almost all the light that reaches them. Black objects absorb almost all the light that reaches them. Only a very small amount of light is reflected back to your eyes from black objects. Notice the gray hat the clown in the picture is wearing. The hat absorbs a little bit of all the colors that hit it. Since the hat absorbs some light, it looks darker than the clown's white glove. The hat also reflects some of all the colors of light that hit it. So the hat looks lighter than the clown's black tie. The drawing shows the rays that are absorbed and reflected by the clown's clothes.

Is a Blue Object Always Blue?

The three pictures all show the same top. In the first picture, you see the top with white light shining on it. The top looks blue. Only the blue part of the white light is reflected to your eyes. The rest of the light is absorbed.

The second picture shows blue light shining on the top. In blue light the top looks blue. The blue light shining on the top is reflected to your eyes.

But notice what happens when you shine red light on the top. The top looks almost black. The top can reflect only blue light. The red light shining on the top is absorbed. When almost all the light shining on an object is absorbed, the object looks black.

Top in white light

Top in blue light

Top in red light

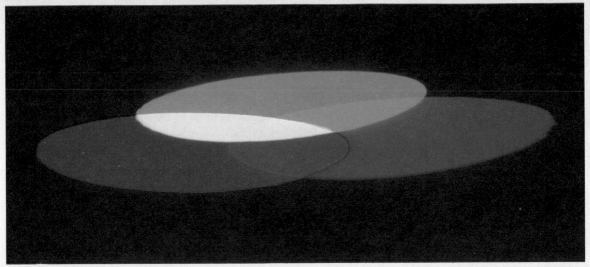

Colors of light can be mixed

What Happens When You Mix Colors of Light?

You may have mixed two colors of paint together to make a third color. But you can mix colors of light too! Red, green, and blue are the primary colors of light. These colors can be mixed together to make other colors. The picture shows beams of red, blue, and green light shining on white paper. Notice that where the beams overlap, you see other colors. The colors made by mixing light are not the same as colors made by mixing paint. Observe the color made by mixing red light with green light. Notice that, where all three primary colors of light overlap, white light is produced. This mixing of light is another way to show that white light is made of colors.

Think About It

1. Why does a leaf look green in sunlight?
2. What colors of light does a white piece of paper reflect? A black piece of paper?
3. Name the primary colors of light.
4. **Challenge** What color would a white top look if you shined red light on it? Explain.

Find Out

How are the colors made by mixing paint different from those made by mixing light? Mix different colors of paint together to find out.

Activity

Observing Color

Purpose
To infer, based on observations, how colored light affects colored objects.

You Will Need
- flashlight
- red and blue cellophane
- 1 sheet of white construction paper
- 1/4 sheet each of red, blue, and green construction paper
- rubber band
- scissors
- tape

Directions
1. Draw and cut out 3 paper circles—1 red, 1 blue, and 1 green, as shown in the picture.
2. Tape the 3 colored circles onto the white construction paper.
3. In a darkened room, shine a flashlight beam on each circle. Observe and record the color each circle appears to be.
4. Cover your flashlight lens with several layers of red cellophane, and fasten with a rubber band, as shown in the picture.
5. Shine the flashlight on the paper. Observe and record the color you see on each circle and on the white paper.
6. Remove the red cellophane, and cover your flashlight with blue cellophane.
7. Shine the flashlight on the paper. Observe and record the color you see on each circle and on the white paper.

Think About It
1. What colors of light did the white paper reflect?
2. What colors of light did each of the circles reflect?
3. Explain why some of the circles sometimes looked black.
4. **Challenge** What color would each circle look if you covered your flashlight with green cellophane?

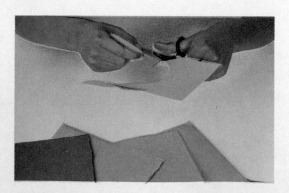

Tie It Together

Sum It Up

1. Draw a rainbow, and color it correctly.

2. Draw and color the spectrum made when sunlight passes through a glass prism.

3. List the colors of light each of the objects below absorbs and reflects.
   a. white tablecloth
   b. green grass
   c. black shoes
   d. blue pants
   e. red sweater

4. Explain two ways you can show that white light is made of colors.

5. List two parts of the spectrum that you cannot see.

6. What part of a light bulb gives off light? What part of a fluorescent light gives off light?

Challenge!

1. What colors of light are reflected by a yellow sweater?

2. If you pass a flashlight beam through a prism, a visible spectrum is made. What do you think would happen if you passed the spectrum you made through a second prism?

3. Why would a blue shirt look brighter in fluorescent light than in light from a light bulb?

4. Would blue light or orange light bend more as it passed through a prism? Explain your answer.

5. Plants need light to grow. But plants do not grow well in green light. Why?

Science Words

filament

fluorescent

visible spectrum

Laboratory

Making a Periscope

Purpose
To infer how mirrors in a periscope (per′ə skōp) help us look at objects that we cannot see with our eyes alone.

You Will Need
- 3 large pieces of cardboard
- centimeter ruler
- scissors
- tape
- 2 7.5-cm × 5-cm mirrors
- protractor

Stating the Problem
Did you ever wish that you could see over people's heads in a crowd? Submarines can "see" above water by using an instrument called a periscope that has mirrors. How can mirrors help us look at objects that we cannot see with our eyes alone?

Investigating the Problem
1. Cut 4 pieces of cardboard, each 30 cm in length and 6 cm in width.
2. Cut 2 squares of cardboard. Each side should be 6 cm long.
3. As shown in picture *a*, draw a 4-cm square about 3 cm from 1 end of one of the long pieces of cardboard that you cut in step 1. Do the same for one of the other long pieces of cardboard. Cut out both squares.
4. Tape a mirror next to each cut-out space as shown in picture *b*. The mirror should be taped to the cardboard at about a 45° angle. Use a protractor to measure the angle.
5. Tape together the cardboard pieces that you cut in steps 1 and 2 to make a box like the one shown in picture *c*.
6. Hold the box long-side-up, as shown in picture *d*,

a

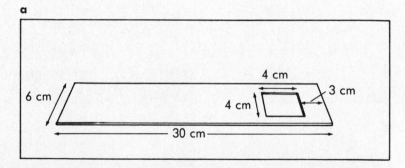

6 cm 4 cm 4 cm 3 cm 30 cm

b

c

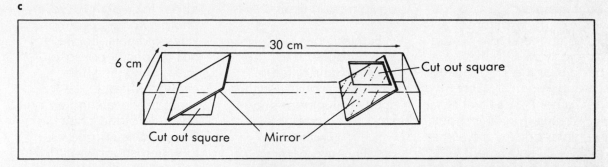

6 cm

30 cm

Cut out square

Cut out square   Mirror

d

and look through the bottom hole. Record what you observe.

Making Conclusions
1. Draw a diagram of the periscope that you made, and show how the light from an object that you observed traveled through the periscope and reached your eyes.
2. What would happen if you lowered the upper mirror about 2 cm toward the middle of the opening?
3. How can you use a periscope to see around corners?

Careers

Photographer

Over thirty different lights fill the studio where Bernie works. In the middle of the studio is an arrangement of sports equipment. Baseball bats, ice skates, running shoes, helmets, and twenty other pieces of equipment lie in the middle of the room. Is Bernie training for the Olympics? "No, I use this equipment in a different way."

Bernie is a photographer. He photographs different kinds of products, such as sports equipment and food. The companies which make these products use Bernie's pictures in their catalogs and advertisements.

"The lighting is one of the most important things about taking a picture. Photographers use many kinds of lights. Each kind has a special purpose. The main light is the strongest. It acts like the sun, casting a shadow on one side of the object. Other lights can be used to soften shadows or to lighten a backround. I also use white umbrellas to reflect the light and spread it out evenly."

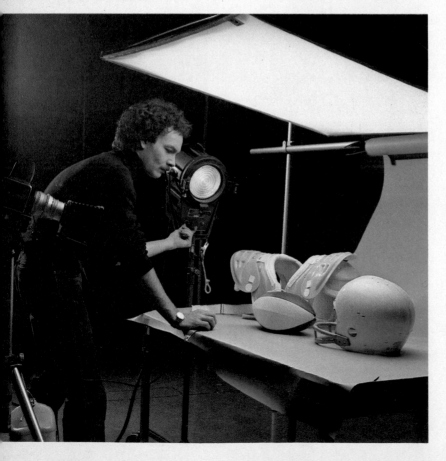

When Bernie was fourteen years old, a camp counselor got him interested in photography. He took some photography classes in school and learned how to develop his own pictures.

"I started taking pictures for the local newspaper. I did not get paid but my name was printed under my pictures. Young people can get good experience with a local newspaper or as a helper in a photo studio."

The newer cameras can do many things automatically. "But having a fancy camera is not enough to get a good picture," says Bernie. "The best photographs are good because the photographer knew how to use light."

Designer

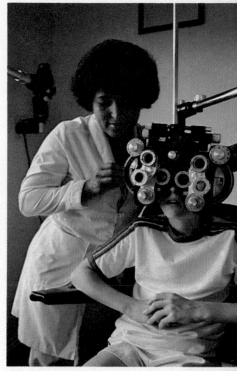

Optometrist

Many pictures that photographers take end up in books like this one. A **designer** helps decide which pictures will be shown. This person also decides where a picture will be placed on the pages. The designer checks the photograph to see that its color and lighting are correct. The designer knows that a good photograph in the right place makes reading more enjoyable.

Students who want to be designers go to a school of design after high school.

Many people interested in light get jobs working with vision.

When you want to get your vision checked, you go to an **optometrist** (op tom′ə trist). This person examines your eyes and tests your vision. The optometrist finds out if you need glasses.

If you do need glasses, you usually have to wait a few weeks for them. The glasses must be made. Each lens in a pair of eyeglasses is specially made for the patient. An **optical mechanic** makes the lenses for glasses.

This worker uses tools to carefully grind and polish each lens. The two lenses are then cut to fit into the eyeglass frames. The optical mechanic takes special care to make sure you get a perfect fit. Some optical mechanics make lenses for cameras and binoculars.

People who want to be optometrists go to college for six years. Optical mechanics train on the job for three years.

On Your Own

Picture Clue

Did you discover what the picture on page 266 shows? If not, go back to the Activity on page 276. What did you use in the Activity that produced images like the ones you see on page 266?

Projects

1. Observe the uses of mirrors in store windows, in cars, in barber shops, and in dentists' offices. Report on the reason the mirrors are shaped as they are, and why they are placed as they are.

2. Find out what color of light is made when you mix blue light and yellow light. Use two flashlights covered with colored cellophane, and shine the lights on white paper.

3. Examine your own or your friends' eyeglasses to find out if they have convex or concave lenses. Look at a magazine page through the lenses to see what the lenses do to the words.

Books About Science

Color, from Rainbows to Lasers by Franklin M. Branley. Crowell, 1978. Explains the basics of color, how color is created, and how it is used.

Living Light: Exploring Bioluminescence by Peg Horsburgh. Messner, 1978. Explains the causes of bioluminescence, and describes plants and animals that exhibit the property.

What Is a Laser? by Bruce Lewis. Dodd, Mead, 1979. Explains what lasers are, how they work, and some of the amazing things they can do.

The Magic of Color by Hilda Simon. Lothrop, Lee & Shepard, 1981. Explains the difference between colored light and pigment, and illustrates the formation of afterimages by the eye.

Unit Test

Matching

Number your paper from 1-5. Read the description in Column I. Next to each number, write the letter of the word or phrase from Column II that best matches the description in Column I.

Column I

1. occurs when light bounces off a smooth surface

2. can act as lenses to make images look larger or smaller

3. the bending of light as it passes from one substance into another

4. layer at the back of the eye that sends messages along the optic nerve to the brain

5. found in both a camera and your eye

Column II

a. refraction

b. reflection

c. retina

d. water drops

e. lens

f. pupil

True or False

Number your paper from 6-10. Next to each number, write *true* if the sentence is correct and *false* if the sentence is incorrect. Make each false statement true by changing the underlined word or phrase and writing the correct word or phrase on your paper.

6. White light contains all colors in the visible spectrum.

7. Fluorescent lights give off more heat that light bulbs.

8. A black piece of paper absorbs less light than a yellow piece of paper of the same size.

9. A piece of cloth looks blue because other colors of light are reflected.

10. The opening that allows light to enter a camera is similar to the pupil of your eye.

UNIT SEVEN
THE SOLAR SYSTEM

The whirlpool gives me the chills
    and I become cold.
It makes me frightened!
The whirlpool in the wide sea
    haunts me.
But I know that I am safe here
    far, far away.

Harold Juan *age 12*

Chapter 18

The Earth, Sun, and Moon

On most days the sun shines in the sky during the daytime. On other days both the sun and moon appear in the sky at the same time. At a glance the sun and moon appear to be the same size. But the difference in their sizes is huge!

The lessons in this chapter describe the earth, sun, and moon and explain how the sun and moon affect the earth.

1 Comparing the Sun and Moon

You can find out how the sun and moon can look the same size. Just hold up a large ball, such as a beach ball. This ball is your "sun." Ask a classmate to hold up a small ball. This ball is your "moon." A third classmate should stand as shown to watch the balls. Be sure the person with the smaller ball stands between you and the person watching. Now, start moving away from the person with the smaller ball. When the balls appear to be the same size, the watcher should tell the other two people to stop.

Think About It

1. In what way does distance affect how large an object looks?
2. Why do you think the sun and moon look the same size?
3. **Challenge** In what other ways are the sun and moon alike? Different?

2 What Is Known About the Sun?

On a summer night the sky might look like the sky in the picture. But the thousands of stars you would see are only a few of the stars in the universe. The sun, like all stars, is a ball of hot, glowing gases. The sun is a medium-sized star with a yellow-white color.

At the sun's surface the temperature is about 5,500° Celsius. This temperature is about 15 times hotter than the hottest temperature needed to cook food. But some stars are even hotter—up to 30,000° Celsius at the surface. Other stars are as cool as 2,500° Celsius at the surface.

The temperature at the center of the sun is 15,000,000° Celsius. At this temperature, atoms break into smaller particles.

The night sky visible away from a city

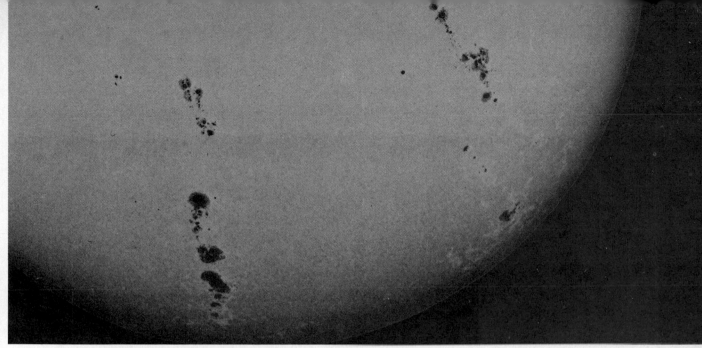

Our sun

The sun's heat and light are produced by processes deep within the sun. Studies of similar processes on earth help scientists understand what happens inside the sun. The studies show that the sun has reached the middle of its lifetime. Scientists predict that the sun should remain about as it appears in the picture for the next five billion years.

Even though the sun is the star closest to us, it is still very far away. Light travels at a speed of 300,000 kilometers per second. But even at this speed, sunlight takes 8.5 minutes to reach us.

The sun is very important to earth because it is the star closest to us. Without the sun's warmth and light, earth would be an icy rock on which nothing could live.

Think About It

1. Describe the sun's temperature, color, and size.
2. In what ways is the sun important to us?
3. **Challenge** If Jupiter is five times as far from the sun as Earth is, how long does sunlight take to reach Jupiter?

Have You Heard?

Very little of the sun's light reaches the earth. Most of the sun's light spreads out into space.

3 How Does the Earth Move?

rotation (rō tā′shən), the act of spinning around a center.

axis (ak′sis), an imaginary straight line through an object and about which the object spins.

Sit very still without moving a muscle. No matter how still you sit, you are moving. You cannot tell that the earth carries you with it as it moves. The earth spins—or rotates—as a basketball spins on the tip of a player's finger. The earth makes one **rotation** when it spins around once. The time for each rotation is 24 hours—what we call a day.

The earth rotates around an imaginary line that runs through its center. This line is the earth's **axis.** Notice in the picture that the axis connects the North and South Poles.

The earth's rotation causes daylight and night. To understand how, follow what happens to point A in the pictures. Point A has night when that part of the earth faces away from the sun. As the earth rotates, point A slowly moves as shown. When point A moves into the sunlight, point A has daylight.

The sun does not really rise in the east or set in the west. The sun only appears to rise and set because the earth rotates from west to east.

How earth's rotation causes day and night

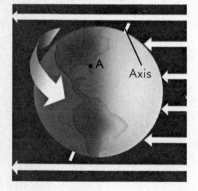

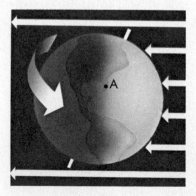

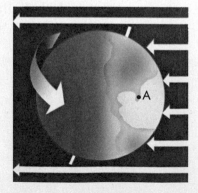

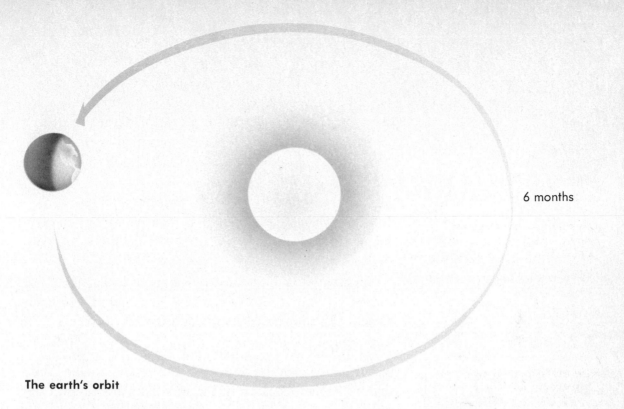

6 months

The earth's orbit

The earth also moves in a path around the sun. This path—an **orbit**—is shaped like an almost perfect circle, as shown. The earth moves along this orbit—or revolves—around the sun.

The earth completes one **revolution** when it has moved once around its orbit. One revolution takes about 365 days—what we call a year.

The earth revolves around the sun for the same reason that objects fall down on earth—gravity. When you throw a ball into the air, you know that it will return to the ground. A high-flying kite will return to earth when the wind dies down. Gravity makes objects return to earth and keeps the earth revolving around the sun. Without gravity, the earth would fly into space, as the drawing shows. But because of gravity, the earth's motion is curved into an orbit.

On earth the force of gravity on an object is the object's **weight.** The more mass an object has, the more gravity pulls on it. So the object weighs more.

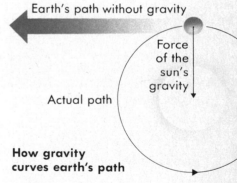

Earth's path without gravity

Actual path

Force of the sun's gravity

How gravity curves earth's path

orbit (ôr′bit), a closed, curved path that an object follows as the object moves around another object.

revolution (rev′ə lü′shən), movement of an object in an orbit around another object.

weight, the amount of the earth's force of gravity on an object.

311

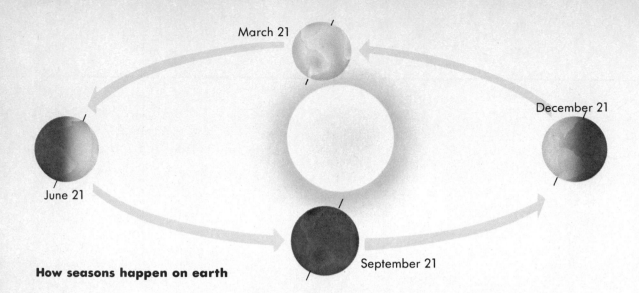

March 21

December 21

June 21

September 21

How seasons happen on earth

What Makes the Seasons Change?

Summer days can be long and warm. But when winter comes, the days become shorter and cooler. The seasons happen because of the way the sun's rays hit the earth.

Notice in the picture that the earth's axis does not stand straight up from the earth's orbit. Around June 21 the northern half of the earth faces into the sun's rays. This half receives more sunlight than the southern half does. It is summer in the northern half and winter in the southern half. During the next six months, the earth moves halfway around its orbit. By December 21 the northern half faces away from the sun's rays. Now this half has winter. The southern half has summer. From December 21 to June 21, the earth moves around the other half of its orbit until the northern half has summer again.

Think About It

1. How long do the earth's rotation and revolution take?
2. What keeps the earth in its orbit?
3. **Challenge** Where on the earth would you notice the least change in seasons?

Activity

Observing Motions of the Earth

Purpose
To demonstrate the earth's rotation and revolution.

You Will Need
- toothpick
- polystyrene or soft rubber ball
- piece of string 2 m long
- light bulb in a socket

Directions
1. Stick the toothpick into the ball to represent earth's axis at the North Pole.
2. Use a pencil to mark an X on the ball. The ball should look like the ball shown.
3. Knot the ends of your string together. Lay the string on a table to make the string look like the earth's orbit.
4. Put the bulb in the orbit as shown.
5. Hold the ball so the toothpick points toward the light somewhat.
6. Rotate the ball from west to east, as marked in the drawing.
7. Notice how the lighting on point X changes.
8. Repeat step 5, and move the ball around the orbit without rotating the ball. (Be sure to point the toothpick as shown on page 312.)
9. Notice how the lighting changes on the top and bottom halves of the ball.

Think About It
1. Explain why half the earth is always in the dark.
2. Can light eventually reach all parts of the earth in step 8?
3. **Challenge** How long does daylight last at the North Pole?

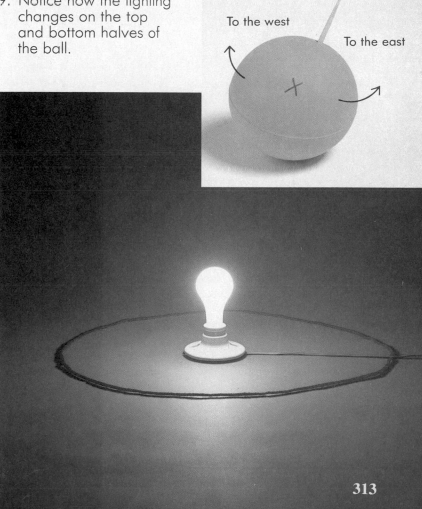

To the west

To the east

4 What Is Known About the Moon?

The moon is the earth's **satellite**—it revolves around the earth. Astronauts took this picture of the moon from space. The dark patches are large, flat plains. The light patches are mountains and rough hills.

The moon is covered with billions of bowl-shaped pits called **craters**. Some craters are as small as dinner plates. Other craters are much bigger. The crater shown is 112 kilometers wide.

Scientists think these craters formed when rocks called **meteorites** struck the moon. Meteorites often contain large amounts of metals.

On July 20, 1969, American astronaut Neil Armstrong became the first person to step onto the moon. Since that first time, several astronauts have walked on the moon. They left the tracks shown. Notice that the moon's surface is made of rocky and glassy bits and chunks.

satellite (sat′l īt), a smaller object that revolves around a larger object.

crater (krā′tər), a bowl-shaped hole ranging in size from tiny to very large.

meteorite (mē′tē ə rīt′), a piece of rock, often containing metals, that strikes a planet or a satellite.

The moon as seen from space

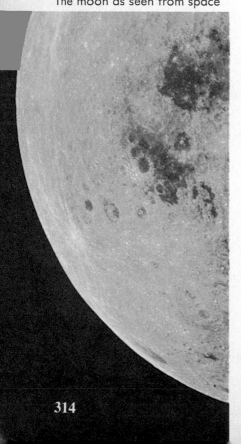

An astronaut's footprint on the moon

Crater Thomson

How the earth looks as seen from the moon

The earth has weather because the sun heats the earth's air and water. Weather wears down the earth's surface. The moon has neither air nor water. So the moon has no earthlike weather to wear down its surface. Instead, scientists think some dustlike powder forms every time a meteorite smashes itself and part of the moon's surface.

The inside of the moon is not active, so meteorites cause the only changes on its surface. Scientists think the moon's mountains and craters are very old.

The moon does not have blue skies as earth does because the moon has no air. Astronauts on the moon saw blackness surrounding the sun, the earth, and stars, as the picture shows. The stars are the same stars that people see from earth.

Without air to protect it from sunlight, the moon's temperatures become much hotter and colder than temperatures on earth. The temperature reaches 127° Celsius in daylight—hot enough to cook an egg. At night the temperature is −113° Celsius.

Crescent moon

Half-moon

phase (fāz), the shape of the lighted part of the moon, as seen from earth.

How Is the Moon Related to the Earth?

Moonlight is just sunlight that is reflected from the moon's surface. We see different amounts of the lighted part on different nights. The moon can look like a circle, a half circle, or a curved sliver called a crescent (kres⁄nt). Sometimes you cannot see the moon at all. The shapes that you see are the moon's **phases.**

You see the moon's phases because the moon revolves around the earth. One revolution of the moon, which we call a month, lasts 29.5 days. As the moon revolves, you can see different amounts of its lighted part. Notice where the earth, moon, and sun are in the new-moon drawing. You see no moon because the part facing you is in shadow. As the moon keeps revolving around the earth, you see first a crescent and then a half of the lighted side.

New moon

Now, notice how the earth, moon, and sun look in the gibbous (gib′əs)-moon drawing. You see almost the whole lighted part of the moon. Finally, you see the full moon—the whole lighted side. The reverse happens as the moon keeps revolving, until you again see no moon.

The moon stays in orbit around the earth because of the force of gravity between the two. This force also causes tides of the oceans on earth. At the seashore the water level rises and falls twice a day.

Think About It

1. Describe the moon's surface.
2. Explain why we see phases of the moon.
3. What causes tides on earth?
4. **Challenge** Draw the three phases between the full moon and the new moon.

Gibbous moon

Full moon

Have You Heard?
The astronauts who went to the moon saw the phases of the earth.

Gibbous moon

Do You Know?

Where Did the Moon Come From?

Even though the moon is our nearest neighbor in space, scientists are not sure how it formed. Four possible explanations have been suggested.

The "capture model" suggests that at one time the moon, like the earth, traveled in its own orbit around the sun. The moon's path may have come close to the earth's orbit, as shown. The earth's gravity pulled the moon out of its original orbit. The moon then began a new orbit around the earth.

The "escape model" suggests that the earth and moon were once a single body. As the sun's gravity pulled on the earth, a bulge may have developed on one side of the earth, as shown. In time, this bulge broke away from the earth, traveled into space, and became the moon.

A third model suggests that the moon and earth were formed separately at about the same time and in the same region of space. This model says that the two bodies formed from huge spirals of tiny particles and hot gases.

The fourth model suggests that the moon was formed when an object, such as a giant meteor, smashed into the earth. A section of the earth might have been blown into orbit around earth.

So far, scientists do not have enough information to say which of these models is correct. Astronauts have brought back moon rocks for scientists to study. These rocks might help scientists find evidence to support one of these models. Further space exploration will probably help us find out more about the moon. Then, scientists of the future might unravel the mystery of the moon's origin.

Capture model

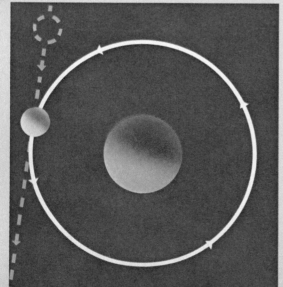

Escape model

Tie It Together

Sum It Up

1. Draw and color a picture of the sun. Mark the temperatures at the surface and deep in the center.

2. Copy the picture below, and label the parts marked with 1- 2. Label the seasons at 3- 6.

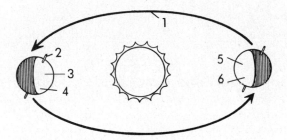

3. Copy the pictures below on a sheet of paper. Beside each picture, write the name of the phase of the moon.

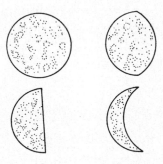

Challenge!

1. Compare the sun with other stars.

2. The sun always appears to be the same size as seen from earth. What information about the shape of the earth's orbit can you infer from this fact?

3. Explain how seasons happen on earth.

4. Explain why the moon gets so much hotter and colder than the earth.

5. In what ways is the moon similar to the earth? Different?

6. If you were on the moon, when would the earth's dark side face you?

Science Words

axis	revolution
crater	rotation
meteorite	satellite
orbit	weight
phase	

Chapter 19
Members of the Solar System

For many years people believed that the earth was the center of the universe. They believed that everything they saw in the sky, including the sun and stars, traveled around the earth. But careful observations helped people change these ideas. One observation was that Jupiter has moons, as the picture shows. Today, we know that the earth is one of nine known planets that orbit the sun. The sun and all the objects that orbit it make up our solar system.

The lessons in this chapter describe the members of the solar system.

1 Measuring Large Distances
2 Which Planets Are Nearest the Sun?
3 Which Planets Are Farthest from the Sun?
4 What Other Objects Are in the Solar System?
5 How Have People Learned About the Solar System?

1 Measuring Large Distances

Distances in our solar system are very large. Measuring these distances in kilometers gives us numbers that are too big to work with easily. For example, Earth is 150,000,000 kilometers from the sun. The planet Saturn is 10 times as far away.

We can invent and name a unit for measuring long distances. Let this unit equal the distance from the earth to the sun. Give the unit a name, such as the *zap*. When you use the zap, you compare other distances to the distance between the earth and the sun.

To get an idea of how far away the planets are, draw a scale model. Let 1 centimeter = 1 zap. This scale is just like a map scale. For example, Venus is 3/4 zap from the sun. So Venus is marked 3/4 centimeter from the sun in the drawing. Use the chart of the distances to the planets to finish your drawing.

Think About It

1. What should you think about when choosing a unit for measuring an object?
2. How many times farther from the sun is Uranus than Earth?
3. **Challenge** Figure the distance to Mars in kilometers.

Distances to the planets

Planet	Distance to the sun in zaps
Mercury	0.5
Venus	0.75
Earth	1
Mars	1.5
Jupiter	5
Saturn	10
Uranus	19
Neptune	30
Pluto	40

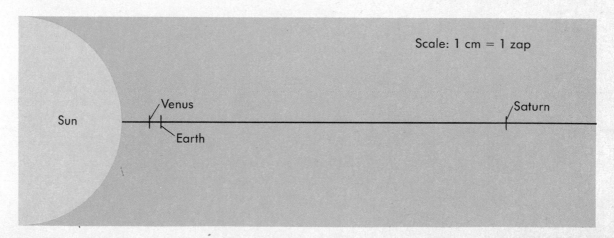

Scale: 1 cm = 1 zap

Sun   Venus   Earth   Saturn

2 Which Planets Are Nearest the Sun?

Have You Heard?

Stars are so far away from us that they appear as points of light. We see their light twinkle because the slightest movement of air can affect how their light reaches us. Planets are so much closer to us than stars that we see planets as steady disks of light.

We can compare the planets in the solar system in many ways. One way is to compare their distances from the sun. The four closest planets are Mercury, Venus, Earth, and Mars. They are fairly near the sun and each other. Also, these four planets are more like each other than they are like the remaining planets. Each one is small and rocky compared with the other planets.

Mercury is the smallest of these four planets. It is less than half the size of Earth. Mercury is also the planet nearest the sun. So Mercury's temperature in daylight can reach 400° Celsius. At night the temperature falls to −183° Celsius.

Mercury seems to have no air around it. So Mercury's surface, shown in the picture, looks like our moon's surface. Craters caused by meteorites, steep cliffs, and flat, dry plains mark the surface.

Mercury

Venus is sometimes called Earth's twin. Venus and Earth are about the same size and have about the same mass. Measurements taken of Venus show that Venus, like Earth, has a very rocky surface. The picture shows some of Venus' surface.

Here, the likeness between Venus and Earth ends. Notice the swirling, yellow-white clouds around Venus. They are mainly an acid mist, not water like Earth's clouds. Venus' air is mainly carbon dioxide gas. We could not live by breathing this gas. It traps any sunlight that gets through the clouds. The trapped sunlight makes Venus' surface hot—475° Celsius.

Our Earth is the largest of the four planets nearest the sun. The picture shows how Earth looks from space. Notice how much water Earth has. Earth's air is mainly nitrogen and oxygen. Earth is the only known planet on which life as we know it can exist.

Venus' surface

Venus

Earth

Mars' surface

Mars

Have You Heard?

Olympus Mons, the largest mountain on Mars, is 24 km high—nearly 3 times as high as Earth's highest mountain, Mount Everest. This mountain is as wide across its base as the whole state of Missouri!

What Is Mars Like?

You can spot Mars, the "red planet," in the night sky by its color. In some ways Mars' surface is similar to Earth's deserts. Notice the scattered rocks and sandy soil in the picture.

Strong windstorms on Mars keep enough dust in the air to make Mars' sky pink. The air also has fewer gases and is much thinner than Earth's air. Mars' air is mainly carbon dioxide, with some oxygen, water vapor, and carbon monoxide—a gas poisonous to people.

A day on Mars can be as warm as 26° Celsius—room temperature on Earth. At night, temperatures can fall to −60° Celsius.

Like Earth, Mars has an icecap at each pole of its axis. Mars' icecaps are mainly frozen carbon dioxide, called dry ice, with some frozen water.

Mars is smaller than both Venus and Earth. Mars' two moons are much smaller than Earth's moon.

Think About It

1. Name the four planets nearest the sun.
2. How are these planets alike? Different?
3. **Challenge** What conditions on the earth make life as we know it possible?

Activity

Making Models of Planets

Purpose
To compare the appearances of the first 4 planets.

You Will Need
- cardboard
- compass for drawing circles
- ruler
- string
- scissors
- paints, crayons, markers, or colored pencils or chalks
- cotton batting (optional)
- glue (optional)
- coat hanger

Directions
1. Use the compass to draw 2 circles for your planet. The chart gives a scale that shows you how big to make each circle.
2. Cut out the circles.
3. Use the ruler to draw a line on each circle as shown.
4. Cut each circle on the line.

5. Push the circles together at the slits as shown.
6. Color your model to look like its picture on pages 322–324. If you have cotton batting, you can use it with glue to show Earth's clouds and Mars' icecaps.
7. Tape a length of string to each model, as shown, to attach the model to the hanger.
8. Attach your models to the coat hanger.

Think About It
1. How are your models like the planets?
2. Which planet has the densest amount of gases around it?
3. **Challenge** Explain why one of Mars' icecaps should be bigger than the other.

Planet	True Diameter	Circle's Diameter
Mercury	4,878 km	3 cm
Venus	12,104 km	7.5 cm
Earth	12,756 km	8 cm
Mars	6,714 km	4 cm

3 Which Planets Are Farthest from the Sun?

Find Out

Methane is also called swamp gas. Look in an encyclopedia to find out why methane is found near swamps.

The five remaining planets are so far from us that we did not know much about them until several years ago. All of them are so cold that everything at their surfaces is frozen. Four of them are giant planets.

Jupiter is the next planet from the sun after Mars. Jupiter, shown in the picture, is the largest of all the planets. If Jupiter were hollow, about 1,300 Earths could fit inside it.

Jupiter's solid center is small compared with the rest of this planet. Jupiter is 99 percent liquid hydrogen and liquid helium.

Imagine a single storm many times larger than the Earth. Scientists think Jupiter's Great Red Spot, shown in the picture, is such a storm. Even though the spot's swirling clouds move from year to year, the spot has been there for hundreds of years. The gases and clouds around Jupiter are mainly hydrogen and helium, which are poisonous to people.

Lightning has been observed in Jupiter's clouds. But if it rains there, it may rain liquid ammonia.

Jupiter has a thin ring of ice chunks around it. About 24 moons revolve around Jupiter.

Jupiter

Saturn

After Jupiter, Saturn is next in line from the sun and second in size. Saturn is known for its beautiful set of hundreds of rings, shown in the picture. Billions of ice chunks make up the rings. The chunks range in size from as small as a speck of dust to as large as 3 meters across. About 21 moons revolve around Saturn.

The gases around Saturn and the materials that make up this planet are very like those of Jupiter. Scientists are eager to learn more about the weather around both Jupiter and Saturn. They hope their studies of these planets will teach them more about weather on Earth.

Have You Heard?

Mercury, Earth, Mars, Jupiter, and Saturn rotate from west to east on their axes. But Venus rotates from east to west. If you could see the sun from Venus, the sun would appear to rise in the west and set in the east.

Uranus

Have You Heard?

Uranus seems to be the only planet that rotates in a north-south direction. Its rings also circle it in a north-south direction.

What Is Known About the Three Outer Planets?

We know little about the remaining planets because they are so far away. Uranus, the next planet after Saturn, is greenish blue. Uranus has a set of icy rings and five moons. The drawing shows how this planet might look.

The planet Neptune is like Uranus in some ways. Both planets are about the same size and mass and are probably made of the same materials. Each planet is about 64 times the size of Earth. Neptune has rings and two moons.

Pluto is the ninth, smallest, and last known planet from the sun. Measurements show that Pluto is about the size of our moon. Pluto is so far away and so small that it was not discovered until 1930. Pluto's moon was not discovered until 1978.

The materials that make up Pluto puzzle scientists. It seems to be an icy rock—more like Jupiter's moons than like the other planets.

Where Pluto came from also puzzles scientists. They think that eight of the planets formed along with the sun. But they are not sure about Pluto, because it is very different from the other planets. Also, Pluto's orbit is stretched-out and long compared with orbits of the other planets.

Think About It

1. Name the five outer planets in the solar system.
2. Which of all the planets is the largest? Smallest?
3. **Challenge** Compare the planets. Be sure to mention each planet's size, its distance from the sun, the materials from which it is made, and the number of moons it has.

Do You Know?

There Are Many Kinds of Moons

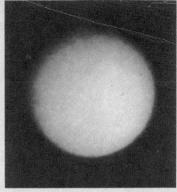

Saturn's moon Titan

Visitors to other planets may someday argue about which planet has the most interesting moons. Besides Earth, six other planets in our solar system are known to have moons—Mars, Jupiter, Saturn, Uranus, Neptune, and Pluto.

The two moons of Mars, Phobos and Deimos, are both much smaller than our own moon. In fact, it would take several thousand objects the sizes of Phobos and Deimos to fill the space taken up by our moon. Phobos and Deimos also have very un-moonlike shapes. The Martian moons are shaped like shoe boxes.

For many years astronomers thought that Jupiter had eleven moons. But the Voyager space probes showed us that at least twenty moons orbit Jupiter. Some of these moons are no larger than Phobos or

Deimos. But four of the moons of Jupiter are much larger. Ganymede and Callisto, the two largest of Jupiter's moons, are each more than twice the size of our moon.

One of the most unusual discoveries was made on Jupiter's moon Io, shown in the picture. Volcanoes have been seen erupting on Io's surface! Io, then, has something in common with our Earth. Io and Earth are the only two objects in the solar system known to have active volcanoes!

The Voyager space probes also sent back information about the moons of Saturn. Of the twenty or so moons discovered so far, one is of special interest. Titan, shown in the picture, is just slightly smaller than Jupiter's moon Ganymede. But Titan has something no other moon has—an atmosphere. Some scientists think that Titan is a place where some form of life could develop.

Who knows how many other surprises we might find as we learn more about the moons of the distant planets—Uranus, Neptune, and Pluto!

Jupiter's moon Io

329

4 What Other Objects Are in the Solar System?

Have You Heard?

More than 200 million meteors are in earth's air every day. People do not see most of them because they are too small to burn very brightly or to reach earth.

The solar system has other objects besides planets, moons, and the sun. Between the orbits of Mars and Jupiter are tiny planets called **asteroids** and other smaller rocks. Asteroids orbit the sun. They are from 1 kilometer to 700 kilometers across. Smaller asteroids do not have a regular shape. Asteroids are rocky and often have large amounts of metals in them.

Sometimes the smaller rocks and bits of dust come close enough to the earth to enter our air. When they do, friction between the air and the dust heats and burns up the rock. We often see these dust bits in the sky as bright streaks of light called **meteors.** If a meteor is big enough, it does not burn up completely before reaching the ground. Meteorites are meteors that hit the earth's surface.

The picture shows Meteor Crater in Arizona. Scientists think that a meteorite struck there about 50,000 years ago. The hole it made is so large it would take more than an hour to ride your bicycle around it. Meteor craters have been found in many other parts of the world.

Meteor Crater, Arizona

The path of Halley's comet through our solar system

Another kind of object passes through the solar system. A **comet** is a dirty snowball of dust and frozen gases several kilometers across. As the comet gets close to the sun, some of the comet melts, forming a cloud. The cloud is blown back into a tail that points away from the sun.

Comets travel around the sun in very long, stretched-out orbits, as shown. Comets can take from a few years to hundreds of years to travel around the sun.

A famous comet is named after Sir Edmond Halley, who studied it. He believed that the comet had appeared about every 75 years at least as far back as 1066. In 1682 Halley predicted that this comet would appear again in 1758. He was correct. The picture shows Halley's comet as it looked in 1910.

comet (kom′it), a ball of dust and frozen gases that orbits the sun in a long, stretched-out path.

Halley's comet

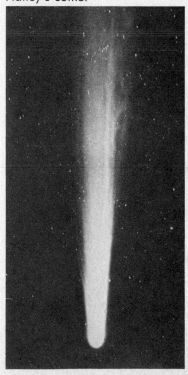

Think About It

1. How do a meteor and a meteorite differ?
2. What object in our solar system do comets orbit?
3. **Challenge** What is the next year after 1910 for Halley's comet to appear?

5 How Have People Learned About the Solar System?

People have always been curious about objects in the night sky. Maps showing the positions of different stars and planets were drawn as many as four thousand years ago.

During the 1600s Galileo became famous for using a telescope to look at the night sky. He found that the moon was not a smooth ball but that mountains and valleys covered the moon's surface.

Galileo observed the phases of Venus, which showed that Venus orbits the sun. He also discovered Jupiter's four largest moons. These discoveries were important because people believed that all objects revolved around Earth. If Venus orbited the sun and four objects orbited Jupiter, Earth was not the center of everything.

Since Galileo's time, people have improved the telescope. Today, different kinds of telescopes are used. The picture shows one of the largest telescopes, in California.

For centuries, people could study the solar system only with a telescope. Now, we can send spacecraft to get more and better information. We learned most of what we know in the last fifty years.

The Hale telescope in the Palomar Observatory

Astronaut on moon's surface

The Apollo flights explored the moon in the 1960s and early 1970s. One of the spacecraft is shown in the picture. The United States landed astronauts on the moon six times. The astronauts did many experiments on the moon and brought back samples of its surface.

The Mariner flights in the late 1960s explored Venus and Mars. The spacecraft sent back many pictures of these planets. Then, in 1976, two Viking spacecraft landed on Mars, sent us pictures, and tested the soil and air. The tests for life on Mars so far seem to show that none exists there.

Voyager 1 flew past Jupiter in 1979 and Saturn in 1980. Then, it continued out of the solar system. *Voyager 2* flew past Jupiter, reaching Saturn in 1981. It continued on to Uranus and Neptune.

Other countries have also explored space. The Soviet Union has sent several Venera spacecraft to land on Venus. Several took pictures of Venus' surface.

Voyager

What Space Flights Are Planned for the Future?

Until 1981, spacecraft were used for only one flight. Then, a space shuttle, shown in the pictures, was built and tested. A space shuttle takes off like a rocket but lands like an airplane. It can be used many times. Space shuttles can carry astronauts and equipment out into space or to orbiting space stations.

The United States has planned to send the spacecraft *Galileo* to orbit Jupiter and to send smaller spacecraft into Jupiter's clouds in the mid-1980s.

We study the solar system for many reasons. By studying the other planets, we can learn more about the earth and about how the solar system formed. We can get a better look at the universe by sending telescopes out beyond the earth's clouds. Studies of the sun are especially important, since the sun affects everything on the earth.

Think About It

1. What tools have we used to learn about the solar system?
2. Why do people study objects in space?
3. **Challenge** What would you like to have people explore in space?

The space shuttle *Columbia*

Tie It Together

Sum It Up

1. List the members of the solar system in order of their distances from the sun.

2. List the members of the solar system in order from smallest to largest.

3. Name the two smallest members of the solar system.

4. What instrument made a big change in what people observed about the planets?

Challenge!

1. Explain why we should no longer call Venus ''Earth's twin.''

2. Compare a planet with an asteroid.

3. What do you think happens to the mass of a comet every time the comet comes near the sun?

4. In what ways is space research useful to us?

Science Words

asteroid

comet

meteor

Laboratory

Demonstrating the Moon's Rotation

Purpose
To infer how the moon can rotate on its axis and yet present the same side to the earth at all times.

You Will Need
- rubber ball or beach ball
- 2 note cards
- marking pen
- masking tape
- string, 1.5 m in length
- chalk
- paper

Stating the Problem
Since ancient times, people have observed and studied the moon. Even without using telescopes people noticed that the surface of the moon does not appear to change. Observers on the earth see the same craters on the moon each night. In other words, the same side of the moon always faces the earth.

Scientists have used this observation to infer that the moon rotates on its axis. How can the moon rotate but always show the same side to observers on earth?

Investigating the Problem
1. Work with a partner. You will represent an observer on earth. Your partner will hold a ball which will represent the moon.

a

2. Make the labels *front* and *back,* and tape them to opposite sides of a ball. See picture *a.* The side of the ball labeled *front* represents the side of the moon that an observer sees from the earth. The side labeled *back* represents the side of the moon that an observer on earth cannot see.

3. Look at picture *b.* Tie a piece of chalk to a string. Hold the loose end of the string while your partner stretches the string and draws a circle around you. This circle represents the moon's orbit around the earth.

4. On separate pieces of paper, write the numbers *1, 2, 3,* and *4.* Tape these pieces of paper on the floor as shown in picture *c.*

5. Ask your partner to hold the ball with the side labeled *front* facing you. Note which wall of the classroom the *front* side of the ball faces. Your partner will walk around the circle without rotating the ball. *HINT: If the ball does not rotate, the side labeled* front *will always face the same wall.* Ask your partner to stop at points *1, 2, 3,* and *4.* Record the side of the ball that you observe.

6. After you record your observations when your partner is at point 4, ask your partner to make sure that the side of the ball labeled *front* faces you. Then,

b

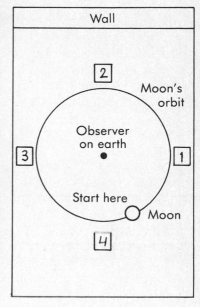

Wall

2

Moon's orbit

3   Observer on earth   ●   1

Start here

Moon

4

c

your partner should walk around the circle, rotating the ball twice. This means that your partner will rotate the ball once before reaching point *2* and again before reaching point *4*. Ask your partner to stop at each of the 4 points. Record the side of the ball that you see at each point.

7. After you have recorded your observations, make sure that the *front* side of the ball faces you. Ask your partner to walk around the circle, rotating the ball once. Your partner will rotate the ball halfway by the time he or she reaches point *2*.

Making Conclusions
1. Which step represents the moon's pattern of rotation? Explain how you know.
2. What would happen in step 7 if you started with the side of the ball labeled *back* facing the observer in the circle?
3. Which side or sides of the moon would an observer near the sun see as the moon revolves around the earth?
4. When the moon is a crescent, sometimes you can see the faint

outline of the rest of the moon. Is this the back of the moon? Explain your answer.
5. Each of Mars' 2 moons always keeps the same side facing Mars. If one moon, Phobos (fō′bôs), revolves around Mars in about 7 1/2 hours, how long does it take this moon to rotate once on its axis? Deimos (dī′môs) Mars' other moon, revolves around Mars in about 30 hours. How long does it take Deimos to rotate on its axis? Explain your answers.

337

Careers

Astronomer

"If you have ever gazed with wonder at a dark night sky dotted with sparkling pinpoints of light, astronomy may be for you."

Jim is an astronomer at a planetarium—a dome-shaped building that uses a machine to project images of stars on the ceiling. "Across the country, people of all ages enjoy astronomy as a hobby. Most of them use telescopes to view the moon, planets, and stars at night. But today, many astronomers use other instruments, such as radio telescopes, to study the stars during the day."

Jim's major job at the planetarium is to design the new exhibits that people come to see. "One of the main exhibits is our Sky Show. Visitors enter a theater with a large, domed ceiling. We turn off the lights and project an image of the night sky on the ceiling. We help people find all of the planets and stars that are visible in this part of the country."

Jim also works on other exhibits, such as moon rocks, spacesuits, sundials, and antique telescopes.

"The field of astronomy is interesting because there are still so many new frontiers in space. The success of the space shuttle has opened some new doors for us. Our next big step will be when the shuttle carries a space telescope into earth orbit. This large telescope will peer deep into space with clearer pictures than ever before."

People wanting to become professional astronomers must go to college for at least four years. They study astronomy, other sciences, and math. "Most astronomers have gone to college for seven years. But astronomers, and other scientists, continue to learn new things throughout their entire careers."

When you think of aircraft and spacecraft, you probably think of **pilots** and **astronauts.** These people are very important. They control many of the movements of the crafts. Astronauts also perform experiments while in space.

People who want to be astronauts or airline pilots must go to college. Airline pilots must have piloting experience in other kinds of airplanes.

Pilots and astronauts know that their jobs are possible because of the talents of thousands of people on the ground. Any rocket or airplane starts as a drawing on an **engineer's** drawing board. The engineer determines how the craft will look and helps decide what materials will be needed to build it. The engineer also helps build scale models of the craft.

The models are tested in a wind tunnel to see how well the actual craft will fly. An **engineering technician** may operate the wind tunnel.

Engineers have gone to college for at least four years. Technicians have spent at least two years in college.

When the craft is ready to be built, the **welders and sheet metal workers** go to work. Many of these workers learn their skills at a two-year trade school.

During a flight, computers often help steer the craft. Computers also help in designing and testing the aircraft. A **computer programmer** gives the computer instructions on how to perform these skills.

A person who wants to be a programmer must have two years of college training.

Astronaut

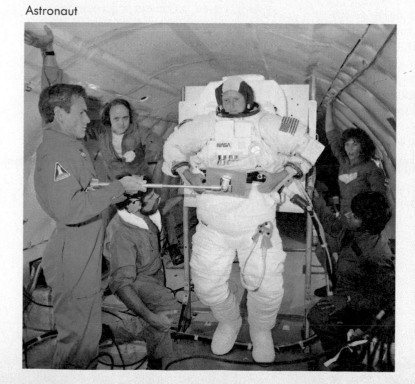

Engineering technician

On Your Own

Picture Clue

Something exciting is going on in the picture on page 304. The object looks like the inside of a volcano surrounded by a sea of waves. To find out the subject of this picture, see page 326.

Projects

1. Find out what an eclipse is. Build a model to show what happens during an eclipse.

2. Pick one planet from the solar system. Find out everything you can about this planet. Then, prepare a talk to give to your class. Use posters to illustrate your talk.

3. Some people wonder whether humans could build a colony on our moon or on one of the other planets or moons. Find out as much as you can about planets or moons on which people could live. Build a model space colony for one of these places. Explain how the conditions there made you design and build the colony as you did.

4. Look in an almanac or on a calendar to learn the times of the year when meteor showers are common. With your family's permission, watch one of these meteor showers.

Books About Science

A Close Look at the Moon by G. Jeffrey Taylor. Dodd, Mead, & Co., Inc., 1980. A description of the moon's origin and of recent discoveries about the moon.

The Earth and Space by David Lambert. Warwick Press, 1979. A guide to the wonders of the universe, from the earth below to the stars above.

Exploring the Sun by William Jaber. Julian Messner, 1980. A description of our understanding of the sun, from ancient legends to our use of the sun's energy today.

The Moons of Our Solar System by David G. Knight. William Morrow & Co., Inc., 1980. A discussion of the origin and characteristics of moons in the solar system, based on recent information.

Unit Test

Matching

Number your paper from 1–5. Read the description in Column I. Next to each number, write the letter of the word or words from Column II that best match the description in Column I.

Column I

1. star closest to the earth

2. force that keeps you on earth and keeps the earth in its orbit around the sun

3. causes day and night on earth

4. lasts one year

5. planet closest to the sun

Column II

a. gravity

b. Halley's comet

c. Mercury

d. the earth's revolution

e. the earth's rotation

f. the sun

Multiple Choice

Number your paper from 6–10. Next to each number, write the letter of the word or words that best complete the statement or answer the question.

6. How is the moon different from the earth? The moon
   a. has no atmosphere.
   b. has a steady temperature near 50° Celsius.
   c. has a blue sky.
   d. has water.

7. What causes high and low ocean tides?
   a. blowing winds
   b. ships moving across the ocean
   c. the moon's gravity
   d. hurricanes

8. Like Earth, Mars has
   a. an atmosphere containing oxygen.
   b. polar caps.
   c. large amounts of water.
   d. only one moon.

9. Why does the moon appear to change shape?
   a. Clouds get in the way.
   b. The earth's shadow falls on the moon.
   c. We see different amounts of the moon's lighted side as the moon revolves around the earth.
   d. Planets and stars often block the moon's light.

10. The largest planet in the solar system is
    a. Saturn.
    b. Uranus.
    c. Earth.
    d. Jupiter.

UNIT EIGHT
THE
ENVIRONMENT

Something spilled
    upon the land
The land it spoiled
    was covered with sand
It is very pretty to the eye
But the damage it makes,
    my oh my!

Tracey Holloway *age 9*

Chapter 20
Keeping Our Water Clean

A few guppies in a large fish tank might not make the water dirty. Snails in the tank may eat small amounts of waste in the water. But when the fish population grows, waste in the water increases and becomes a problem. To keep the fish alive, you must either clean the water or reduce the fish population.

The lessons in this chapter tell about water pollution, so you will know how you can help keep water clean.

1 Recording How You Change the Water You Use

2 How Do People Cause and Correct Sewage Pollution?

3 How Can Heat Pollute Water?

4 How Can Chemicals Pollute Water?

5 Why Is Oil Pollution a Major Problem?

1 Recording How You Change the Water You Use

Just as fish change water around them, people change the water they use. We use water in homes, factories, and on farms. We add chemicals, heat, or waste materials to the water.

About 570 liters of water are used each day for each person in the United States. About 380 liters of that water are used by industries that make the products we need. We each use about 190 liters of that water in our homes.

Divide a piece of paper into two columns. In the first column make a list of the ways you use water in just one day. In the second column, record the things you add to the water as you use it. To get started, think about what the boy in the picture adds to the water as he washes his bicycle.

Think About It

1. About how much water do you use for each activity on your list? Do you use more or less than 190 liters?
2. What do you add to the water you use?
3. **Challenge** Figure out how much water is used and changed by all the students in your class in just one day. How much water does your class use in one year?

Turn to Page 400

2 How Do People Cause and Correct Sewage Pollution?

pollutant (pə lüt′nt), waste material harmful to living things.

pollution (pə lü′shən), the dirtying of any part of the environment, especially with waste material.

sewage (sü′ij), waste water and human wastes.

Clean water is important to all life on earth. Water **pollution** is any change in water that makes the water harmful to living things. Many **pollutants,** such as added heat or waste, can harm the earth's water.

People cause most water pollution. When fewer people lived on earth, water pollution was not as serious a problem as it is now. As our population grew, we used and changed more and more water. Many cities were settled around rivers. People drank the river water. They also dumped human wastes into the river. To get clean water, people built pumping stations up the river from the city. They poured their wastes into the river downstream from the city. The picture shows that, as more cities were built along river banks, the problems of water pollution became greater.

Human wastes—or **sewage**—from cities have polluted many rivers and lakes. Tiny organisms that cause diseases grow well in sewage. If polluted water were used for drinking water, the whole population of a town could become ill.

Pollution along a river

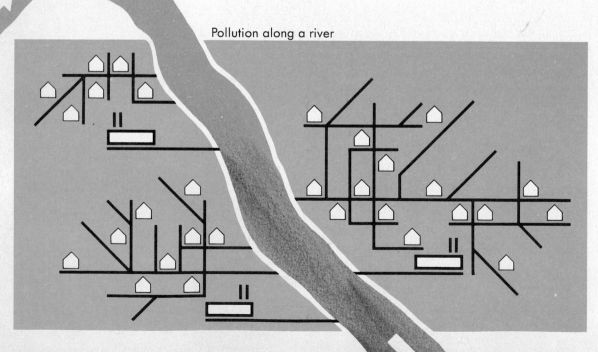

346

Pollution spreading down a river

At one time people thought rivers and lakes could clean themselves. They knew rivers and lakes held huge amounts of water. They thought all that water would weaken—or **dilute**—the pollutants and make them harmless. We now know that just a little pollution can damage even a large body of water. Rivers and lakes can not clean themselves as fast as people pollute them.

Notice in the picture how water can spread pollution. People have learned that, once the pollution has spread, it is difficult to clean up. Now people work hard to keep our lakes and rivers clean.

dilute (də lüt′), to make weaker by adding water.

Have You Heard?

Dripping faucets and other leaks in New York City waste as much water as a city of 100,000 people uses.

How Have We Reduced Sewage Pollution?

Water-treatment plants help reduce sewage pollution. At one time, sewage polluted many water sources. Today most waste water is piped to water treatment plants. The picture shows how the used water is cleaned. First, the sewage moves through screens that remove any large solid objects. Next, the sewage moves into settling tanks for several hours. During this time, suspended material, known as sludge, settles to the bottom. Bacteria eat the sludge, changing it into a harmless substance. The remaining waste water then enters a tank where air is bubbled through it. Then, it moves into another settling tank, where more sludge settles. The remaining waste water passes through a sand filter to remove any remaining solid particles. Finally, chemicals are added to kill the bacteria, and the clean water can be returned to rivers and lakes.

Think About It

1. What is water pollution?
2. How does a water-treatment plant help reduce water pollution?
3. **Challenge** Are people the only cause of water pollution? Explain your answer.

Water treatment

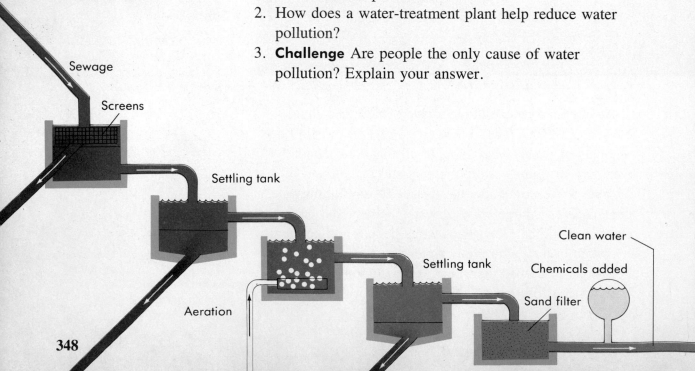

Sewage

Screens

Settling tank

Aeration

Settling tank

Clean water

Chemicals added

Sand filter

Activity

Observing Dilution

Purpose
To observe that a small amount of pollution can affect a large amount of water.

You Will Need
- 4-L jar
- 10 small jars
- water
- food coloring
- marking pencil

Directions
1. Fill the large jar with water. Add 1 drop of food coloring to the water. Observe the color of the water.
2. Add 30 more drops of food coloring. Notice how dark the water becomes now. If the food coloring were pollution, predict how much water you would need in order to dilute the food coloring enough to make the color disappear.
3. Number the small jars 1 through 10.
4. Fill jars 1 and 2 half full with the colored water you made.

5. Add clean water to jar 2 until it is full. Compare the color of the diluted water in jar 2 with the color of the water in jar 1.
6. Pour half the water from jar 2 into jar 3. Add clean water to jar 3 until it is full. Observe any change in the color of the water.
7. Divide the colored water and add clean water until you have filled jar 10. Observe the color of the water in each jar.

Think About It

1. How did the color of the water in a jar change when you added clean water?
2. How much clean water did it take to dilute the food coloring? How is dilution a poor way to reduce water pollution?
3. **Challenge** Does the water in jar 10 look clear? Could there be any food coloring left in the water even if the water looks clean?

3 How Can Heat Pollute Water?

Many people enjoy swimming in a heated pool or a warm lake. But heat can also pollute water and harm living things. You know how uncomfortable you get when you are very hot. Many animals are also uncomfortable when they are too hot. Some animals cannot stand even small temperature changes.

Heat is added to water in many ways. You heat water to bathe and to wash dishes and clothes. Many factory machines use water to make the products people need. Factories take in cool water and pump out heated water. The picture shows heated water from a factory dumping into a river. Notice the vapor rising from the water.

Power plants produce large amounts of heat when they make electricity. All power plants need large supplies of water to cool their machines. If the water is not cooled before it is returned to lakes and streams, the heat can destroy many plants and animals.

Heat pollution from factory

Cooling pond

Heat pollution has several effects on water. It reduces the amount of oxygen in the water. You may have noticed that when aquarium water becomes warm, fish swim near the surface where there is more oxygen. Fish and plants that need a lot of oxygen may die in warm water. Heat pollution also disturbs the life cycles of many water plants and animals. Brook trout lay their eggs in the fall or early winter. The eggs hatch in about 5 months if the water temperature stays at 3° Celsius. If the temperature rises to 12° Celsius, the eggs hatch too soon, in only 32 days. At temperatures above 15° Celsius, the eggs do not hatch at all.

One solution to heat pollution is to use towers to cool hot water. The warm water stays in the tower until the water cools to the same temperature as the lake or stream. Then, it is released. Some factories use ponds, like the one in the picture, to cool water. In northern areas these ponds also provide an ice-free feeding area for water birds.

Think About It

1. Describe two effects of heat pollution.
2. How do cooling towers help solve the problem of heat pollution?
3. **Challenge** How could conserving electricity reduce heat pollution?

4 How Can Chemicals Pollute Water?

Mercury passes from one organism to another

Bacteria

Protists

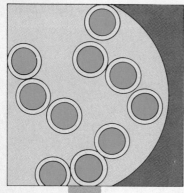

People use chemicals every day in soaps and other home products. In time these chemicals end up in waste water. Farmers use some chemicals to help crops grow. They use others to kill weeds and insects. Rain and melting snow wash these chemicals into lakes and streams.

Factories make many products from chemicals. Cars run on chemicals made from oil. Medicines that keep you healthy come from chemicals. Even some of your clothes are made from chemicals. In the past, factories dumped many of these chemicals into lakes and streams. It was not known how the chemicals could damage organisms.

Some chemicals are poisons that harm living things in the water. These chemicals are a threat to people and animals that eat food from polluted water. Mercury is one poison that has polluted water. Some factories dump chemicals with small amounts of mercury in them into lakes or streams.

The picture shows how mercury can pass from one organism to another. Bacteria in the water absorb mercury along with their food. The bacteria cannot digest the mercury, so mercury builds up in their bodies. Tiny protists eat thousands of bacteria. These protists end up with a lot of mercury in their bodies. Small fish eat many of these protists, and big fish eat the small fish. Big fish may also end up with large amounts of mercury in their bodies. People who eat the fish may suffer from mercury poisoning. Even small amounts of mercury can cause serious brain damage.

Small fish

Big fish

People

Some chemicals in sewage and household detergents reduce the amount of oxygen in the water. These chemicals act like fertilizers. They speed the growth of certain protists. When the protists die, bacteria cause them to decay. The bacteria use up oxygen from the water. Water plants and animals that also need oxygen may die.

Chemical pollution is a difficult problem because each kind may require a different solution. Some governments have passed laws to stop factories from dumping poisons into lakes and rivers. As a result, many factories are building their own waste-water-treatment plants. Many states have stopped the sale and manufacture of chemicals that have polluted our water. Chemical companies are also developing new chemicals that cause less pollution.

Chemicals used for farming cannot be easily removed from water supplies. Farmers are using new methods to reduce the chemical pollution of streams and lakes. One way to reduce some types of chemical pollution is to use natural fertilizers such as manure or compost.

Instead of spraying fields with chemicals, farmers put natural enemies of insect pests in the fields. Some farmers are using wasps and ladybird beetles, shown in the picture, to rid their crops of insect pests.

Have You Heard?
The use of salt on roads to melt ice and snow can cause water pollution. Melting snow can wash the salt into the ground and pollute wells that provide people with drinking water.

Ladybird beetle

Think About It

1. What are three sources of chemical pollution?
2. List two ways that chemicals affect water.
3. What are three solutions to the problem of chemical pollution?
4. **Challenge** If the use of farm chemicals were reduced, farms might produce less wheat, corn, and other crops. What problems might be caused by using this method of reducing chemical pollution? Explain.

5 Why Is Oil Pollution a Major Problem?

Have You Heard?

Oil pollution is not limited to oceans. You have probably seen small oil slicks on parking lots and along streets. Rain can wash this oil into lakes and streams.

Oil-soaked bird

Oil spills from offshore wells and tanker accidents are a major cause of water pollution. After an oil spill, oceans and beaches are covered with oil. In the picture you can see the coat of oil that covers the bird.

Oily water can poison animals and plants. Oil can cover plants and animals and keep them from getting food or oxygen. For example, oil might stick to a seagull's wings and make it unable to fly or swim. Getting food would be a problem for the gull, because the oil would cover its food. The seagull might swallow some of the oil and become poisoned.

Cleaning up oil spills is difficult. When beaches are polluted, tons of oily sand must be bulldozed and carried away. Dumping the oily sand somewhere else pollutes the land.

Oil floating on water can be cleaned up in several ways. Burning the floating oil gets rid of the oil. But burning causes air pollution and adds heat to the water. Spraying chemicals on floating oil breaks up the spill but also damages sea life. One of the best ways to clean up oil is to surround the oil with floating collars like those in the picture. The oil is then pumped from the surface of the water into barges.

Floating collars

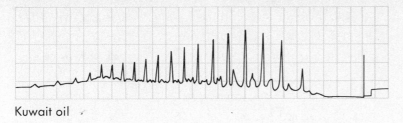
Kuwait oil

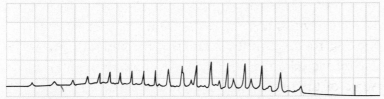
East Texas oil

Cleaning up oil spills is expensive. Governments are working on laws to keep ships from dumping oil into the oceans. Scientists have found one way to help enforce those laws. Oil is a mixture of different chemicals. Oil from different areas contains different amounts of these chemicals. Scientists recently found a way to "fingerprint" oil spills. By studying a sample from the oil spill like the one in the picture, the scientists can find out where the oil came from. The pictures show two of these oil "fingerprints." This "fingerprinting" makes it easier to find out who is responsible for the oil spill. Government officials can then make them pay for the cleanup.

People still need to find better ways to clean up oil pollution. As with other forms of pollution, the best solution is prevention.

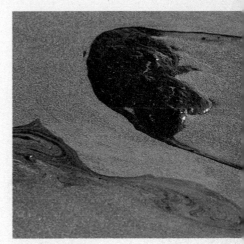
Oil on beach

Think About It

1. What are the major causes of oil pollution?
2. How does oil pollution affect living things?
3. How have people tried to solve the problem of oil pollution?
4. **Challenge** What new laws would you propose to deal with the problems of oil pollution?

Find Out

Read magazine or newspaper articles from the summer of 1979 to find out about one of the largest oil spills in history—the blowout of the oil well Ixtoc I in the Gulf of Mexico.

Discover!

An Oil-Eating Bacterium

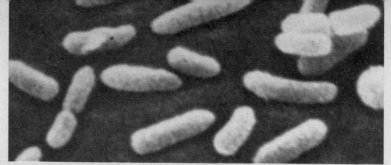

Oil-eating bacteria

Meet the newest weapon in the battle against oil spills— bacteria! The biologist Ananda Chakrabarty developed the tiny organisms shown here. The picture shows the bacteria many times larger than real life.

Chakrabarty put together genetic material from four different kinds of bacteria until he came up with a new bacterium that dined on oil.

Oil spills in the ocean are a major problem. Between 20 and 40 million liters of crude oil are spilled or dumped into the earth's waters each year. And this problem might get worse. Oil wells are being drilled into the ocean bottom. If these wells leak, oil will spill into ocean water. Then, ocean water and beaches are badly damaged.

People have tried many ways to get rid of oil slicks that damage beaches. Often people work together to scoop oil globs from the water and beaches, as the picture shows. The clean-up is slow, and the method only works well in small areas.

Imagine the excitement when Chakrabarty announced a new way to clean up oil spills. Chakrabarty predicted an added bonus with his new bacterium. After the organism eats its fill of oil, it will die and become harmless food for fish.

Cleaning up oil on a beach

Tie It Together

Sum It Up

The map below shows the path Clear River follows to the ocean. Use the map to answer the questions below.

1. List five ways in which pollutants might be added to Clear River and the ocean.

2. Describe what could be done to prevent each type of pollution.

3. Which town—Waterville or Rivertown—needs a water-treatment plant more? Why?

4. How might the sources of pollution you listed in the first question affect the fishing village?

5. Dead fish have been found in the river near Rivertown. What could have killed the fish?

Challenge!

1. Look at a large map of the United States. See how many large cities are located on Lake Erie. Why do you think Lake Erie has had a pollution problem?

2. Explain how pollution in rivers can damage life in the oceans.

3. A large company wants to build a paper mill along a river in your town. What would you want the company to do to make sure the river did not become polluted?

4. The poisonous chemical arsenic is found in some insect sprays used on farms. How could using this chemical harm fish?

5. Many oil companies are drilling offshore oil wells beneath the ocean. Describe what could happen if one of these wells began leaking oil.

Science Words

dilute   pollution

pollutant   sewage

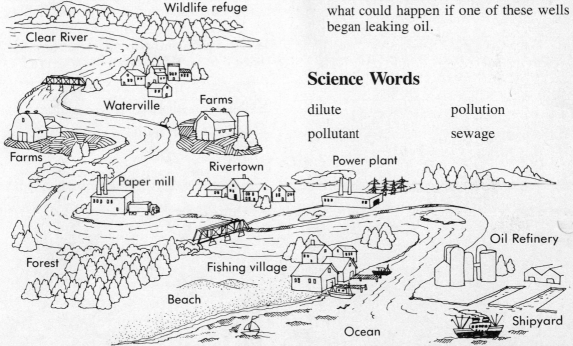

Chapter 21
Breathing
Clean Air

You could live without many things.
But you could not live without the layer
of air that surrounds the earth. If food
tasted spoiled, you could put off eating
for several days. If water had a strange
taste or smell, you could put off drinking
for a while. But what could you do if the
air smelled bad? You could not just stop
breathing until the air smelled better.

The lessons in this chapter will identify
the causes of air pollution and describe
what is being done to keep the air
clean.

1 Testing Your Sense of Smell

The man in the picture is cleaning fish. If you walked along the pier, you would notice the odor of the fish. If you asked the man about his job, he might say that you get used to the odor after a while. You can test your sense of smell to find out what the man meant.

Pour a few drops of oil of peppermint into a jar that has a lid. Place your open jar near your nose. Time and record how long it takes until you can no longer smell the odor. Next, put the lid on the jar, and breathe normally for five minutes. Remove the lid, and sniff the oil of peppermint again. Can you smell the odor now?

Think About It

1. How long did it take until you could no longer smell the oil of peppermint?
2. Would your sense of smell always be a good way to determine what odors might be in the air? Explain.
3. **Challenge** If you can "get used to" the odor of oil of peppermint, can you also get used to the odor of polluted air?

Man cleaning fish

2 How Can Air Pollution Be Natural?

You might not think of dust, ash, and pollen as pollutants. But when these particles, or small bits of matter, float through the air, they add to air pollution. This kind of air pollution is thought of as natural pollution, since it is not caused by people. Some events that cause natural pollution can also be helpful.

Windstorms, like the one in the picture, blow large amounts of dust into the air. But wind also spreads pollen—the tiny grains in flowers—over large spaces. Even though pollen in the air can make some people sneeze a lot, it is needed for plants to reproduce.

Fires started by lightning cause natural air pollution. Burning produces ash and gases that enter the air. But fires can be helpful, because they burn out dead wood from the forest. They also clear away the thick ground cover that would choke off many small trees.

When a volcano erupts, another kind of natural air pollution occurs. The volcano throws dust, ash, and harmful gases into the air. The Mount St. Helens eruption covered more than 380 square kilometers of land with a thick layer of dust and ash. Notice that the man in the picture is wearing a mask to keep from breathing in the dust and ash in the air. Natural pollution from Mount St. Helens traveled around the world. Winds carried the dust and ash far from the volcano.

Although volcanic eruptions can cause great damage, they also produce some useful effects. The earth around active volcanoes becomes very hot. Steam and hot water form inside the earth. Some countries with active volcanoes, such as Iceland, use the hot water and steam to heat homes and make electricity.

The volcanic ash and dust that settle on the ground around a volcano fertilize the soil. Two years after an eruption on a small volcanic island near Alaska, the island was covered with flowers.

Think About It

1. What kinds of air pollution are thought of as natural pollution?
2. **Challenge** Do you think natural pollution is a serious part of the air pollution problem? Explain.

Have You Heard?

In 1815 the Mount Tambora volcano in Indonesia erupted, spreading 150 cubic km of ash through the atmosphere. The ash affected the climate around the world. In Britain the summer of 1816 was the coldest on record, because ash clouds blocked out the sunlight.

Cleaning volcanic dust off car

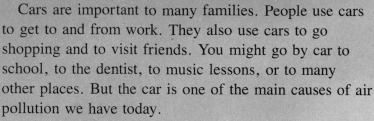

3 How Do Automobiles Cause Air Pollution?

carbon monoxide (kär′bən mo nok′sīd), colorless, odorless, poisonous gas.

smog (smog), a layer of pollutants in the air caused by exhaust gases reacting in sunlight.

Have You Heard?

Studies of seawater, snow, and sediments show that the air in the Northern Hemisphere contains 1,000 times more lead than would occur naturally.

Cars are important to many families. People use cars to get to and from work. They also use cars to go shopping and to visit friends. You might go by car to school, to the dentist, to music lessons, or to many other places. But the car is one of the main causes of air pollution we have today.

When cars burn gasoline, they give off large amounts of gases into the air. One of these gases is **carbon monoxide,** which is poisonous and has no color and no odor. Even small amounts of carbon monoxide can cause headaches and dizziness. Carbon monoxide takes the place of oxygen in the blood. The heart has to work harder to supply oxygen to the body. This strain on the heart can be dangerous for elderly people or people with heart or breathing problems.

Cars also give off other gases that add to air pollution. Sunlight changes some of these gases into chemicals that irritate your eyes, nose, and lungs. The result is a blanket of harmful gases known as **smog.** The picture shows smog in the air around a large city. Notice the color of the air.

Many cities have large numbers of cars. Since so many people now drive cars, smog is found in many large cities around the world. In many cities, people use car pools or public transportation to decrease the number of cars on the road. By decreasing the number of cars, we can decrease the amount of exhaust gases put into the air.

Another pollutant given off by some cars is lead from leaded gasoline. Newer cars have engines that use lead-free gasoline. As older cars are replaced with new ones, lead pollution will decrease.

Car makers are developing cars that cause less pollution. Newer cars have control devices that greatly reduce the amount of pollution they give off. These devices change carbon monoxide and other pollutants into carbon dioxide and water vapor.

Think About It

1. List three ways that cars cause air pollution.
2. How does smog form?
3. What can be done to reduce pollution caused by cars?
4. **Challenge** In what ways could electric and steam-powered engines reduce the amount of air pollution from cars?

Find Out

Talk to an auto mechanic to find out how pollution-control devices on cars work.

4 How Can Burning Be a Problem?

sulfur dioxide (sul′fər dī ok′sīd), compound of sulfur and oxygen.

To many people, autumn means raking beautiful, crunchy leaves. Autumn used to mean the smoky smell of burning leaves. Now, few people are allowed to burn piles of leaves on the street. A look at the picture will tell you why.

Open burning of leaves or trash can spread air pollution over a large area. Smoke from burning contains particles and harmful chemicals. Many cities have passed laws, making such burning illegal.

Burning fuels causes a large part of our air pollution. Many factories and homes burn fuels, such as coal, oil, or natural gas, in their furnaces. These fuels contain varying amounts of sulfur. When the fuels burn, sulfur combines with oxygen to form **sulfur dioxide** gas. This gas is released in the smoke from chimneys and smokestacks. Once in the air, winds can carry the gas hundreds or thousands of kilometers.

Air polluted with sulfur dioxide can irritate people's skin and eyes. Sometimes people have difficulty breathing.

Statue damaged by acid rain

Sulfur dioxide dissolves easily in water. People used
to think that rain would get rid of sulfur dioxide by
washing it out of the air. Rain does wash sulfur dioxide
out of the air, but rain does not get rid of it. When
sulfur dioxide combines with rain, a weak acid forms.
This weak acid joins with oxygen to form a stronger
acid. Rainwater combined with sulfur dioxide is **acid
rain.**

Acid rain can harm plants and animals. It can kill fish
and other water life. It can hurt the growth of new
leaves or buds on plants. Acid rain even damages
buildings and statues by dissolving the building
materials. The picture shows some of the damage done
by acid rain.

Have You Heard?
Air pollution is a worldwide
problem. Acid rain could erase
4,000-year-old hieroglyphics on
Egyptian buildings within the
next 100 years.

acid rain (as′id rān), rain
containing acids.

365

What Can We Do About Acid Rain?

Finding ways to reduce acid rain is not easy. One simple way is to use less fuel. Another way is for power plants to use coal with less sulfur. Some plants are treating coal to remove the sulfur before burning. Many factories are adding **scrubbers,** like those in the picture, to their smokestacks. Inside the scrubbers the sulfur dioxide gas is removed by chemical treatment.

Scientists are experimenting with ways of avoiding acid rain damage. Some scientists are trying to raise fish and crops that will not be damaged by acid rain. Other scientists are trying to find ways of coating buildings and statues to protect them.

Think About It

1. How does the burning of fuels produce acid rain?
2. What are three methods of dealing with the problem of acid rain?
3. **Challenge** Explain how acid rain can damage lakes that are hundreds of kilometers from the nearest city.

scrubber (skrub′ər), a device attached to a factory smokestack to remove pollutants.

Have You Heard?
A large, coal-fired power plant can give off as much as 400,000 metric tons of sulfur dioxide in 1 year.

Scrubbers reduce air pollution

36

Activity

Collecting Evidence of Air Pollution

Purpose
To recognize particles as a type of air pollution.

You Will Need
- 4 large lids from jars or plastic lids from coffee cans
- black construction paper
- white construction paper
- scissors
- petroleum jelly
- hand lens

Directions
1. Take 4 lids from jars or coffee cans. Line half of each lid with black construction paper. Line the other half with white construction paper, as shown in the picture.
2. Cover the construction paper with a thin layer of petroleum jelly.
3. Put the lids in different places around the room, such as on the floor, on a table, on a windowsill, and in a drawer.
4. Predict which lid will collect the most particles. List reasons for your predictions.
5. Allow the particle collectors you made to sit for 2 days.

6. Use a hand lens to observe the amount of particle pollution collected on each lid. Notice the size, shape, and color of the particles.

Think About It

1. Which lid collected the most particles?
2. Was your prediction correct? If not, explain why a different lid collected more particles.
3. Why did the number of particles vary from place to place?
4. Describe the different kinds of particles you collected.
5. **Challenge** Where do you think the particles came from?

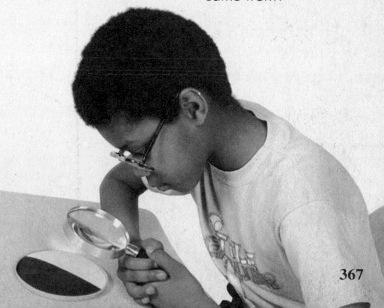

Do You Know?

Air Pollution Can Occur Indoors

Smoking causes air pollution. Cigarettes might seem like a small problem compared with cars, power plants, and factories. But that is true only if you are thinking about outdoor pollution.

What about indoor air pollution—inside a house, a restaurant, or an office? In these places tobacco smoke can cause a serious pollution problem.

Scientists have known for many years that cigarette smoke can be dangerous to people who smoke. The rate of heart and lung disease is higher among smokers than among nonsmokers. But the idea that nonsmokers can be harmed by someone else's smoke is fairly new. Some studies have shown that tobacco smoke in a closed place, such as a house or a store, can have harmful effects on everyone in the room.

One study was done in California in 1980. It showed that nonsmokers' lungs were less healthy if they breathed smoke from someone else's cigarette.

Another study was done in Japan. A group of women married to men who smoked was compared with a group of women married to nonsmokers. The women who were married to smokers had a higher rate of lung cancer.

Other studies have not shown the same results. So, many scientists are still not sure how harmful cigarette smoke is to nonsmokers.

Some people are asking whether anything can be done about indoor pollution from smoking. Some think there should be laws to protect nonsmokers. They want to ban smoking in all public places.

Other people do not agree. They think that everyone who wants to smoke should have the right to do so. People who do not want to breathe cigarette smoke should go somewhere else.

If you had to decide what to do about this problem, what would you do?

Tie It Together

Sum It Up

Number your paper from 1 to 12. Copy the chart below. Complete the statements to fill in the chart.

1.
2.
3.
4.
5.
6.
7.
8.
9.
10.
11.
12.

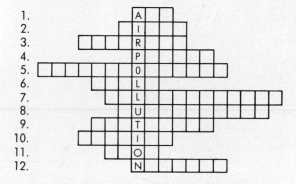

1. Dust and :::::: from the Mount St. Helens eruption covered a large area.

2. Air pollution can be carried far from its source by :::::: .

3. Plants, animals, and buildings can be damaged by :::::: .

4. Natural pollution that can cause some people to sneeze a lot is :::::: .

5. :::::: is a colorless, odorless, poisonous gas given off by car exhausts.

6. You cannot depend on your sense of :::::: to determine if the air is polluted.

7. When mixed with rain, :::::: forms acid rain.

8. In large cities a major source of air pollution is :::::: .

9. :::::: are a type of air pollution that can be seen.

10. :::::: trash or fuels puts particles and harmful gases into the air.

11. When pollutants from car exhausts react with sunlight, :::::: forms.

12. Dust, ash, and pollen are all types of :::::: pollution.

Challenge!

1. Do the positive effects of natural air pollution outweigh the negative effects? Give reasons for your answer.

2. How do you and your family create air pollution?

3. Why has the air pollution problem gotten worse in the last hundred years?

4. The electric company wants to build a coal-powered generating plant near your house. What should your community do to keep air pollution to a minimum?

5. How is your home heated? Are there other ways your house could be heated that would cause less air pollution?

Science Words

acid rain

carbon monoxide

scrubber

smog

sulfur dioxide

Chapter 22
Changing the Land

On a holiday weekend people in the United States throw away enough garbage to fill a line of garbage trucks that is 67 kilometers long. Some garbage is burned. But most garbage ends up in open dumps or landfills.

As our population grows, so does the problem of what to do with all our garbage.

The lessons in this chapter will describe how people change the land so that you will be able to do your part to protect the land.

1 Classifying Trash
2 How Is Waste Disposal a Problem?
3 What Is Polluting the Land?
4 How Is Land Being Changed?

1 Classifying Trash

People make trash. But what kind of trash do they make? Your activities at school are different from your activities at home. So the trash you make at school is different from the trash you make at home.

Divide a piece of paper into four columns. Label the first column *paper*, the second column *plastic*, the third column *metal*, and the fourth column *other*, as shown below. Predict what kind of trash you will throw away most during a school day.

During the day, list in the correct column everything you throw away. At the end of the day, study your list. Compare it with lists made by other class members.

Think About It

1. Which column had the longest list? Was your prediction correct?
2. Identify items thrown away that could be used again.
3. How could your class reduce the amount of trash it makes?
4. **Challenge** How would the trash produced at home be different from the trash at school?

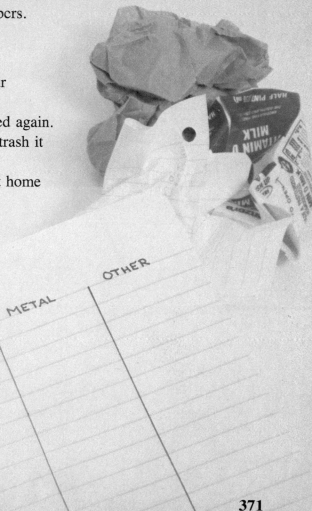

2 How Is Waste Disposal a Problem?

Over 4 billion people live on earth. The population of earth now doubles about every 35 years. An increasing population causes many problems. As more people live on earth, they use more of the earth's resources. They also produce more wastes.

People have always produced wastes. Even if there were no wastes from the packaging of food, people would still produce wastes from food. Eggshells, skins of fruits and vegetables, and bones from meat are natural waste products. The chart shows you what kinds of wastes people produce.

Wastes people produce

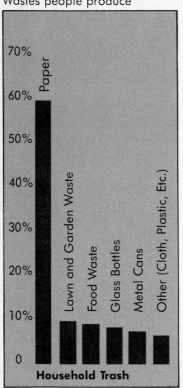

Household Trash

Biodegradable wastes

Plant matter and animal matter are examples of **biodegradable** substances—those that can be broken down by the action of bacteria. The picture shows examples of biodegradable wastes. These substances decay and enrich the soil.

biodegradable
(bī′ō di grā′də bəl), able to be broken down by the action of bacteria.

Old-fashioned store

The picture on the right shows examples of wastes that are not biodegradable. They will not break down, or decay, to enrich the soil. They just keep piling up. Each year we must find a place for more of these materials.

To understand one reason our trash problem has grown, look at the picture above. The picture shows an old-fashioned store. Products were sold without a lot of packaging. Stores did not give out paper bags. People usually brought their own shopping bags to carry what they bought. Most things people bought were made of biodegradable materials.

Non-biodegradable wastes

Trash in the streets

Building built on landfill

How Can We Solve the Trash Problem?

In the past, when people wanted to get rid of their trash, they just threw it out. Sometimes they threw it into the streets or alleys. Sometimes they packed it into a wagon and dumped it near the edge of town. Open dumping caused many problems. The trash was ugly and often smelled bad. It attracted rats and other animals that carried diseases.

Over the years people have changed the way they dispose of trash. Now trash is often crushed and deposited in open areas. A layer of trash is dumped and smashed down. Then, it is covered with a layer of dirt. Another layer of trash is dumped and covered with dirt. This method of trash disposal is called **landfill.** The building in the picture was built on an area that was once a landfill.

landfill (land′fil′), site where wastes are disposed of by burying them under layers of earth.

374

Burning trash is another way to dispose of wastes. Often, when trash was burned, smoke filled the air. Burning trash added to air pollution. Today, new furnaces for burning trash—or **incinerators**—have been developed. These new incinerators have scrubbers on their smokestacks. The scrubbers reduce air pollution. The new incinerators also collect some of the heat energy produced by burning trash. This energy can be used to heat homes and businesses.

incinerator (in sin′ə rā′tər), furnace for burning trash.

The picture shows a plant in Dade County, Florida. The plant produces fuel from trash. This fuel is burned to produce electricity. Using trash as fuel can save nearly one million barrels of oil each year.

Producing electricity from trash

How Does Recycling Help?

recycle (rē sī′kəl), treat or process something so it may be used again.

Another way of dealing with the trash problem is **recycling,** or changing waste products so they can be used again. Waste products made of paper, glass, or aluminum can be recycled. These people are taking newspapers, bottles, and cans to be recycled. The glass bottles can be crushed, melted down, and made into new bottles. Recycling reduces the amount of trash. It also takes less energy to recycle glass than to make new glass from raw materials.

Wastes can be recycled

Think About It

1. How does a growing population affect our trash-disposal problem?
2. List three things that are biodegradable. List three things that are not biodegradable.
3. How can recycling help our trash-disposal problem?
4. **Challenge** List three things your family could do to reduce the amount of trash it throws away.

Have You Heard?

Recycling aluminum cans uses only one-tenth of the energy it would take to make new cans.

Do You Know?

Treasures Can Come from Trash

To many people, old tires are just a problem. People throw away 200 million tires each year. How can the tires be anything more than just another part of our waste-disposal problem?

One way tires can be used is to make a habitat for fish. Old tires are dumped into the ocean near the shoreline. Soon, sea plants and animals begin to grow on the tires. An artificial coral reef forms. More than two thousand tire-reefs like this have been built. The largest one, near Fort Lauderdale, Florida, is made of several million old tires.

Boat owners often find old tires useful. They fasten parts of tires to the boat docks. The tires protect the boat from damage when it bumps into the dock.

One inventor is using old tires for playgrounds. He has built more than two hundred playgrounds like the one in the picture. So far, he has used more than sixty thousand tires. Swings, jungle gyms, playhouses, and other equipment can be put together from car and truck tires.

Perhaps the most unusual use of tires is as an energy source. Tires can be changed into an oil-like liquid. When this "tire oil" is burned, it produces as much energy as an equal amount of coal. The heat produced can be used to run power plants or to warm office buildings. In New York City the tires thrown away in one year could supply enough energy for fifteen thousand people.

The new uses that people are finding for tires remind us that many treasures may be hiding in our trash.

Using old tires to build a playground

3 What Is Polluting the Land?

groundwater, water that seeps downward and soaks the soil; the source of wells and springs.

Have You Heard?

About half the drinking water in the United States comes from wells and springs supplied by groundwater.

People dispose of most wastes from homes by burning or burying them. Many of these wastes are not harmful. But factories must also dispose of waste products. Some of these wastes are chemicals that are dangerous to living things. These wastes can be poisonous or can catch fire. The chart shows some other sources of harmful wastes that can pollute our land.

In the past many liquid wastes were poured into pits and allowed to soak into the ground. Often, the fresh water under the earth's surface—or **groundwater**—was polluted by these wastes.

Some solid and liquid wastes were placed in large metal drums. These drums were stored at dumps like the one in the picture. Sometimes the drums were buried in landfills. After a few years many of the drums started leaking. Chemicals polluted the land and the groundwater.

Waste dumps can cause pollution

Sources of harmful wastes

Source	Wastes
military bases	explosives
hospitals	disease-carrying wastes
laboratories	poisonous chemicals
gasoline stations	waste oil
power plants	ash
nuclear power plants	radioactive wastes

Disposing of nuclear wastes

People are dealing with the problem of chemical wastes in several ways. Wastes are being buried in special plastic-coated drums that resist leaking. Some factories are changing their manufacturing processes to reduce the amount of chemical wastes. Scientists are trying to find ways to recycle wastes or make them harmless.

Wastes from nuclear power plants and industries are another source of land pollution. These wastes are usually sealed in large containers, as shown, and buried or stored underground. Many people are concerned that some **radiation**—or energy that is harmful to living things—can escape from the buried containers. Scientists are trying to find ways to recycle radioactive wastes. They are also looking for safe ways to store the wastes that cannot be recycled.

radiation (rā′dē ā′shən), energy and particles given off by atoms undergoing nuclear decay.

Think About It

1. List two ways air and water pollution affect the land.
2. Name four sources of land pollution.
3. List three ways land pollution can be reduced.
4. **Challenge** How does the pollution of groundwater affect people?

Find Out

Read about the problems people faced when a school and houses were built near a chemical-waste dump at Love Canal in Niagara Falls, New York.

4 How Is Land Being Changed?

Land is as important to our lives as clean air and water. The land gives us a place to build houses, schools, roads, and factories. We plant crops, graze livestock, and grow trees on land. We mine chemicals, minerals, and fuels from the land.

As more people live on the earth, it is necessary to grow more food and make more products. We must also build more houses, schools, roads, and factories. These increases in population change the way we use land. Towns grow into cities, and cities expand into the country. Houses and factories are built on lands that were forests, farms, or deserts. Each time we build new homes, farms, factories, or roads, we change the land, as the picture shows.

Rain falls on forests, farms, and cities. In the forest some water seeps into the ground, while some flows into rivers and lakes. Since most of the forest soil is covered by plants and trees, little soil washes away. The leaves protect the ground from heavy rain, and the roots hold the soil in place.

Changing the land to build houses

Logging removes trees from hillsides

On farms some water seeps into the ground. This water is needed to grow crops and to replace groundwater. Since parts of the soil have no plants, rain can wash away some soil. Muddy water flows into streams and lakes from farms. Much soil can wash away when there are no crops on the farm. The wearing away of land—or **erosion**—on farms removes soil needed to grow crops and also pollutes water.

In a city, with large paved areas, almost all the water goes down the sewers and into rivers and lakes. Very little water seeps into the ground. Flooding, which increases erosion along rivers, can result. When water flows into rivers and lakes, the amount of groundwater in wells is reduced.

Mining and logging are necessary to provide fuels, paper, and wood products. Land areas are needed to store waste products. These uses of land also affect the environment.

Look at the picture of the hillside that has been logged. If this area is not replanted, erosion will cause more land damage. Gullies, like the ones in the picture, will form as water washes away more and more soil. Water pollution will also increase as soil washes into streams.

Gullies caused by erosion

erosion (i rō′zhən), wearing away of land by water, wind, or glaciers.

How Do People Protect the Land?

reclamation (rek′lə mā′shən), returning to a useful or good condition.

People often try to restore damaged land by **reclamation,** a process that returns land to a useful, good condition. There are many kinds of reclamation. Sometimes people try to return an area exactly to the way it was. The forest in the picture is owned by a lumber company. Notice the areas where new trees have been planted to replace the ones cut down. After a time the logged hillside will look the way it did before the trees were removed. Other kinds of reclamation try to reduce the erosion, pollution, and damage to plants and animals.

Many reclamation projects find other uses for mined, logged, or damaged land. Strip mines can be used for waste disposal. The waste is used to fill the huge hole. Other strip mines are allowed to fill with water. The lakes that form are used for fishing, swimming, and sailing. The picture below shows a reclaimed strip mine.

Usable land is as important to people as clean air and water. Mining and logging do not need to ruin the land. Since people will need the land in the future, it is best to plan reclamation before mining or logging an area. It is easier to keep an area healthy than to clean up badly damaged land.

Reclaimed strip mine

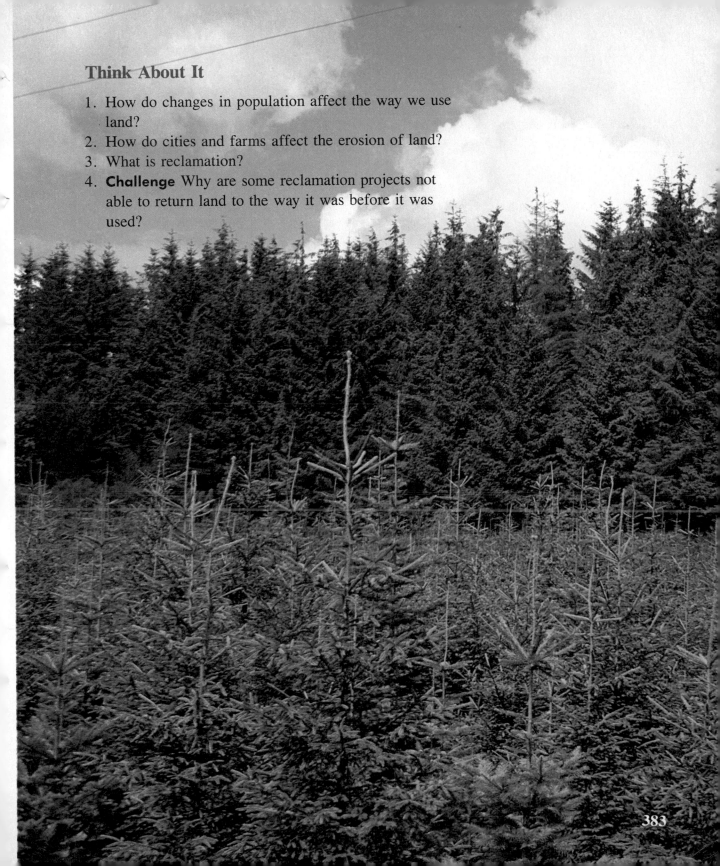

Think About It

1. How do changes in population affect the way we use land?
2. How do cities and farms affect the erosion of land?
3. What is reclamation?
4. **Challenge** Why are some reclamation projects not able to return land to the way it was before it was used?

Activity

Designing a City of the Future

Purpose
To describe how land use is important in planning a city.

You Will Need
- large sheet of paper
- crayons
- colored markers

Directions
1. Every city needs places for people to live, work, go to school, and play. Draw a map of a city of the future when land is used very carefully.
2. Draw places where the people will live.
3. Draw schools where the children will go.
4. Draw and label factories and office buildings where people will work. Decide whether you will put factories near the houses and schools. Will workers need parking lots for their cars?
5. Draw stores where people will shop. Decide where stores should be located.
6. Include parks and playgrounds in your city.
7. Draw other things that are important to a city, such as waste-disposal sites, farms, mines, or forests.

Think About It
1. How is your future city different from the cities of today?
2. What problems did you think about when you were drawing the city?
3. **Challenge** How did you protect the land from pollution and damage?

384

Tie It Together

Sum It Up

1. Which of the following are biodegradable wastes?
   a. plastic bag
   b. chicken bone
   c. paper bag
   d. glass bottle
   e. nylon stocking
   f. grass clippings

2. Which of the following can be safely disposed of in a landfill?
   a. tin cans
   b. waste oil
   c. newspapers
   d. chemicals
   e. nuclear wastes
   f. wood crates

3. Which of the following items can be recycled?
   a. newspapers
   b. plastic cups
   c. soft-drink cans
   d. glass bottles
   e. old clothes
   f. books

4. Which of the following can help reduce land damage?
   a. building factories
   b. planting trees
   c. strip-mining coal
   d. building roads
   e. refilling strip mines
   f. planting flowers on a hillside

Challenge!

1. List three of your family's activities that do not produce any waste.

2. How many different ways could you reuse a peanut butter jar?

3. Your neighbor wants to get rid of some old tires. What would you suggest he do with them?

4. A company wants to use an old farm near your town as a landfill for chemical wastes. What questions would you ask before deciding whether to approve the plan?

5. New houses are being built on a hillside. The builder cut down all the trees and bushes. How could this damage the land?

Science Words

biodegradable

erosion

groundwater

incinerator

landfill

radiation

reclamation

recycle

Laboratory

Filtering Water

Purpose
To infer how the sizes of particles mixed in water determines how well the water can be cleaned by filtering.

You Will Need
- water
- 2 baby-food jars with lids
- spoon
- soil
- medicine dropper
- red food coloring
- 2 paper cups
- absorbent cotton
- centimeter ruler
- sand
- charcoal paste
- pebbles
- 2 clear glasses

Stating the Problem
Muddy water contains small particles of soil. A water filter cleans muddy water by trapping the soil particles as the water passes through the filter. Does a water filter trap some particles better than others? Would a water filter clean muddy water better than it would water colored with food coloring?

a

Investigating the Problem
1. Half fill 2 baby-food jars with water.
2. Add some soil to one of the jars. Close the jar. As shown in picture *a*, shake the jar until the soil is mixed well with the water. Observe the size of the particles in the muddy water that you made. Save the muddy water.
3. Add a few drops of red food coloring to the other jar of water. Close the jar, and mix the food coloring in the water.
4. Observe whether particles are visible in the red-colored water. Record in your notebook whether the particles were larger in the colored water or in the muddy water. Save the colored water.
5. Make a water filter by poking 4 holes

through the bottom of a paper cup, as shown in picture *b*.

6. Place a clean layer of cotton on the bottom of the cup.
7. Add a 1-cm layer of sand over the cotton.
8. Your teacher will give you some charcoal paste. Layer the paste about 1 cm thick over the layer of sand.
9. Add a 1-cm layer of pebbles over the charcoal paste. Picture *c* shows how the layers of the water filter should look.
10. Repeat steps 5–9, using another paper cup to make a second water filter.
11. Slowly pour the muddy water over the filter. Use a clear glass to collect the water that passes through the filter. Observe and record the appearance of the water.

Pebbles
Charcoal
Sand
Cotton

c

12. Slowly pour the red-colored water over the other filter. Use a clear glass to collect the water that passes through the filter. Observe and record the appearance of the water.

Making Conclusions
1. How did the size of particles in the water affect how well the water was cleaned by the filter? How do you know?
2. How were the layers of cotton, sand, charcoal, and pebbles in the water filter different from each other?
3. Why were different layers of materials used to make the water filter?
4. Do you think a water filter could remove all the harmful particles that muddy water from a river or lake might contain? Explain.

b

387

Careers

Recycling-Plant Manager

One of the biggest problems that people have to deal with is garbage. What do we do with all our garbage? Carolyn is doing her part to battle the garbage problem. She is a manager at an aluminum recycling plant.

"At our plant alone," says Carolyn, "we are able to recycle about 45,000 kilograms of aluminum each week. We collect aluminum from citizens and from large companies.

"The first thing we do is separate the steel from the aluminum with a large magnet. Next, the aluminum is weighed and shredded into pieces the size of popcorn. These pieces are melted and can then be reshaped to make aluminum products again."

Besides helping solve our garbage problem, Carolyn points out many other advantages to recycling.

"In recycling aluminum cans, we are saving over 9/10 of the energy needed to produce new cans. Recycling also helps to conserve our natural resources. Since we can recycle aluminum many

times, people do not need to mine as much aluminum ore. Also, people who collect aluminum cans are helping to keep America beautiful. They make money, too. We pay people for bringing in aluminum."

Besides cans, people bring in pie plates, frozen-dinner trays, and foil. "Last year a tornado struck here. People gave us a lot of the aluminum siding that came off their houses."

After high school, Carolyn took several business courses before working at the recycling plant. "I really like knowing that what we do here is important to the community."

Garbage and other kinds of pollution are a major concern of people all around the world. Many people use their skills to control or stop pollution.

A **sanitary engineer** designs water-treatment plants, sewage-treatment plants, and sanitary landfills. The engineer spends a lot of time at the building site. He or she makes sure the plant or landfill is being constructed properly. This person also advises people in industry on how to safely dispose of oil, chemicals, and other wastes.

Like other engineers, sanitary engineers have gone to college for at least four years.

Once a sewage or water-treatment plant is designed and built, it must be put to use. **Waste-water plant operators** work at the plant. These operators run the machinery that removes pollutants from sewage. Operators also test water samples to make sure the water that is leaving the plant is clean enough.

Environmental technicians also collect water samples. They collect air and water samples near factories, forests, and other places. The technicians test the samples to be sure they do not contain harmful pollutants.

People who want to be technicians learn their skills during two years of college. Operators learn most of their skills on the job. But many operators attend college for one or two years.

Before you can help solve a problem, you must learn about the problem. In this unit, you learned about the problem of pollution with the help of your **teacher.** You learn a lot about different subjects from your teacher. A teacher can help people understand the world around them. Most teachers go to college for four years.

Sanitary engineer

Environmental technician

On Your Own

Picture Clue

Did you find out what the picture on page 342 shows? Look closely at the picture on page 355. Notice how the pictures are alike.

Projects

1. Find out how trash is disposed of in your community.

2. Report on new kinds of automobile power designed to prevent smog.

3. Talk to someone who works at a local water-treatment plant. Find out how your water supply is treated.

4. Organize a recycling committee to collect bottles, newspapers, and aluminum cans.

5. Find out how acid rain can destroy building materials. Test samples of building materials, such as granite, limestone, or marble, with vinegar.

Books About Science

Pictures and Pollution by Barbara Slavin Kataoka. Childrens Press, 1977. Learn how pollution affects all our lives.

Poisoned Land: The Problem of Hazardous Waste by Irene Kiefer. Atheneum, 1981. Chemical-waste dumps pollute many areas of the United States.

Three Drops of Water by Sigmund Kalina. Lothrop, Lee & Shepard Company, 1974. Follow the journey of three water drops down a river to the sea. Find out what happens to them along the way.

Water by Alun Lewis. Franklin Watts, 1980. Compare the amount of water you use with the amount used by people in western Europe.

Unit Test

Matching

Number your paper from 1–5. Read the description in Column I. Next to each number, write the letter of the word or phrase from Column II that best matches the description in Column I.

Column I

1. using something over again
2. reduces sewage pollution
3. produces acid rain
4. caused by car exhausts
5. helps identify oil spills

Column II

a. sulfur dioxide
b. recycling
c. "fingerprinting"
d. smog
e. cooling towers
f. water-treatment plant

Multiple Choice

Number your paper from 6–10. Next to each number, write the letter of the word or words that best complete the statement or answer the question.

6. What is the *best* way to reduce water pollution?
   a. dilute polluted water with clean water
   b. use less water
   c. prevent pollution from getting into the water
   d. store polluted water in old lakes

7. Which of the following cause air pollution?
   a. cars
   b. factories
   c. volcanoes
   d. all the above

8. Why can air pollution spread out more quickly than land or water pollution?
   a. Winds can easily move polluted air.
   b. Air pollution is easier to see.
   c. There is more air pollution.
   d. Air pollution occurs in more places.

9. Which of the following cause land pollution?
   a. trash
   b. farming chemicals
   c. materials from power plants
   d. all the above

10. Which of the following statements is *most* correct?
    a. Pollution is not a serious problem.
    b. Air pollution is a more serious problem than land or water pollution.
    c. Water pollution is a more serious problem than air or land pollution.
    d. All kinds of pollution are serious problems.

Glossary Index

a hat	**i** it	**oi** oil	**ch** child		a in about
ā age	**ī** ice	**ou** out	**ng** long		e in taken
ä far	**o** hot	**u** cup	**sh** she	ə =	i in pencil
e let	**ō** open	**ů** put	**th** thin		o in lemon
ē equal	**ô** order	**ü** rule	**ŦH** then		u in circus
ėr term			**zh** measure		

absorb (ab sôrb′), 50: to take in

absorb (ab sôrb′), 240, 292–294: to take in without reflecting

acid (as′id), 216–218, 323: substance with a sour taste that turns litmus red

acid rain (as′id rān), 365–366: rain containing acids

adaptation (ad′ap tā′shən), 126–129: a trait that makes an organism well suited to its environment
and extinction, 134–137
and natural selection, 129–130
See also genes, heredity, trait

air
and evaporation, condensation, 198–199, 208, 212
as mixture of gases, 209, 211
on planets, 322–324, 326
and sound waves, 232–233, 234

air pollution
and acid rain, 365–366
and automobiles, 362–363
and burning matter, 364, 375
natural, 360–361
and smoking, 368

algae (al′gə), 55, 57

ammonia, 214, 216, 326

amphibian (am fib′ē ən), 24: an ectothermic vertebrate with uncovered skin that usually lives part of its life in water and part on land

amplifier (am′plə fī′ər), 257: a device that magnifies changes in electrical signals

amplitude (am′plə tüd), 236–237: the distance a vibrating object moves from its resting position

animals, 15, 18, 19: organisms that have many cells and that cannot make their own food. Most animals can move
ectothermic, 24–25
endothermic, 22–23
invertebrates, 21, 26–31
kingdom, 11, 14, 15, 20–21
sending, receiving sounds, 242, 250–251
traits of, 20
vertebrates, 21, 22–25
See also invertebrates, vertebrates

arthropod (är′thrə pod), 26–27: an invertebrate with jointed legs and an exoskeleton

asteroid (as′tə roid′), 330: any of the thousands of very tiny planets that are found between the orbits of Mars and Jupiter

astronauts, 314–315, 333–334

atom (at′əm), 172–174: a particle that is the building block of matter
and compounds, 177
and elements, 176–177
and molecules, 174–175
parts of, 172–174

auditory nerve (ô′də tôr′ē nėrv), 248: nerve that carries sound signals from the inner ear to the brain

axis (ak′sis), 310: an imaginary straight line through an object and about which the object spins

axis

backbone, 21

bacteria
in moneran kingdom, 16, 58
and water pollution, 348, 352–353, 356

base, 216–218: substance with a bitter taste that turns litmus blue

biodegradable (bī′ō di grā′də bəl), 372–373: able to be broken down by the action of bacteria

birds, 21, 23, 124, 136

blood
and digestion, 86–87
diseases of, 113

blood cells, 72–73, 113

blood tissue, 78–79

blood vessels, 80, 86, 91, 113

boiling, 197: rapid change of state from liquid to gas that takes place within the liquid as well as at its surface

boiling point, 197, 209, 211: the temperature at which a substance exposed to the air rapidly changes from liquid to gas

bone cells, 72, 91

bones, 23, 80, 142

brain, 72, 80, 248, 278–279, 352

budding (bud′ing), 52: a type of reproduction in which a tiny cell grows out and breaks away from another cell

camera, 280–282

carbon, 172, 174, 178, 202

carbon dioxide, 36, 169, 200, 204, 323–324: a colorless, odorless gas formed when fuel containing carbon is burned. It is used by plants in photosynthesis.

carbon monoxide (kär′bən mo nok′sīd), 324, 362: colorless, odorless, poisonous gas

cast, 147: a fossil that forms when a mold fills with sediment

cell (sel), 7–8, 72–73: a small unit that makes up living things
  characteristics of, 72–73
  and chromosomes, 75, 100–101
  and cytoplasm, 74–75, 76, 92, 93
  and diseases, 112–113
  energy of, 90–91, 92, 94–96
  moneran, 58
  nucleus, 54, 74–75, 100
  offspring, 93, 95, 101
  parts of, 74–75
  plant, 36, 76
  protist, 54–55
  reproductive, 42, 44, 50–52, 106
  spores, 44, 50
  and tissues, 78–79, 80–81, 93
  types of, 72
  and viruses, 60
  yeast, 52–53

cell wall

nucleus

cytoplasm

onion cell

cell activity
  growth, reproduction, 59, 92–93, 95, 101, 110
  and metabolism, 96
  and nutrients, 86–88, 90–91
  and respiration, 90

cell division (sel də vizh′ən), 93, 95, 101, 110: cell reproduction in which a parent cell divides into 2 offspring cells

cell membrane, 74–75, 76, 88, 90, 92

cell respiration (sel res′pə rā′shən), 90: the cell process that uses energy and oxygen to break down nutrients and to gain energy

cell wall, 36, 76: the stiff outer covering of a plant cell

chemical (kem′ə kəl) **change,** 200–204, 217: a change in which 1 or more new substances are formed

chemical pollution, 352–353, 378–379

chemical properties (kem′ə kəl prop′ər tēz), 171: properties that tell how a substance will act in the presence of another kind of matter

chloroplast (klôr′ə plast), 76: an egg-shaped cell structure that holds chlorophyll

chlorophyll (klôr′ə fil), 36, 50, 59, 76, 110: green material found in plants and used for making food

chromosome (krō′mə sōm), 75, 92–93, 95, 100–101: a stringlike part in the nucleus that stores the directions for the activities of the cell

cilium (sil′ē əm), 55: a short, hairlike part that grows out from a cell. [Plural: cilia (sil′ē ə)]

classification, 10–13
  five kingdoms, 14–16
  by genus and species, 11
  See also five kingdoms, species

classify (klas′ə fī), 10: to arrange in groups, according to some system

cochlea (kok′lē ə), 248: the fluid-filled, snail-shaped part of the inner ear that sends sound signals to the auditory nerve

color
  and light, 274–275, 285–288, 290–296
  in chemical change, 202
  and melanin, 103, 108
  as physical property, 170–171
  of sun, 308
  See also light

comet (kom′it), 331: a ball of dust and frozen gases that orbits the sun in a very long, stretched-out path

communication
  of animals, 250–251
  by deaf people, 249
  and listening, 245
  and speech and hearing, 246–249
  See also sound

compound (kom′pound), 177: a substance made of 2 or more elements that are chemically joined

compression (kəm presh′ən), 230–231: the place in a sound wave where particles are squeezed together

concave (kon kāv′), 273: curving inward

concave lenses, 273–274

condense (kən dens′), 199: change from gas to liquid

conduction (kən duk′shən), 188: the flow of heat due to the transfer of energy from one particle striking another

conifer (kon′ə fər), 42–43: a cone-bearing plant

connecting tissue, 78

continents, movement of, 149

contract (kən trakt′), 184–187, 194: to become smaller in size; to take up less space

convection (kən vek′shən), 189: the flow of heat due to the flow of hotter material in a liquid or gas

convex (kon veks′), 273: curving outward

convex lenses, 273–274, 279, 280

cornea (kôr′nē ə), 278: the clear part of the outer coat of the eyeball

crater (krā′tər), 314, 322: a bowl-shaped hole ranging in size from tiny to very large

cytoplasm (sī′tə plaz′əm), 74–75, 76, 92–93: the part of the cell that is inside the membrane but outside the nucleus

a hat	i it	oi oil	ch child	(a in about
ā age	ī ice	ou out	ng long	e in taken
ä far	o hot	u cup	sh she	ə = { i in pencil
e let	ō open	ù put	th thin	o in lemon
ē equal	ô order	ü rule	ᴛʜ then	(u in circus
ėr term			zh measure	

decibel (des′ə bəl), 237: unit used in measuring the strength of a sound

dicot (dī′kot), 40: a flowering plant with two seed leaves in its seeds

digestive system, 79, 80

dilute (də lüt′), 347, 349: to make weaker by adding water

dinosaurs, 140–145

disease, 27
diabetes, 112
from fungi, 50, 52
hemophilia, 113
from monerans, 16, 58–59
from protists, 56
sickle-cell anemia, 113
from viruses, 60

dissolve (di zolv′), 212–215: cause a substance to become part of a solution

dog breeds, 109, 125, 126

dominant (dom′ə nənt) **gene,** 106–109, 112: a gene that causes a trait to appear even though a gene for a variation of the trait is present

eardrum (ir′drum′), 247: a thin tissue in the outer ear that vibrates when sound waves strike it

ears, 247–248, 251

earth, 322, 323
atmosphere of, 323
distance from sun, 321
and moon, 314–317
motions of, 310–313
See also moon, planets, solar system, sun

echo (ek′ō), 240–242: a sound reflected after an original sound

echolocation (ek′ō lō kā′shən), 242: method of finding objects by using sound waves that are reflected off the objects

ectothermic (ek′ta thėr′mik), 24–25: having a body temperature that changes with the surroundings

eggs
amphibian, 24
bird, 23
fish, 25
mammal, 22
reptile, 24

electron (i lek′tron), 173–174: a part of an atom with a negative charge of electricity that moves about in the space an atom occupies

element (el′ə mənt), 176–178: a substance that cannot be broken down into a simpler substance by ordinary means

endothermic (en′dō thėr′mik), 22–23: able to keep a constant body temperature by producing one's own body heat

energy
of cells, 90–91, 92, 94–96
organisms use of, 89, 94–95
radiant, 190

environment (en vī′rən mənt), 7: the living and nonliving surroundings of an organism
and adaptation, 126, 128, 134
and extinction of species, 134–135
and habitat, 135–136, 145
and land, 371–384
and natural selection, 129–132
and organisms' response to, 7, 8
and water, 345–355

erosion (i rō′zhən), 381, 382: wearing away of land by water, wind, or glaciers

evaporate (i vap′ə rāt′), 198–199, 208, 212: slow change from liquid to gas, occurring at the surface of the liquid

exoskeleton (ek′sō skel′ə tən), 26: a hard outside covering that protects and supports an arthropod

expand (ek spand′), 184–187, 194: to become larger in size: to take up more space

extinct (ek stingkt′), 134–138, 140, 144, 148: no longer existing

eyes, 103, 105, 278–279, 280–281, 289, 292

ferns, 44, 46

filament (fil′ə mənt), 290–291: very slender, threadlike part

fish, 21, 25, 80, 94, 241, 250, 344, 351, 352

five kingdoms, 14: system of classification of animals, plants, fungi (fun′jī), protists (prō′tists), and monerans (mə nir′ənz)

flagellum (flə jel′əm), 55: a long, whiplike part that grows out from a cell. [Plural: flagella (flə jel′ə)]

flatworms, 29

flowering plants, 15, 37, 38–40
dicots, 40
monocots, 40

fluorescent (flù res′nt), 291: able to give off light when exposed to ultraviolet rays or X rays

focus (fō′kəs), 274: point at which rays of light meet

food
and digestion of, in cells, 86–87
and photosynthesis, 36, 76
transport of, in plants, 37, 39, 42, 44–45, 81
use of by organisms, 6

formula (fôr′myə lə), 177: a group of symbols that is used to write the name of a compound

fossil (fos′əl), 146–154: remains or traces of an organism that once lived on earth
determining age of, 154
record, 148, 151–153

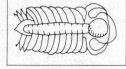

trilobite fossil

freezing point, 196: the temperature at which a substance changes from liquid to solid; same temperature as the melting point

frequency (frē′kwən sē), 238: the speed at which something vibrates

frogs, 21, 24, 95, 130

fruit, 39, 216

fungi (fun′jī), 16, 48–53, 57: organisms, such as mushrooms and molds, that are not green and cannot make their own food. Most are many-celled organisms that absorb food from organic matter. [Singular: fungus (fung′gəs)]
kingdom, 14, 16, 50–53
and tissues, 80
See also molds, mushrooms, yeasts

gas
and boiling point, 197, 211
in chemical change, 202
and convection, 189
and evaporation, condensation, 198–199
and expansion, contraction, 184–187
in mixture, 208–211
in solution, 214
and sound, 233
as state of matter, 169

gene (jēn), 100: a direction for a trait. Genes are found along the bands of a chromosome
affecting traits, 106–109
and chromosomes, 100–101
dominant, 106–109, 112
influence on, 112–114
and mutations, 110–111
recessive, 106–109, 112, 113
and variations in traits, 102–105
See also heredity, trait

genus (jē′nəs), 11: a group to which closely related species belong

gravity (grav′ə tē), 311, 317: a force that pulls all things together

groundwater, 378, 379: water that seeps downward and soaks the soil; the source of wells and springs

growth, 6, 8
and cells, 73

habitat (hab′ə tat), 22, 135–136: a place where an organism lives

hearing, 247–248

heat (hēt), 182–183: a flow of energy from warmer objects to cooler ones
and changing state of matter, 196–197
and conduction, 188
and convection, 189
as energy from cell, 90
and expansion, contraction, 184–187
and radiant energy, 190
and temperature, 183
of sun, 309
and water pollution, 346, 350–351

heredity (hə red′ə tē), 101: the passing of genes from parent to offspring
and diseases, 112–113
and traits, 99–104
See also adaptation, genes, trait

hollow-bodied animals, 30

homogeneous (hō′mə jē′nē əs), 213: distributed evenly or uniformly throughout

horses, 152–153

human beings
causing extinction of species, 136–137
and pollution, 345–347, 349–355, 362–368, 370–384

hydrogen, 174, 176, 202

incinerator (in sin′ə rā′tər), 375: furnace for burning trash

indicator (in′də kā′tər), 217–218: substance that changes color when touched by an acid or base

infer (in fer′), 12: using what you already know to make a decision

infrared rays, 288

inherit (in her′it), 101: to receive a set of genes from 1 or 2 parents

insects, 21, 27, 126, 250–251

insulin (in′sə lən), 112: a substance made in the body that helps sugar enter cells

invertebrate (in ver′tə brit), 21, 26–31: an animal without a backbone
organs, systems in, 80
See also animals, organisms, vertebrate

iris (ī′ris), 278–279, 281: the colored part of the eye around the pupil

iron, 171, 202, 203

reflected light

metabolism (mə tab′ə liz′əm), 96: all the activities of an organism that either break down substances or make new substances

meteor (mē′tē′ər), 330: streak of light in the sky caused by a chunk of rock burning up in the earth's air

meteorite (mē′tē ə rīt′), 314–315, 322: a piece of rock, often containing metals, that strikes a planet or a satellite

methane, 326

microscopes, 77

middle ear, 247: space containing 3 small bones that pass sound waves from the eardrum to the inner ear

mirage, 277

mirrors, 269–271

mixture, 208: 2 or more substances that are placed together but are not chemically joined
homogeneous, 213
and solutions, 213–215
types of, 208–210
See also solutions

mold, 147: a hollow shape left when an organism decays

molecule (mol′ə kyül), 174–175: a combination of 2 or more atoms
and changing state of matter, 196–199
and evaporation, condensation, 198–199, 212
and expansion, contraction, 185
and heat, 183, 188–190
in solutions, 213

mollusk (mol′əsk), 28, 31: an invertebrate with a muscular foot, a soft body, and usually, a hard shell

monerans (mə nir′ənz), 14, 16, 58–59: organisms, such as bacteria, made of very small cells that lack nuclei
helpful, harmful, 59
kingdom, 58–59
one-celled, 16, 72
and viruses, 60

monocot (mon′ə kot), 40: a flowering plant with one seed leaf in its seeds

moon
and earth, 316–317
origin of, 318
phases of, 316–317
properties of, 314–317
and sun, 307
See also earth, planets, solar system, sun

crescent moon

moons, 324, 326–329, 332: of planets

mosses, 45, 46, 80

motion
of earth, 310–313

of molecules, 183, 185, 188, 189
of moon, 316–317

Mount St. Helens, 361

moving pictures, 282

muscle cells, 72–73, 90

muscle tissue, 78–79

muscles, 79, 80

mushroom, 14, 16, 50–51, 80

musical instruments, 252–254

mutation (myü tā′shən), 110–111: a change in the directions for a trait that produces a new trait which can be inherited

natural selection, 129–132: process by which organisms of a species are able to survive and reproduce because they are adapted to their environment

Neptune, 328, 333

nerve cells, 72

nerve tissue, 78–79

neutral (nü′trəl), 217, 218: neither acid nor base

neutralization (nü′trə lə zā′shən), 217, 218: chemical change in which an acid and a base combine to form substances that are neither acids nor bases

neutron (nü′tron), 173–174: a particle with no charge of electricity that is part of the nucleus of an atom

nitrogen, 209, 211, 214, 323

nucleus (nü′klē əs), 54, 58, 74–75, 100: the control center of a cell. [Plural: nuclei (nü′klē ī)]

nucleus (nü′klē əs), 173–174: the central part of an atom [Plural: nuclei (nü′klē ī)]

nutrient (nü′trē ənt), 87, 89, 90–91, 94, 95: a food or water particle that organisms need in order to grow and to stay alive

octopus, 31

odor, as physical property, 170–171

offspring, 99–100, 101, 104, 106–107, 111, 130–131

offspring cells (ôf′spring′ selz), 93, 95, 101: the cells that result from cell reproduction

oil pollution, 354–356

one-celled organisms, 16, 54–55, 58, 72

optic nerve (op′tik nėrv), 279: the nerve that goes from the eye to the brain

orbit (ôr′bit), 311: a closed, curved path that an object follows as the object moves around another object

organ (ôr′gən), 79, 80–81: a group of different tissues working together

organic (ôr gan′ik) **matter,** 51: material that is part of a living or dead organism

pine tree

skin

a hat	**i** it	**oi** oil	**ch** child	(a in about
ā age	**ī** ice	**ou** out	**ng** long	e in taken
ä far	**o** hot	**u** cup	**sh** she	ə = { i in pencil
e let	**ō** open	**ù** put	**th** thin	o in lemon
ē equal	**ô** order	**ü** rule	**ŦH** then	(u in circus
ėr term			**zh** measure	

muscle tissue

water molecules

Acknowledgments

Positions of photographs are shown in abbreviated form as follows: top (**t**), bottom (**b**), left (**l**), right (**r**), center (**c**). All photographs not credited are the property of Scott, Foresman and Company. Cover, illustration by William Peterson, photograph by Lynn M. Stone; **2**, Giuseppe Mazza; **4**, Charlie Sumners/Tom Stack & Assoc.; **5**, Bettmann Archive; **6**, (**tl**) Ian Beames/Ardea London; **7**, (**l**) Kenneth W. Fink/Root Resources, (**tr**) E. R. Degginger, (**br**) Giuseppe Mazza; **8**, (**tl**) Sigurjón Einarsson, (**c, br**) Sigurdur Thorarinsson; **9**, NASA; **14**, (**tl**) Manfred Kage/Peter Arnold, Inc., (**l**) H. Chaumeton/Nature Agence Photographique, (**c**) Martin W. Grosnick/Ardea London, (**tr**) Hans Reinhard/Bruce Coleman Ltd., (**br**) Zig Leszczynski/Animals Animals; **15**, (**t**) Joe Branney/Tom Stack & Assoc., (**b**) A–Z Collection; **16**, (**t**) L. Lacoste/Jacana, (**bl**) Frieder Sauer/Bruce Coleman Ltd., (**r**) Evelyn Tronca/Tom Stack & Assoc.; **18**, Mike Coltman/Seaphot; **19**, (**tr**) Y. Lanceau/Nature Agence Photographique, (**cr**) James M. Cribb, (**br**) Robert A. Tyrrell, (**b**) Varin-Visage/Jacana; **22**, (**tl**) Werner Curth/Ardea London, (**bl**) E. R. Degginger, (**br**) Alice Su; **23**, (**l**) Henry R. Fox/Animals Animals, (**tr**) Jonathan Scott/Seaphot, (**br**) Brian Hawkes/Jacana; **24**, Breck P. Kent; **25**, (**tl**) Salvatore Giordano III, (**tr**) Giuseppe Mazza, (**b**) Ed Robinson/Tom Stack & Assoc.; **28**, (**t**) Heather Angel/Biophotos, (**c, b**) E. R. Degginger; **29**, (**r**) Martin M. Rotker/Taurus, (**l**) Giuseppe Mazza; **30**, (**t**) Richard Murphy/After-Image, (**c**) M. Timothy O'Keefe/Tom Stack & Assoc., (**bl**) Chuck Nicklin/Woodfin Camp & Assoc., (**br**) P. Morris/Ardea London; **31**, (**t**) Zig Leszczynski from Breck P. Kent, (**b**) Giuseppe Mazza; **34**, Malcolm S. Kirk/Peter Arnold, Inc.; **36**, (**l**) Rod Planck/Tom Stack & Assoc., (**r**) Harald Sund; **37**, (**l**) Eric Carlé/Shostal, (**tr**) Sdeuard C. Bisserôt, (**br**) Salvatore Giordano III; **38**, (**l**) Breck P. Kent, (**r**) E. H. Herbert/Natural Science Photos; **41**, (**t, c**) E. R. Degginger, (**b**) Hans Reinhard/Bruce Coleman Ltd.; **43**, (**l**) Brian Parker/Tom Stack & Assoc., (**r**) John Kohout/Root Resources; **44**, John Kohout/Root Resources; **45**, (**t**) Larry West, (**b**) E. R. Degginger; **48**, John Kohout/Root Resources; **50**, Eric V. Grave/Photo Researchers; **51**, (**l**) E. R. Degginger, (**bl**) Breck P. Kent, (**tr**) John Kohout/Root Resources; **52**, Anheuser-Busch Cos., Inc.; **54**, (**r**) Howard Hall/Tom Stack & Assoc., (**l**) Michael Abbey/Photo Researchers; **55**, (**l**) H. M. Canter-Lund/N.H.P.A., (**r**) Kim Taylor/Bruce Coleman Ltd., (**br**) M. Walker/N.H.P.A.; **56**, (**tl**) Dr. G. Leedale/N.H.P.A., (**bl**) Manfred Kage/Peter Arnold, Inc., (**r**) Biophoto Assoc./Science Photo Library; **57**, (**t**) Fred Bruemmer, (**b**) C. R. Knights/Ardea London; **58**, (**tl**) Gene Cox/Science Photo Library, (**bl**) Michael Abbey/Photo Researchers, (**r**) Manfred Kage/Peter Arnold, Inc.; **59**, (**t**) Dr. G. Leedale/N.H.P.A., (**b**) John Kohout/Root Resources; **60**, (**l**) Omikron/Photo Researchers, (**r**) Photo Researchers/DC; **63**, (**tl**) Herbert Lanks/Globe Photos from Stockphotos Inc., (**tc**) Leonard Lee Rue III/Photo Researchers, (**tr**) Laura Riley, (**bl**) Rod Planck/Tom Stack & Assoc., (**bc**) Wayne Lankinen/Bruce Coleman Ltd., (**br**) John Gerlach/Tom Stack & Assoc., (**r**) Edward S. Ross; **65**, (**b**) Andrew Rakoczy/Bruce Coleman Inc.; **68**, Alice Su; **70**, Giuseppe Mazza; **72**, (**t**) Dr. G. Leedale/Biophotos Assoc. from N.H.P.A., (**b**) From *A Text-Atlas of Scanning Electron Microscopy,* by Richard G. Kessel and Randy H. Kardon. Copyright © 1979 by W.H. Freeman and Company. All rights reserved.; **73**, Courtesy of Chas. Pfizer & Co., Inc.; **74**, (**l**) Manfred Kage/Peter Arnold, Inc.; **75**, (**tl**) Dr. G. Leedale/Biophoto Assoc. from N.H.P.A., (**tr**) John Walsh/Science Photo Library, (**b**) Manfred Kage/Peter Arnold, Inc.; **76**, (**l**) Biophoto Assoc./Science Photo Library, (**r**) John Walsh/Science Photo Library; **77**, (**t**) Courtesy Dr. A. E. Vatter, (**bl**) John Walsh/Science Photo Library, (**br**) Manfred Kage/Peter Arnold, Inc.; **78**, Kim Taylor/Bruce Coleman Ltd.; **80**, Breck P. Kent; **81**, E. J. Cable/Tom Stack & Assoc.; **84**, Robert A. Tyrrell; **89**, Don Ornitz/Globe Photos from Stockphotos Inc.; **91**, (**t**) J. M. Labat/Jacana, (**b**) Manfred Kage/Peter Arnold, Inc.; **93**, (**bl**) Manfred Kage/Peter Arnold, Inc.; **94**, Oxford Scientific Films Ltd./Animals Animals; **95**, Oxford Scientific Films Ltd./Animals Animals; **96**, Stouffer Productions/Bruce Coleman Ltd.; **98**, Charles McDougal/Ardea London; **100**, (**l**) E. R. Degginger, (**r**) Hans Reinhard/Bruce Coleman Inc.; **101**, (**t**) Grant Heilman, (**b**) E. R. Degginger; **102**, (**l**) Jean-Paul Ferrero/Ardea London, (**r**) Sdeuard C. Bisserôt; **103**, (**l, tr**) Alice Su, (**br**) Jean-Paul Ferrero/Ardea London; **106**, Dale & Marian Zimmerman/Bruce Coleman Inc.; **109**, Walter Chandoha; **110**, George Whitely/Photo Researchers; **111**, (**l**) Herb Gehr/Life Magazine © 1947 Time Inc., (**tr, br**) Photo Researchers; **113**, (**t**) Manfred Kage/Peter Arnold, Inc., (**b**) Dr. G. Leedale/N.H.P.A.; **119**, (**l**) E. R. Degginger, (**r**) Jacqueline Durand; **122**, Chaumeton-Samba/Nature Agence Photographique; **124**, Leonard Lee Rue III/Atoz Images; **125**, (**tr**) Bill Bachman/Photo Researchers, (**l**) Robert H. Glaze/Artstreet, (**br**) E. R. Degginger; **126**, (**l**) Breck P. Kent, (**r**) William Calvert from E. R. Degginger; **127**, Fred Bruemmer; **128**, E. R. Degginger; **129**, (**l**) Udo Hirsch/Bruce Coleman Ltd., (**r**) A. Greensmith/Ardea London; **130**, (**t**) E. R. Degginger; **131**, Fred Bruemmer; **132**, Tony C. Caprio from Breck P. Kent; **135**, Arthur Hayward/Ardea London; **136**, Courtesy of The Cincinnati Zoo; **137**, Fred Bavendam/Peter Arnold, Inc.; **137**, Dale & Marian Zimmerman/Bruce Coleman

Inc.; **140,** Vince Abromitis/Carnegie Museum of Natural History; **142,** University of Nebraska State Museum; **145,** Paula Chandoha; **146, (tl)** E. R. Degginger, **(bl)** Edward S. Ross, **(r)** C. Berry/Shostal; **147,** Speciman from North Museum—Franklin and Marshall College; Runk/Schoenberger from Grant Heilman; **148,** Smithsonion Collection from Breck P. Kent; **149,** Robert M. Hicks/Dept. of Earth Sciences, University of California, Riverside, from M. O. Woodburne; **150, (t)** Grant Heilman, **(b)** Betty Crowell; **152,** Nick & Gidge Drahos; **154,** Michael Collier; **158,** Paula Chandoha; **159, (l)** Barbara Van Cleve/Atoz Images, **(r)** Paula Chandoha; **162,** J. P. Conrardy/Tom Stack & Assoc.; **164,** E. R. Degginger; **168,** Roger Archibald/Earth Scenes; **176,** Obodda Collection from Breck P. Kent; **178, (tl)** E. R. Degginger, **(bl, r)** Salvatore Giordano III; **180,** W. E. Ruth/Bruce Coleman Inc.; **181,** Rick Myers/Tom Stack & Assoc.; **182,** Donald Dietz/Stock, Boston; **184,** Augusts Upitis/Shostal; **190,** A. Azzarello/ Shostal; **192,** E. R. Degginger; **194,** Robert Frerck/Odyssey Productions; **195,** Adam Woolfitt/ Woodfin Camp & Assoc.; **199,** Dan Morrill; **201,** Salvatore Giordano III; **211,** Milton & Joan Mann; **214,** Lee Boltin; **223, (l)** Bill Gilette/ After-Image, **(r)** Tom Pantages; **228,** E. R. Degginger; **232,** M. Timothy O'Keefe/Tom Stack & Assoc.; **234,** Carl Roessler; **239,** Anne Schullstrom; **241,** Photri; **242,** Ted Farrington/Root Resources; **244,** Geg Germany/© Daily Telegraph Magazine from Woodfin Camp & Assoc.; **249, (t)** Joan Menschenfreund/International Stock Photo, **(b)** Robin L. Hight; **250, (tl)** Anthony Healy/Bruce Coleman Ltd., **(bl)** Carl Roessler, **(r)** Udo Hirsch/Bruce Coleman Ltd/; **251 (l)** Phil & Judy Sublett, **(r)** Stephen J. Krasemann/N.H.P.A.; **263, (r)** Victoria Bellersmith from E. R. Degginger; **266,** Hans Pfletschinger/Peter Arnold, Inc.; **268,** Mike Mazzaschi/Stock, Boston; **270,** Robert Frerck/Odyssey Productions; **272, (l)** Bill Ross/West Light, **(r)** Jane Burton/Bruce Coleman Ltd.; **273,** Bill Ross/West Light; **277,** Phil Degginger; **282,** Shep Abbott/Animals Animals; **285,** J. P. Saint-Marc/Explorer; **287,** Abramson-Culbert Studio; **288, (t)** Courtesy of Dr. Harvey White, Radiology Dept., Children's Memorial Hospital, Chicago, **(bl)** Lee Balterman/Marilyn Gartman Agency, **(cl, br)** Milton & Joan Mann, **(cr)** Jacqueline Durand; **289,** M. Iger/Shostal; **304,** NASA; **306,** Robert H. Glaze/Artstreet; **308,** H. Armstrong Roberts; **309** Mount Wilson and Palomar Observatories; **314,** NASA; **315,** NASA; **316,** Mount Wilson and Palomar Observatories; **317,** Mount Wilson and Palomar Observatories; **320,** Dr. Hans Vehrenberg; **322,** NASA; **323, (tr)** Vernadsky Institute through the U.S. Geological Survey (Lunar Planetary Institute), **(l, br)** NASA; **324,** NASA; **326,** NASA; **327,** NASA; **329, (t)** NASA, **(b)** Jet Propulsion Laboratory/NASA; **330,** Collier/Condit from Collier Photographics; **331, (art)** © 1975 The New York Academy of Sciences, **(br)** Hale Observatories; **332,** L. L. T. Rhodes/Atoz Images; **333,** NASA; **334, (l)** Jim Tuten/Black Star, **(b)** NASA; **338,** Michael Collier; **339, (l)** NASA, **(r)** Shar Feldheim; **342,** Tom Myers; **347,** Dan Budnik/Woodfin Camp & Assoc.; **350,** Daniel Brody/Stock, Boston; **351,** Annie Griffiths; **353,** Edward S. Ross; **354, (l)** Michael W. Richards/Bruce Coleman Ltd., **(b)** Shostal; **355, (l)** Courtesy of Woods Hole Oceanographic Institute, Woods Hole, Massachusetts, **(r)** Ray Hunold; **356, (t)** General Electric Research and Development Center, **(b)** D. Berretty (Rapho)/Photo Researchers; **358,** Salvatore Giordano III; **359,** Berg & Assoc.; **360–61,** Pierre Aucante/Nature Agence Photographique; **361, (r)** James Mason/Black Star; **363,** Peter Fronk/Atoz Images; **365,** Francis Laping/DPI; **366,** Salvatore Giordano III; **373, (l)** Historical Picture Service; **374, (l)** Bettmann Archive; **375,** Resource Recovery (Dade County), Inc.; **377,** Richard Choy/Peter Arnold, Inc.; **378,** Gary Milburn/Tom Stack & Assoc.; **379,** Aronson Photo/Stock, Boston; **380,** Stock, Boston; **381, (t)** D'Arazian/Shostal, **(b)** Jerome Wyckoff; **382,** Pete Pearson/Atoz Images; **383,** Vance Henry/Taurus; **388,** Harald Sund; **389, (l)** Lou Jones, **(r)** Ted Horowitz/The Stock Market.

Ligature Publishing Services, Inc.: design implementation, internal art and photographic direction.

We wish to express our appreciation to the following schools for their contributions:

Poems for the series were written by children at Fairfield Public Schools, Fairfield, Connecticut; Greeley School, Winnetka, Illinois; Howland School, Chicago, Illinois; Indian Oasis Elementary District, Sells, Arizona; and Model Laboratory School, Eastern Kentucky University, Richmond, Kentucky.

Cloze reading tests for the series were administered at Banting Elementary School, Waukesha, Wisconsin; and Gospel Lutheran Grade School, Milwaukee, Wisconsin.

Photographs for Book 5 were taken at Orrington School, Evanston, Illinois; and Martin Luther King Lab School, Evanston, Illinois.

Using Metric

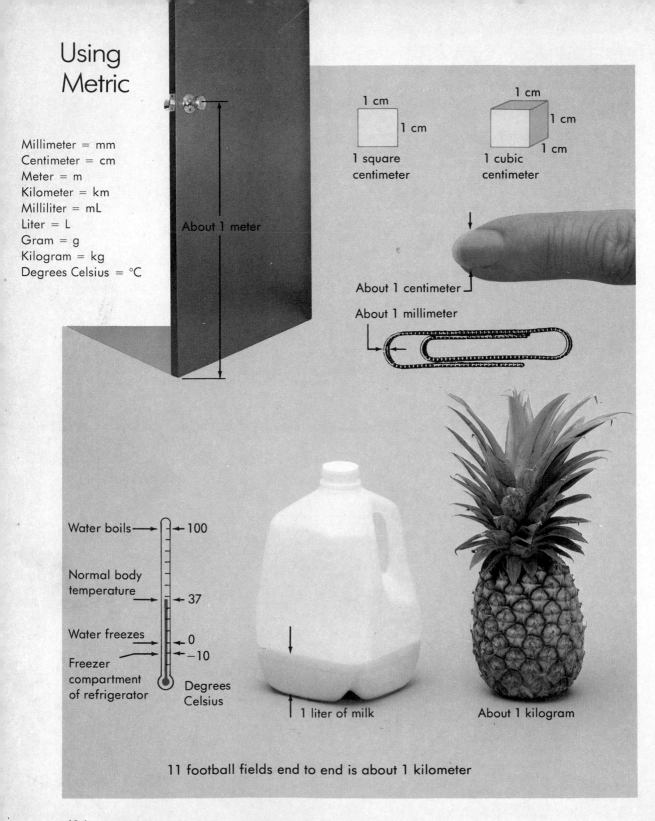

Millimeter = mm
Centimeter = cm
Meter = m
Kilometer = km
Milliliter = mL
Liter = L
Gram = g
Kilogram = kg
Degrees Celsius = °C

About 1 meter

1 cm
1 cm
1 square centimeter

1 cm
1 cm
1 cm
1 cubic centimeter

About 1 centimeter

About 1 millimeter

Water boils → 100

Normal body temperature → 37

Water freezes → 0
→ −10
Freezer compartment of refrigerator

Degrees Celsius

1 liter of milk

About 1 kilogram

11 football fields end to end is about 1 kilometer